A Comedian *Sees* the World

A Comedian Sees the World

CHARLIE CHAPLIN

Edited by Lisa Stein Haven

UNIVERSITY OF MISSOURI PRESS
Columbia

Introduction, notes, and appendices by Lisa Stein Haven,
copyright © 2014 by
The Curators of the University of Missouri
University of Missouri Press, Columbia, Missouri 65201
Printed and bound in the United States of America
All rights reserved
5 4 3 2 1   18 17 16 15 14

Cataloging-in-Publication data available from the Library of Congress
ISBN 978-0-8262-2040-0

∞ This paper meets the requirements of the
American National Standard for Permanence of Paper
for Printed Library Materials, Z39.48, 1984.

Jacket design: Mindy Basinger Hill
Interior design and composition: Richard Farkas
Typefaces: Adobe Caslon Pro, Mostra Nuova

Contents

Acknowledgments   vii

Introduction   1

A Comedian *sees* the World

    Part I   23

    Part II   49

    Part III   75

    Part IV   105

    Part V   131

Appendix A: Tour Itinerary   145

Appendix B: From the Archive Pressbooks. Receiving the Légion d'Honneur Medal   153

Appendix C: From the Archive Pressbooks. The Command Performance Debacle   167

Appendix D: Notes and Correspondence. Syd Chaplin's Contribution   175

Notes   187

Works Cited   223

Index   229

Acknowledgments

This project would have been impossible without the kind assistance of many great people. Kate Guyonavarch and Josephine Chaplin of Association Chaplin in Paris offered access to any and all manuscripts, documents, etc., housed at Progetto Chaplin in Bologna, without which I could not have completed this project. Kate went above and beyond her call of duty to offer me tireless support, hospitality, and friendship. Thanks also to her assistants, Claire Byrski and Charlie Sistovaris. My thanks to Celia Cenciarelli of Cineteca di Bologna for her enthusiasm and commitment to helping me complete this project, and to Gian Luca Farinelli for his vision of what this book should feel and look like. My thanks to Evelyn Lüthi-Graf of the Archives de Montreux who provided much needed assistance and support during my research of the Chaplin archives housed in that facility. And, finally, thanks to Kris Teters, Betty Pytlik, Carey Snyder, Lori Rieder Lammerding, and Carl Wilson for offering their continued comfort and support over the course of this project.

Introduction

The World Crisis in Dumb Show. The genius for using sound without syllables, which was so effective in his last film, can adapt itself to any locality, any necessity for expression. One imagines the little comedian in his usual picture make-up pleading soundlessly at Geneva for custard pies instead of poison gas. Or at Harbin he sits on a keg of powder and kicks his big, flat shoes against it while he shows a few Generals how to win. The Chinese "sound effects" in this scene should be good. Riding a Soviet tractor in the Russian fields, wearing a loin cloth and carrying his flexible cane in India, taking off his battered derby to an American bank that never failed, he can remain as silent, wistful and funny as ever in his old character.

—*New York Times*, 15 April 1932

As the *New York Times* news writer suggests in this excerpt, Charlie Chaplin was (1) often conflated with his film persona, the Little Tramp, and (2) viewed as seemingly "at home" in diverse locations and situations across the world's landscape. Chaplin took advantage of the juxtaposition of these two phenomena twice[1] during his long forty-year residence in the United States, in 1921 and in 1931–32. Each of these trips followed the completion of a film that marked significant risk on Chaplin's part, as well as a period of some personal scandal publicized in the press.

When Chaplin left for London in September 1921, he had recently completed his first feature comedy, *The Kid*. The film was important for several reasons. First, as Charles Maland points out, it followed close on the heels of two relative failures, *Sunnyside* (1919) and *A Day's Pleasure*

(1919) (55). Second, articles began to crop up in the press at this time, such as "Is the Charlie Chaplin Vogue Passing?" (Farmer 249) in which the author asserts that Chaplin's appeal was the result of repetition and that he objected to "styling Charles Chaplin a great artist when he's nothing of the sort" (249). Also, not only was the film six reels long, but it took the risk of juxtaposing scenes of comedy with those of pathos in a bold new way.[2] In addition, Chaplin was just recovering from his first divorce scandal; his divorce from actress Mildred Harris became final in August of that year. Despite Maland's suggestions that the press treated Chaplin with gentleness (44) in their handling of the divorce, *The Des Moines Sunday Register* devoted two full pages of their Sunday magazine to Mildred Harris's court testimony during the proceedings.[3] Copyrighted by the International Features Service, the article would have appeared in newspapers throughout America's heartland, thereby presenting Chaplin as a "real" person who contradicted his film persona.

His 1931-32 trip was propelled by much the same set of conditions. *City Lights*, the film he released just before his departure, despite its synchronized sound track, was essentially a silent film. By 1931, sound technology had been in place in the film business for more than five years.[4] Proof of the risk involved here for Chaplin is evidenced by the fact that he was compelled to secure venues for showing the film himself in both Hollywood and New York. He contributed significantly to the completion of H. L. Gumbiner's Los Angeles Theatre on Broadway in Los Angeles in order to show his film there. And in New York, he rented the George M. Cohan Theatre against the advice of his associates.[5] In his personal life, Chaplin had recently undergone two scandals—the long and tortuous divorce suit of his second wife, Lita Grey, and his debt of back taxes to the Internal Revenue Service. One closely followed the other in 1927. Whatever revelations the press had provided during the Chaplin-Harris divorce, the Chaplin-Grey divorce made them pale in comparison. Most scholars agree that the public was divided on the issue along the lines of education level and economic status—at least in the United States.[6] After the publication of Lita Grey's divorce complaint in a small brochure-sized document sold on street corners like any scandal sheet, the public began to choose sides.[7] For Chaplin were his colleagues in the arts and academia (including many members of the press); against him were the women's clubs and self-righteous moralizing middle America. In Europe, there was no split, for most refused to judge Chaplin's art on the basis of this particular human frailty. In an essay entitled "Hands Off Love," printed in *transition* in September 1927, a group of thirty-one European artists and intellectuals, including Louis Aragon, André Breton, Marcel Duhamel, Max Ernst, Man Ray, and others transmitted their own comments on Chaplin's situation to the public:

> A Dog's Life. That is at the very moment the life of a man whose genius won't win him his case; of one on whom everyone's back will be turned, who will be ruined with impunity, from whom all of his means of expression will be taken, who is being demoralized in the most outrageous fashion, for the benefit of a miserable, spiteful little bourgeoisie, and for the sake of the grandest public hypocrisy possible to imagine. A dog's life. Genius is nothing to the law when matrimony is at stake, the blessed state of matrimony. And anyway as we know, genius is never anything to the law, never. (10)

The American government chose this inconvenient moment (20 January, to be precise) to sue Chaplin for back taxes, seizing and sealing all of his assets, including the studio (Maland 97). By 1931, though, despite the predictions listed in the essay cited above, public rancor had largely been shelved, but the specter of its ability to arise at any moment must have added to the tense atmosphere that surrounded the production of *City Lights*. As I have tried to show, both junctures (the release of *The Kid* in 1921 and the release of *City Lights* in 1931) were tentative ones in Chaplin's career and might make or break him professionally. As such, these junctures demanded strong and innovative promotional texts. At each of these points, the travel narrative comes to the rescue, for following each tour, Chaplin released a "promotional" travel book: *My Trip Abroad* (1922) and "A Comedian Sees the World" (1933-34) respectively.

Historical Context

The world Chaplin decided to tour in early February 1931 was in crisis, both economic and political. In Germany, Hitler had been agitating the populace against the tenets of the Treaty of Versailles since the late 1920s. The British ambassador in Berlin, Sir Horace Rumbold (who was to accompany Chaplin to the theater in Berlin in March 1931), in a memo to his financial adviser in March 1929, warned that if war reparations were set at the rumored two million marks, "'there may be a pretty good row over here leading perhaps to the holding of fresh elections'" (qtd. in Gilbert 757). Nazis and other political groups in Germany became less and less willing to bear the brunt of World War I guilt on their shoulders. Also, the country itself became less and less able to pay. In fact, the gold standard was causing major problems to the economies of countries across the world. As Carroll Quigley suggests, "it was estimated that the world's stock of gold money needed to increase by 3.1 percent per year in the 1920s to support the world's economic development with stable prices on the gold standard. The production of new gold after 1920 was below this rate" (340). This, combined with the League of Nations' recommendation that all countries get on the gold standard, caused a "gold rush" and subsequent gold shortage. The fact that gold was no longer being distributed evenly among countries—as occurred before World War I—suggested as well that the economic system of that prewar period was no longer adequate. In fact, the United States' practice of extending credit indiscriminately at this time caused the Federal Reserve to curtail this practice, with the result that more credit was extended to stock market speculators than before, even though the Reserve's measure was supposed to alleviate this problem. The resulting stock market crash on 24 October 1929 in New York sent shock waves around the world. Possibly one of the worst years for Europe and especially for countries like Austria and Britain was 1931.

What is so intensely interesting about "A Comedian Sees the World" is that Chaplin, when the historical context is investigated, was on the heartbeat of many of the major events and people of 1931. When Chaplin expressed to Ramsay MacDonald his approval of the effects of the dole on his beloved Cockneys during a visit to Chequers in February (pt I: 86-87), he was speaking to the first Labour Parliament prime minister of a parliament that Carroll Quigley argues sealed the fate of the American stock market crash in 1929 because British citizens immediately sent their money to America after its election. On 26 February, at dinner at Churchill's Chartwell in which several young members of Parliament were present, Chaplin remarked that "Lenins and Ghandis do not make revolutions" (pt II: 15) when Gandhi himself was just days away (4 March) from being released from prison by the viceroy, Lord Irwin, after promising to cease his campaign of civil disobedience. Nor could Chaplin have predicted that the financial crisis of 1931,[8] when it reached London by late summer, forced a repeal of this same public assistance that he had touted to MacDonald and demanded the installment of a National government for the first time, composed of four Conservative, three Labour, and two Liberal ministers. As Quigley relates,

> the pound sterling was very vulnerable. There were five principal reasons: 1) the pound was overvalued; 2) costs of production in Britain were much more rigid than prices; 3) gold reserves were precariously small; 4) the burden of public debt was too great in a deflationary atmosphere; 5) there were greater liabilities than assets in short-term international holdings in London (about £407 million to £153 million). (345)

France and the United States lent £130 million to Britain in July and August to fight the depreciation of the pound by circulating more dollars and francs. Still the gold continued to leave the country, totaling £200 million in two months. By 18 September, when Chaplin was back in London, New York City and Paris, France refused further credits to the British Treasury (Quigley 345-46). The crisis also forced Britain off the gold standard on 21 September, just a month before the election Chaplin witnessed in the company of Conservative Lady Astor. The Conservatives won the majority in the election, but decided to keep the National government with Ramsay MacDonald at the helm to allow for greater stability.

Hereafter, the world was no longer unified by one economic system for all; it tended to be organized into the sterling bloc about Britain and the gold bloc about the United States, France, Belgium, The Netherlands, and Switzerland (Gilbert 347). However, recovery from the Depression did not result from the abandonment of gold in Britain because of the deflationary policy it instituted. Neither prices nor employment rose until 1933 and from then on, improvement was slow (Gilbert 348).

When Chaplin visited Berlin from 9-16 March 1931, Hitler sent (on the 15th) this directive to all Nazi Party officials: "'The natural hostility of the peasant against the Jews, and his hostility against the Freemason as a servant of the Jew, must be worked up to a frenzy'"(qtd. in Gilbert 793). Did Chaplin witness the violence of the Brown Shirts against the Jews, which had been going on with greater violence and frequency since 1930? Did he realize that unemployment in Germany had reached five million? Just days after Chaplin's departure from Berlin to Vienna, German Chancellor Brüning announced his intention to form a Customs Union with Austria, a proposal that was rejected by The League of Nations and The Court of Arbitration at The Hague. This decision caused a financial crash of similar proportions to Black Thursday in the United States because with the announcement of a possible *anschluss*, France removed all of its deposits from Austria's Creditanstalten. On 11 May, the Creditanstalten notified the Austrian government that it could no longer meet its obligations. As Martin Gilbert relates, "first Austria, and then, in rapid succession, Germany and Hungary, were plunged into a banking crisis that left millions of small investors penniless" (795). Coincidentally, Chaplin had visited a few members of the Reichstag, Reichsminister Dr. Joseph Wirth among them (Gersch 91-92), just a few short weeks before Chancellor Brüning was forced to close it (on 31 March) for seven months after a vote of no-confidence narrowly missed passage.

Gandhi was attending the Round Table conference, which opened at St. James Palace on 8 September when he met with Chaplin on 22 September 22. When the conference ended inconclusively on 1 December, "he intimated that the Indian national movement and the British government had come to a parting of the ways, and that nonviolent civil disobedience might soon be revived" (Gilbert 799). Interestingly, it was Gandhi's people who suggested and arranged the meeting[9] with Chaplin, even though Gandhi had never even seen a Chaplin film. What did he expect to gain from such a meeting? Did Chaplin gain or suffer further British consternation from it? Back in India by 28 December, Gandhi was arrested once again on 4 January 1932 for further civil disobedience.

Although Chaplin never mentions it in "A Comedian Sees the World," Japan was beginning to cause problems already in 1931 through its constant aggressiveness toward China. On 18 September, just a few months before Chaplin's arrival with his brother in Kobe and following the assas-

sination of Captain Nakamura, the Japanese troops in Manch
mobilized and took Mukden (Gilbert 806). During Chaplin's visi
liberal Prime Minister Inukai was assassinated (he had hoped to
policy of friendly relations with China) and Chaplin was soon to fi
that his life was also in danger there during his stay. Still, he manag
meet the new premier, Satai, just before he departed on 2 June.

Finally, as Chaplin arrived back in Los Angeles on 16 June, an int
national conference on reparations opened in Lausanne, Switzerland. On
July, the conference approved everything the Germans asked for; "The onl
reparations that were retained were a final and nominal demand for 3000
marks" (Gilbert 815). While Lloyd George and Philip Sassoon may have
yawned and looked at their watches during some of Chaplin's economic
diatribes during the tour, it's uncanny how many of his suggestions were
adopted.[10] Getting off the gold standard, as Chaplin advised,[11] did turn
out to be the best thing for Britain. Ending war reparations for Germany
was also sound advice, although by mid-1932, this measure failed to calm
the already riled and vengeful German populace as agitated by Hitler and
others.

Chaplin's Published Travel Narratives

Chaplin's two travel narratives are essentially promotional vehicles—a fact
that should not be surprising if one considers his affinity for the business
side of film, surmised from an anecdote included in his autobiography about
early business inclinations: "There was a strong element of the merchant in
me. I was continuously preoccupied with business schemes. I would look
at empty shops, speculating as to what profitable businesses I could make
of them, ranging from fish and chips to grocery shops" (60). Neither is it
surprising, then, that Chaplin was in Europe on each tour to promote his
newest film—*The Kid* (1921) and *City Lights* (1931), respectively. *My Trip
Abroad* reveals the fact that Chaplin carried his films into Germany for the
first time on this trip and that he also attended the first of many premieres
of his work. The Charles Chaplin Film Corporation correspondence during
this time demonstrates that the second tour's venues were chosen with the
intention of staging premieres of *City Lights* in the chosen city, which then
would be enhanced by a personal appearance of Chaplin himself.[12] Letters

to Chaplin and Arthur Kelly, his representative at the United Artists' New York office, from Boris Evelinoff, Chaplin's European United Artists representative, written and sent the same day (12 December 1935), promise that "ce ne sera pas difficile de reconstruire la grande popularité et l'enthousiasme autour de génie de notre grand Patron 'Charlie,'"[13]—the same publicity as Chaplin had during the 1931-32 tour on what Evelinoff calls "un voyage de propagande en faveur de Charlie." Chaplin managed to get in a little rest and relaxation on the beaches of the French Riviera and the slopes of St. Moritz, but it is clear that these occasions are beside the point. Both the 1921 and 1931-32 tours were clearly arranged for promotional reasons.

However, *My Trip Abroad* seems, at first glance, to be a book recounting Chaplin's exploits on his first trip home to England in 1921 since his great cinematic success.[14] The book was so unimportant to him late in life that, although it is clear that he borrowed from it nearly verbatim for relevant passages in *My Autobiography* in 1964 when Chaplin was in his seventies, he fails to mention the book or the writing of it at all in that text. Chaplin scholars largely dismiss the work as well. Wes D. Gehring, in *Charlie Chaplin: A Bio-Bibliography*, offers a typical review of the work:

> Discarding his "literary" aspirations, in *My Trip Abroad* Chaplin merely records the significant events of his 1921 trip to Europe. The result is a seemingly endless repetition of the important books he read or took along, the important people he met, and the generally unprecedented public response he received. (23)

However, print reviews of the book at its release in 1922 were overwhelmingly complimentary and favorable.[15] Chaplin's most respected biographer, David Robinson (*Chaplin: His Life and Art*) provides some information surrounding *My Trip Abroad*'s genesis:

> Chaplin's record of the trip was mostly written in the course of the train journey back to California, and was taken down at his dictation by a young newspaperman, Monta Bell [. . .]. The account originally appeared as a series of articles in *Photoplay* before publication in book form as *My Trip Abroad* (*My Wonderful Visit*, for the English edition). (290-91)[16]

The book then came to be serialized additionally in *Movie Weekly*, *Screenland*, and twenty-nine newspapers around the country (mostly second-string papers, such as the *Chicago News* and the *New York Evening World*), as well as being translated into twelve languages other than English within ten years of its initial publication.

Robinson states that "some Chaplin biographers have suggested that the text was 'ghosted' by [Monta] Bell, but the style is too distinctive and the analysis of Chaplin's reactions and sensations far too personal for that" (305). My research in the Charlie Chaplin Archive, however, suggested that *My Trip Abroad* was more likely a collaborative effort. Although the contract for it lists as its second point that the "author is sole author and proprietor of said work," the author being listed as Charles Chaplin, Louis Monta Bell[17] is listed as due to receive 1.5 percent of Chaplin's 10 percent of the profits in the fifth point of the contract "for services rendered by him in connection with the writing of such work."[18] Correspondence between P. C. Eastment of McClure Newspaper Syndicate dated 19 October 1921 suggests the details of the financial deal regarding the serialization of *My Trip Abroad* (which was to predate the publication by Harpers & Bros.). It should be noted that Chaplin's press agent at the time was involved:

> In accordance with our conversation with you and your representative Mr. Carlyle Robinson, it is agreed that you will furnish material for a story of your trip abroad, to be written over your signature to us. [. . .] This story is to consist of approximately 50,000 to 60,000 words and is to be prepared by a thoroughly trained newspaper man and submitted to you and your representative for revision and approval before [being] published in the newspapers.

A later letter, also from Eastment, dated 16 February 1922, reveals some information on the way Bell may have become involved. Eastment writes: "I have no doubt that you are finding Mr. Bell both very delightful and very useful to you and I feel pleased for your mutual sakes that our little business deal brought you together." Bell himself, writing to Chaplin in November 1921, reveals this about his writing project: "I have sent 3 batches of copy back for you to read, through Robinson. I still have about thirty thousand words to write and expect to be finished with it in about a week." According

Cover art from the debut installment of "A Comedian Sees the World," in *Woman's Home Companion*, September 1933. (*Author's collection*)

to Chaplin Studios correspondence, Bell then submitted the final chapter in early December 1921. More important, though, is an unpublished typescript found late in my research. It was a typescript dated 24 May 1960 and titled "Monta Bell"—a typescript found among Chaplin's draft and manuscript material for *My Autobiography*. Chaplin's first line of this typescript serves as his admission in print of Bell's role. It reads "Monta Bell, the newspaper man who ghost wrote my book *My Trip Abroad*." This evidence clearly shows that Chaplin did not write the book alone. It was essentially a solicited and paid-for promotional product. Not surprisingly, there are no drafts of any kind for this work in the archives.

For "A Comedian Sees the World," on the other hand, there are several. Its published form comprises five parts, which appeared starting with the September 1933 issue of *Woman's Home* Companion[19] (Crowell Publishing, Springfield, Ohio) and ended with the January 1934 issue. The managing editor for this series was Willa Roberts.[20] While Timothy Lyons and Charles Maland (128) are among the scholars who state that the series appeared in book form, my close examination of the "book" listed on *Worldcat*, a database of library collections around the world, showed that a volume listed as part of the Museum of Modern Art's collection was nothing but a manual compilation of the five *Woman's Home Companion* installments bound into one volume. In fact, the series was never published in book form, despite Chaplin's original desire that this should happen.[21] Due to this fact, it never reached the world outside the United States and, therefore, had neither the financial nor promotional impact of *My Trip Abroad*. It differs from *My Trip Abroad* in several other important ways. First, from the primary documents in the Charlie Chaplin Archive, it can be ascertained that this series was largely Chaplin's own and as such it is perhaps the first instance of his own writing to appear in print, except for the "economic policy," which he released to the papers on 27 June 1933—a document that also resulted from the 1931-32 trip.

Chaplin is unique in the film business for utilizing the travel narrative as a promotional tool. His close companions, Douglas Fairbanks and Mary Pickford, also tried their hands at writing; Fairbanks wrote two men's self-help books, *Laugh and Live* (1917) and *Making Life Worthwhile* (1918), and Pickford made her debut with *Rendezvous with Life* (1935). The travel narrative, however, proves to be the perfect exploitation tool for the Little Tramp character, whether Chaplin realized it or not. Because toys, postcards, and other Little Tramp items often showed the persona in the guise of a typical tourist, accompanied by "luggage" of one type or another, golf

Belgian postcard published to commemorate Chaplin's visit, 1931. (*Author's collection*)

clubs, or collections of postcards and viewing typical tourist sites, Chaplin's audience would easily have accepted the travel narrative as a likely venue for him. Either Chaplin himself or possibly his press agent at the time, Carlyle Robinson (who dabbled in producing travel films after his departure from Chaplin's employ), made that connection and then masterfully exploited it.

Archival Materials

"A Comedian Sees the World" exists in several partial drafts in the Charlie Chaplin Archive. There is a manuscript draft that, when transcribed, is only thirteen pages long and makes up only a small portion of Part I, up only to the point at which he recounts the dinner at Lady Astor's. Several pages of this manuscript are written over and over with nearly the same wording, much the way Chaplin is known to have worked in the medium of film. As Anna Fiaccarini and Cecilia Cenciarelli write in "Chaplin as Author," "writing is for Chaplin an exercise, a job, feverish craftsmanship: its pleasure lies in the search for perfection, through its rigour and discipline" (22). Even with this very small amount of the whole in manuscript form, though, I can begin to see Chaplin's initial foci for the series, including rhetorical strategies he would use throughout the work.

Next, a typescript draft that appears to have some integrity (it has numbered pages to page 76 and follows the sequence of the published series fairly closely) exists, also in the archives. This document would appear to be the studio secretary's (Catherine Hunter's) attempt to translate an often difficult-to-read manuscript into typed form. However, more importantly, this draft has evidence of Chaplin's handwritten deletions and annotations, some written right on the page and others on the back of the preceding page. In most cases, he is clear about where such additions should be located in the text, even numbering changes in some places in order to help with clarity.

This draft deals only with the content of what would be Part I, Part II, and about half of Part III. It ends with Chaplin's first few days spent on the French Riviera, which is essentially June 1931, and it is missing pages 47-53. In addition to this typescript, there is another one—also 76 pages— that appears to be a draft later than the one just described. It contains the changes Chaplin demands in his handwriting on the first typescript. Handwritten comments on this draft are in someone's hand other than Chaplin's (perhaps Hunter herself) and are confined to questions of spelling, punctuation, and getting names, dates, and places correct. In addition to this material, I found one typescript page that was on letter-sized paper, unlike the other typescript drafts, which are on 8 ½ inches by 14 inches, an indication to me that at least one other typescript draft existed at one time. This seems to be the only surviving page from this manuscript (page 63). It was also filed in with the "economic policy" papers.

Interestingly, even though he would be abroad for another entire year, only half of the series dealt with this period (June 1931-June 1932). In addition, the existence of a typescript draft for only this half of the series is consistent with correspondence between Syd Chaplin and Alf Reeves, the Chaplin Studios manager, who noted in a letter dated 30 March 1933 that Miss Roberts, the managing editor of *Woman's Home Companion* and the individual who courted Chaplin's work for her publication, "whilst she was laudatory in her comments on the first half of the story, [. . .] does not appear quite so pleased with the second half remitted later, and has asked Charlie to make some changes, which, however, he does not feel inclined to do." However, in the archives, I was able to locate several pages and partial pages of typescripts that ended up being included at points in the final version of the second half. One of these was a three-page typescript entitled "BALI," which contained what would be the first few paragraphs of Part V of the series. This typescript had a handwritten page that contains the only evidence I found of an outline, or a brainstorm, for the work. Because it's so unique and may provide some concrete evidence of Chaplin's composition process, I include a transcription of it here in its entirety:

Bali

Different from other Tropic mixtures

Captain talks of other islands as wilder—Bali more romantic—Isle of rats—Isle of white people—very few cannibals left—my first reaction—North Bali—South Bali—while progressing more Natives—my brother nudges me—our quest—the meals of the Hotel the food—Hirshfeld the artist ??—The House ?? furnished—music that night—I meet Hirshfeld Landsend—what they drew—

they describe their ways—the present & the beauty—tea at the ??—the native girls' covering—

I found other "pieces" of the second half as well. A two-page typescript filed in with the "economic policy" typescripts, entitled "Depression #1," appears in the final version as an addition to the scene in Einstein's apart-

Manuscript page from "A Comedian Sees the World." (*Charlie Chaplin Archive*)

Theater. The season's showmen of our business said it was a
bad location, off the beaten path of movie goers, the rent
was too exorbitant, etc.   All this was very discouraging as
I had had enough trouble making the picture without having ~~seeit~~
the ~~ixx~~ task of exploiting it, but I was determined to ~~go~~ through
~~it.~~

  Upon my arrival in New York, I discovered that ~~hardly~~
~~a word had been mentioned about the opening.~~ Nobody seemed to
know when or where "City Lights" would play - and only five
days before the opening. What little advertising had been done,
was not informing enough. Such phrases as "Our old favorite is with
us again," etc., were useless. What was necessary ~~was~~/to tell the
public ~~was~~ that "City Lights" would open at the Cohen Theater
at popular prices and continuous performances. So I got busy
giving instructions to my staff. I insisted that when advertising:
Cohen Theater, Popular prices, and Continuous performances were
to be featured as big as my own name. ~~I added another $12,000.00~~
~~to the advertising budget. Again the wiseacres shook their~~
~~heads. They said I should take the terms of the movie~~
~~houses even if it was less. However, having spent $1,800,000.00~~
~~of my own money and two years of nerve wracking work, I was~~
~~determined it was to be a make or break proposition. So I spread~~
~~myself over full page ads in every important New York Journal.~~
Having adjusted the advertising the next problem was the
Theater. I discovered the screen was too large for the size of the
house. Half of the seats would be useless and uncomfortable with
such a size screen so we reduced it ~~with the~~ as a result ~~when~~ we got better
vision and sharper photography. I might say they were five anxious
days ~~before.~~ Everything depended upon this opening. Fortunately it
was a success. The press were unanimous ~~x~~ in their praise and
contrary to all gloomy prognostigations, we broke all records for a
New York engagement and made four time the amount of money I had ever
received from a previous engagement. This

Typescript page from "A Comedian Sees the World." (*Charlie Chaplin Archive*) ment in Berlin in Part III. Another three-quarter-page typescript entitled "Japan #27" appears in the last few paragraphs of Part V and is Chaplin's description of the Japanese tea ceremony for that section. In addition, a single untitled, short typed paragraph on one sheet of paper becomes the final paragraph for the series in its published version. And finally, there is a typescript several pages in length, entitled "Notes for the Final Chapter," none of which was included in the final version. This proposed final chapter for the series was an overview of the effects of the economic Depression on Europe and Asia and Chaplin's own suggestions for solving the problems he saw and described.

The *My Autobiography* Version

Chaplin relates in his 1964 *My Autobiography* that:

> After my arrival in London, [...] I wanted change, new experiences, new faces; I wanted to cash in on this business of being a celebrity. I had just one date, and that was with H. G. Wells. After that, I was freelancing, with the dubious hope of meeting other people.
>
> "I have arranged a dinner for you at the Garrick Club," said Eddie Knoblock.
>
> "Actors, artists, and authors," I said jokingly. "But where is this exclusive English set, these country homes and house parties that I'm not invited to?" I wanted that rarer sphere of ducal living. Not that I was a snob, but I was a tourist, sight-seeing. (271)

So begins a franker version of Chaplin's 1921 tour. In fact, a comparison of his version of the two tours in this volume shows just how different they are from the versions contained in *My Trip Abroad* and "A Comedian Sees the World." Chaplin explains shortly after the passage cited above that it was only his inauspicious meeting with Sir Philip Sassoon that provided his entrée into the circle of society he wished to experience, another fact never provided by the travel narrative version. Included in Chaplin's autobiography but not in his travel narratives are elements of his behavior that his audience would have considered un-Little-Tramp-like, such as his frank opinions about celebrated individuals, which make him seem too much a sort of verbal commentator, and sexual exploits that make him seem successful with women—something the Little Tramp rarely was. Also, his receipt of the Légion d'Honneur medal, his frequent visits with the Prince of Wales, his material acquisitiveness, as well as his tireless efforts for charitable causes are all evidence of a level of affluence that would conflict with the Little Tramp's apparent poverty. In addition, the Europe of the 1930s he experienced was not entirely a venue of high and lascivious living but instead is best represented by Chaplin's final words on the subject: "I saw food rotting, goods piled high while people wandered hungrily about them, millions of unemployed and their services going to waste" (377). This great disparity between the two versions of these tours (from *My Autobiography* and from *My Trip Abroad* or "A Comedian Sees the World") again supports an unstated promotional agenda for the travel narratives' versions, one that seems to include a deliberate conflation of Chaplin's public and filmic personae.

Aftershock

The social consciousness that Chaplin's world tours helped him to develop demonstrably affected his later creative work. The rise of the machines and the fall of the worker as portrayed in *Modern Times*, the palpable and destructive nationalism of Hynkel's minions in *The Great Dictator*, and the tacit desperation of the lowly bank clerk forced to kill the weak and trusting in order to feed his own family in *Monsieur Verdoux* are three obvious examples of this consciousness. Maland notes that by the end of his world tour, "Chaplin was beginning to speak out more often on political affairs, and reporters found them newsworthy" (141). By the mid-1930s, his political opinions "became an inextricable part of his star image" (Maland 133) and his next three films especially (listed above) were more didactic, perhaps due to this fact. David Robinson writes about the effect the tour had on the film *Modern Times*, for instance. He points to Chaplin's "diatribe against complacent acceptance of the growth of the machine age" in a speech following a lunch at Lady Astor's Cliveden early in the tour as "the genesis" of the film (424). More than just the social commentary present in *Modern Times*, though, influences of the tour can be seen in all of Chaplin's remaining films. In *The Great Dictator*, the viewer sees the same "ridiculous figures that stand upon the edge of the roof [. . .] for all the world like bal-

ancing acrobats" ("A Comedian Sees the World" pt. II: 16) adorning the
buildings lining the "Unter den Linden" of Adenoid Hynkel's capital city.
In the scene in which Napaloni meets with Hynkel in his palace for the first
time, we see echoes of his experience with King Albert of the Belgians in
which the towering King offers the diminutive Chaplin a tiny seat during
an audience in Paris ("A Comedian Sees the World" pt. II: 108). *Monsieur
Verdoux* cannot be separated from the effects of Chaplin's 1931-32 world
visit. He witnessed Verdouxs firsthand there; he visited the same cities in
which Verdoux has "wives." Even his anecdote about Hetty Kelly, which
begins Part I of the series, finds its way almost verbatim into the film. The
young woman Verdoux spares from the poisoned wine has now become
rich and prosperous. She is Hetty, several years after Chaplin's first failed
relationship with her:

> I was crossing Picadilly when the screech of an automobile made
> me turn in the direction of a black limousine, which had stopped
> abruptly. A small gloved hand waved from the window. There must
> be some mistake, I thought, when a voice unmistakably called,
> "Charlie?"
>
> As I approached, the door of the car opened and there was
> Hetty beckoning me to get in. She had left the troupe and had been
> living on the Continent with her sister. Oh, yes, her sister had mar-
> ried an American multimillionaire. All this as we drove along.
>
> "Now tell me something about yourself," she said eyeing me
> kindly.
>
> "There is very little to tell," I answered. (pt. I: 8)

Limelight, a film set in London, surely came, not just from Chaplin's
own memories of childhood, but also from his return trips to Kennington in 1921 and 1931. In "A Comedian Sees the World," Chaplin notes to
Ramsay MacDonald that he is pleased to see none of "the old gray-haired
ladies sleeping on the Thames embankment" (pt. I: 87). In *Limelight*, the
viewer sees such a lady when Terry and Calvero walk the embankment
after midnight in one scene; in another Calvero predicts a similar fate for
himself. Also, Chaplin encountered "Calveros" everywhere in London. The
media picked up one such moment when Chaplin meets his old nemesis

from his days with the Karno Company in America, Arthur Dandoe, now working as a lowly sidewalk artist and slips him some money. His visit to a meeting of the Water Rats in November 1931, a sort of fraternity of old music hall performers, must have provided even more material for developing this character.

The tour's influence continued even when Chaplin relocated in Europe and began to make films there. Certainly, King Shadov of *A King in New York* is a caricature of European royalty such as he met on the tour and his hotel suite similar to many he stayed in. The society dame, Mona Cromwell, could easily be Lady Deterding at the Hotel Crillon, Elsa Maxwell, or half a dozen others. The boys' school may have been suggested by Chaplin's visit to the Ballard Institute with Lady Astor in November 1931. And, as Robinson reports, *A Countess from Hong Kong* was at its genesis a script written for Paulette Goddard in the later 1930s, most likely from Chaplin's long relationship with May Reeves over the course of the tour.

There was another important change taking place in Chaplin's creative life as well. He was fast developing an interest in writing, one that would continue throughout his life. Robinson reveals Chaplin's writing process fairly accurately, noting that "he would first write everything out in longhand, and then dictate it to his secretary. Afterwards he would work over the typescript, and successive secretaries were astonished at how he would labour over a word, trying different positions or variations" (453). While there is no evidence left that the process of getting the handwritten manuscript to the typescript page was through dictation, there can be no doubt that Chaplin's writing process was every bit as arduous as his filmmaking one. Even so, because he devoted all of 1932 and 1933 through to 22 February to the task of writing "A Comedian Sees the World," he became both familiar with and somewhat confident of the writing process. The overwhelming volume of written material Chaplin produced from this period onward must be proof of that. In essence, his epiphany, which marked the close of "A Comedian Sees the World"—"a desire for accomplishment—not in the old way but in something new; perhaps in another field of endeavor" (pt. V: 86)—resulted in Chaplin the writer.

A Comedian Sees the World [1]

Part I[2]

By Charles Chaplin (1933)[3]

The most popular actor in the world pieces together the fragments of his youth and his struggles, recapturing the past in today's glory

In the past twenty years I have made seven trips from Los Angeles to New York and one memorable visit to Europe. These excursions were for business reasons only and were never without the sword of Damocles above my head. No wonder, when living in Los Angeles for twenty years, that in the interim of work I became an easy victim to sentimental lapses. Hence all my troubles.

The disillusion of love, fame, and fortune left me somewhat apathetic. There seemed nothing, to turn to outside of my work, and that, after twenty years, was becoming irksome. I needed emotional stimulus.

I am tired of love and people and like all egocentrics, I turn to myself. I want to live in my youth again, to capture the moods and sensations of childhood, so remote from me now—so unreal—almost like a dream. I need to turn back time,; to venture into the blurred past and bring it into focus.

Thrilled with this adventure I buy maps of London and here in my California home I retrace road lines, bringing back memories of places that affected me as a boy.

High factory walls that depressed me, houses that frightened me, bridges that saddened me. I want to capture some of the hurt and joy again. To see the orphan asylum where, as a child of five, I lived two long years. Those cold bleak days in the playground! I want to see the drill hall where on rainy days we were sheltered, sniveling around half-heated water pipes; the large dining-room with its long tables and forms; the smell of sawdust and butter as we entered the kitchen.

These memories have landmarks and I want to stand in the midst of them before it's too late. Something may have happened. The school may be pulled down. I cannot bear to be disappointed this time.

My first trip to England was a disappointment. Not my reception. On the contrary. Friends and everyone were kind to me. But in another respect, which reason I shall explain.

It is necessary to digress and go back to a spiritually starved youth of nineteen earning a sporadic living as a vaudeville sketch artist,[4] as we termed ourselves. In those days life was lonely. My social precincts were limited. I yearned for more than my environment could give me. Those were melancholy days without romance or beauty until one August night something happened.

We were playing a suburban theater. I was standing in the wings, waiting my turn to go on. A troupe of girls was dancing. One of them slipped and the rest smiled—one especially, a brunette with big brown laughing eyes.

She turned to the wings and caught my gaze. Never had I beheld such beauty. I was enthralled. She was conscious of my admiration for her smile became a look of embarrassment.

When she came off to change, however, she asked me to mind her wrap. It had a perfume of lavender. I have liked this perfume ever since.

When they had finished she came for it.

"Thank you," she said and we both stood smiling, but the moment was interrupted by the manager of the troupe.

"Come on, girls, we're late." They were working in another theater. She turned to pick up her things.

"Let me help you," I exclaimed taking her makeup box and opening the exit door.

"See you tomorrow night," she said eagerly.

I could only nod, not trusting myself to speak. As she was leaving through the outer door, she looked back over her shoulder. "Don't forget," she said shyly.

"I won't forget," I replied.

That was the beginning. Each night we would meet for a few moments. We never saw each other during the day, both being busy with rehearsals, and so we arranged to meet at Kennington Gate Sunday afternoon at four o'clock.

I was all dressed up for the occasion; a double-breasted coat pinched at the waist, derby hat, cane, and gloves. I rattled my thirty shillings impatiently.

The Sunday was a typical one. Discarded tram tickets littered the deserted streets and a news sheet blew aimlessly in the road. It was four minutes to four. I was wondering what she looked like without her stage make-up. Somehow I couldn't visualize her features. The more I tried, the more vague my impressions became. Perhaps she was not so beautiful off-stage.

At last I saw someone approaching who answered her description. My heart sank as she came nearer. Not a trace of the beauty I had imagined. I was despondent. However, I braced up. I must give the impression of being enthused, I thought. It would be cruel to display signs of disappointment.

She was almost up to me now. She was looking directly my way. I was about to smile. But she turned her head and passed on. It was not she! Thank heavens, it was not she! I breathed a sigh of relief. The suspense was terrific. It was one minute past four.

A street car slowed up. The occupants were getting off. At last a slender-looking girl, neatly dressed in blue serge and looking radiantly beautiful, alighted and came toward me. I recognized her at once. It was Hetty, more lovely than I had dreamed. What a wonderful day that was!

That night after seeing her home I walked the Thames Embankment. I was all choked up with emotion. I wanted to express my happiness. I wanted to make a gesture. There were nineteen shillings left in my pocket. I lined up a crowd of derelicts to a near-by coffee stall and handed out tea and sandwiches until the money was spent. Such was the reaction of a youth in love.

What happened was the inevitable. After all, the episode was but a childish infatuation to her, but to me it was the beginning of a spiritual development, a reaching out for beauty. I suppose I must have burdened her with my unabated attentions, for she tired quickly and we parted.

I went through the youthful misery of unrequited love. Later she left with the troupe for the Continent and I lost sight of her for two years, but the next time we met it was in a curious way.

I was crossing Piccadilly when the screech of an automobile made me turn in the direction of a black limousine, which had stopped abruptly. A small, gloved hand waved from the window. There must be some mistake, I thought, when a voice unmistakably called, "Charlie!"

As I approached, the door of the car opened and there was Hetty, beckoning me to get in. She had left the troupe and had been living on the Continent with her sister. Oh yes, her sister had married an American multimillionaire. All this as we drove along.

"Now tell me something about yourself," she said eyeing me kindly.

"There is very little to tell," I answered. "I am still doing the same old grind—trying to be funny. I think I shall try my luck in America."

"Then I shall see you there," she interposed.

"Oh, yes, I'll fix that up with my secretary," I laughed ironically.

"But I mean it," she insisted. "You know I've thought of you a good deal since the old days."

Again I was lifted into paradise, yet in the back of my mind I knew it was more hopeless than ever now.

That evening we spent visiting her brother and mother; Hetty was to leave the following day for Paris. We said good-bye and she promised to write. But after one letter she ceased corresponding. Later I left for America.

Soon after I read of her arrival there with her sister. The thought of meeting her now embarrassed me. The affluence of her position added to my sense of inferiority complex. Yet I would often walk by the house on Fifth Avenue where she lived, hoping to meet her accidentally, but nothing ever came of it. Eventually I gave up the idea of ever seeing her again.

Then came my adventure into motion pictures—my sudden rise to popularity.

I had arrived in New York to sign million-dollar contracts. Now is my opportunity to meet her, I thought, but somehow I cannot do it normally. I couldn't go to her house or send a letter. I am too shy. However, I stayed on in New York, hoping to meet her accidentally.

A New York paper had a headline: "Chaplin in Hiding—Nowhere to be Found." Nothing of the kind. If they had noticed a taxi waiting on the opposite side of a certain house on Fifth Avenue, they would have found the culprit.

At last I ran across her brother. I invited him to dinner. He was always aware of my devotion to his sister and was a little shy about discussing her. So during the meal we talked of my affairs.

Eventually I broached the subject. "By the bye, how's your sister?"

"Oh, she's quite well. Of course you know she's married and living in England."

I immediately made up my mind to leave New York and all the nonsense and get back to work.

During the year that intervened, I would occasionally glance over my mail on the chance of finding a particular "e" that was characteristic of her writing. One day a letter came.

I recognized it at once. I tore it open immediately. It was signed "Mrs.—" and in brackets, "Hetty."

She began: "Do you remember me after all these years? I have often thought of you, but never had the courage to write."

What irony! She never had the courage to write!

In conclusion she stated: "If ever you come to London, look me up."

The contents seemed strange and far off. But I was going to London. How wonderful it would be to see her again—this time without the inferiority of my youth. It would be an intellectual adventure.

Whatever happens, I thought, I will not be disappointed. I am too philosophical for that.

I had several weeks before the completion of my picture, but at last my affairs were in shape and I was on my way to England.[5]

The boat arrived in Southampton. There was a tremendous reception. I was received by the mayor. Hundreds of telegrams and wirelesses were waiting, inviting me to banquets and parties. The excitement was intense.

Hetty's brother was on the dock. Perhaps Hetty is with him, I thought. We greeted each other warmly. But she was not there! After the interviews with the press and the crowd demonstrations at the train, we were at last on our way to London.

Sonny, Hetty's brother, was in the carriage sitting beside me, telling me of the excitement in London and what a welcome I was to expect there. I listened politely, but I was preoccupied with other thoughts—. The thrill of meeting Hetty, what she would say, how she would act. I intended to be disarming, simple, and natural. You can afford to be yourself when you're successful.

Sonny and I were alone in the carriage. I hadn't noticed until then. There was something strange about his appearance. As usual, he avoided any mention of Hetty. There was a pause in the conversation. I looked out of the window at the revolving panorama of green fields. At last I ventured to remark: "Is your sister Hetty in town?"

"Hetty?" he said quietly. "I thought you knew. She died three weeks ago."

I was prepared for every disappointment but this. I felt I had been cheated out of an experience and my holiday had suddenly become aimless.

Up to that time I had lived with a vague ideal, a faint hope—never definitely analyzed—but always in the back of my mind. My success I had looked upon as a bouquet of flowers to be addressed to someone, and now the address was unknown.

So I have made up my mind not to be disappointed this time. It is dangerous to depend too much on people. They grow up and become other persons or pass out of our lives.

London, I feel, will remain the same. What little change has taken place will not affect my general impression and if I can capture some fragments of my youth, I shall feel amply rewarded.

The day I completed my current picture, *City Lights*, was one of extreme relief. After fretting and stewing for almost two years, to see the end in sight was like the finish of a marathon.

Usually after each picture I go to bed for a day or two to replenish my nerves, but this time there was another task ahead—the composing of the music and synchronizing it to the picture.[6] I can assure you it was a most nerve-racking experience, . But eventually everything was ready for the premiere showing in Los Angeles.

All first nights are terrifying. On these occasions I always feel that the picture was a mistake and should never have been made. The audience is excited and enthusiastic waiting for it to start.

If only I can sustain this enthusiasm, for there's always that lurking fear

Left to right: Albert Einstein, Chaplin, and Mrs. Einstein at the Los Angeles premiere of *City Lights,* January 30, 1931. (*Charlie Chaplin Archive*)

that they may be disappointed after they've seen it. However, I must walk the plank and accept what the gods have in store for me. When the first laugh comes, what music it is to my anxious ears.

Professor Einstein and his wife dined at my house that evening and went to the theater afterward. I sat between them during the performance. Occasionally I glanced at the professor. What a simple man he is! To think that with his mind he could enjoy a movie with the enthusiasm of a child.

He would laugh and exclaim, "Ach, das ist wunderbar! Das ist schön!" I shall write of the professor, but in a later chapter.

My friends convinced me that I had a success and after the ordeal of that first night in Los Angeles, I made plans to leave the following evening for New York.

Upon my arrival there[7] I invited the late Ralph Barton, the famous caricaturist and writer,[8] to come as my guest to Europe. He confessed to me that he had been feeling depressed, and that recently he had attempted suicide. Poor Ralph! I remember I tried to appeal to his ego.

"Life could never defeat me," I said. "Nothing matters, only physical pain. Our tragedies are only as big as we make them."

Ralph was creatively exhausted. This, I think, preyed on his mind and was partly the cause for his later killing himself.

I tried to cheer him up. "All artists experience a lull in their work. It is a period of replenishing the soil—of plowing in and turning under our past experiences and watering them afresh with new ones. But later you'll reap a creative harvest," I laughed. "What you need is adventure, so come to Europe."

He accepted my invitation, and we sailed for England on the *Mauretania*.

All journeys are long if you're in a hurry, and I counted the hours. My entourage consisted of my friend Ralph Barton, Carl Robinson,[9] my secretary, and Kono, "my man Friday," as I call him. He is everything—nurse, valet, private secretary, and bodyguard. He is Japanese and jack-of-all-trades.

Ralph was feeling better. I was "selling" him England. He was pro-French some three years ago and during my divorce troubles, he would implore me to leave America and come and live with him in France. "America is not civilized," he said. "Artists' lives are too much exposed to the scrutiny of the puritanical. But in France it is different. They are more intelligent about such matters."

Ralph had only recently returned from France, giving up his residence there because he felt he was too far away from his work.

He confessed he had never cared for England or the English. "They are a strange cold people, all bound up in archaic traditions and prehistoric customs. They are snobbish."

But I remonstrated. "Snobbishness is the national fault of all countries. Republics are the same. Take America—for example, its social register and its exclusive clubs, busy excluding. Your occupations and your sports come under a snobbish category. If you can claim two generations of polo-playing in your family, your social position is usually unassailable."

And so the time would pass, sitting up far into the night, discussing the pros and cons of everything.[10]

We were to land at Southampton, but I discovered Sir Malcolm Campbell[11] was getting off there, and thinking that the celebrated should divide the celebrating, we decided to get off at Plymouth and leave Southampton to Sir Malcolm.

It is seven in the morning when we arrive, but there are friends to greet us. After the preliminary interview with the press, we are safely installed in a private carriage on our way to London. Several journalists are on the train, some wanting special interviews, but I have to decline. If I started that sort of thing, I should never have a moment to myself.

However, they are very considerate and let me take a few minutes' nap. On awakening I find I am looking into three cameras. I have been snapped in every known position, both asleep and awake.

The English countryside looks sedate with its red brick houses and green fields, snugly hedged on all sides. There are new types of houses, similar to our small California bungalows. England has done a great deal of building since my last visit. Ralph is going into raptures over the beauty of the Devonshire countryside.

London at last! There is an enormous crowd at the station. As I get out I face a battery of fresh cameras. The police are trying to keep the crowds back. They are frenzied with excitement and I am enjoying it all. We are being carried along in the crush and they are all pushing and shoving. But I love it! It feels like an affectionate embrace.

I am looking into eager faces, eyes that dance with excitement, eyes that reveal the warmth of their affection. We are all caught up in the same emotions. It is their welcome as well as mine.

Why is it that London always wrings my heart? Is it the love of my people? They are my people, these Cockneys. I am one of them. As I look into their faces I see that spiritual hunger, that inner craving. Their emotions have made them inarticulate. They are only expressed by the eager clutching of my sleeve. How little must come into their lives! How appreciative they are for the trivial thing that I've done.

I turn to look at Ralph. There are tears in his eyes. Good heavens! If he starts that I'll be doing it also. But I check myself. This would appear maudlin. So I smile, pressing a finger and clutching a hand as we are bundled into a waiting limousine.

There is a rousing cheer as we leave. "God bless you, Charlie!" and we're on our way to the Carlton Hotel.

JAN 10 1934

Edited by
Gertrude B. Lane

VOL. LX NO. 9

Companion

WOMAN'S HOME

September 1933

WILLA ROBERTS
Managing Editor
HENRY B. QUINAN
Art Director

A Comedian

©A 5 56415

Sees the World

CHARLES CHAPLIN

The most popular actor in the world pieces together the fragments of his youth and his struggles, recapturing the past in today's glory

IN THE past twenty years I have made seven trips from Los Angeles to New York and one memorable visit to Europe. These excursions were for business reasons only and were never without the sword of Damocles above my head. No wonder, when living in Los Angeles for twenty years, that in the interim of work became an easy victim to sentimental lapses. Hence all my troubles.

The disillusion of love, fame and fortune left me somewhat apathetic. There seemed nothing to turn to outside of my work, and that, after twenty years, was becoming irksome. I needed emotional stimulus.

I am tired of love and people and like all egocentrics I turn to myself. I want to live in my youth again, to capture the moods and sensations of childhood, so remote from me now—so unreal—almost like a dream. I need to turn back time; to venture into the blurred past and bring it into focus.

Thrilled with this adventure I buy maps of London and here in my California home I retrace road lines, bringing back memories of places that affected me as a boy.

High factory walls that depressed me, houses that frightened me, bridges that saddened me. I want to capture some of the hurt and joy again. To see the orphan asylum where, as a child of five, I lived two long years. Those cold bleak days in the playground! I want to see the drill hall where on rainy days we were sheltered, sniveling around half-heated water pipes; the large dining-room with its long tables and forms; the smell of sawdust and butter as we entered the kitchen.

These memories have landmarks and I want to stand in the midst of them before it's too late. Something may have happened. The school may be pulled down. I cannot bear to be disappointed this time.

My first trip to England was a disappointment. Not my reception. On the contrary. Friends and everyone were kind to me. But in another respect, which reason I shall explain.

7

Chaplin signing for fans atop the Ritz Carlton Hotel, London. (*Charlie Chaplin Archive*)

My companions are visibly affected. My own emotions are mixed. I have an intense feeling of joy and pity that leaves a vacuum under my ribs. I sit back in the car, telling myself that I am in London—telling myself that ten years have intervened since my last visit. But too much is going on within me to fully drink in the realization of it. Things all appear two-dimensional. My impressions are surfaces. I sit back, numbed with excitement.

Crowds are waiting at the hotel. Again I am stirred. People's affection hurts me but it's a beautiful pain.

The Carlton Hotel! How many times I have looked through its doors as a boy and wondered at its grandeur, never realizing that I should ever engage a suite of rooms there. As I enter its portals these inner thoughts flash quickly through my mind, yet on the surface I seem to take it all for granted.

We are shown into a spacious suite of rooms. Letters and invitations are waiting for us. That night we dine at Sir Philip Sassoon's[12] house in Park Lane.

Wealth is usually a handicap to initiative. Nevertheless Sir Philip is one of the rich young men who have made careers for themselves in the government. I've always admired him for his active part in public affairs and the efficient service he renders his country.

The next morning I am up with the lark and before breakfast, I take a long walk over to the West End and then taxi over to Kennington, my old home.

The morning is bright and promising. As I pass each familiar spot I get a thrill. Dear old London! It is still the same. Here it is eight o'clock in the morning and I find myself all emotional, weeping on street corners.

It is no self-pity. It is the beauty of realization. The past seems to stand revealed, smiling and friendly. Feelings and sensations recur like strange dreams.

As I stand in Kennington Park a woman is sitting on a bench, and a little child runs lambent about the grass before her.

I see myself playing like that little child. I was about five at the time. A woman is sitting on that very same bench. My mother.

I remember there was something hopeless about that day. I never understood the situation. I had been playing in the Children's Gymnasium and decided to return and surprise her. As I approached quietly from behind, I became aware that she was softly weeping. I was so shocked that I ran to her side and wept also. It was hours before she could pacify me.

Soon after, we went to the poorhouse, and parks have always depressed me ever since.

I had left Ralph in bed and when I returned, he had almost finished breakfast. Delicious English sole, toast, and marmalade were his fare, but I wanted fresh herrings. I had yearned for these for the past ten years. So I ordered them rolled in flour and fried in butter.

After breakfast letters were segregated and those that needed answering personally I put aside. During my stay it was necessary to engage three extra secretaries for this work.

Ralph and I had been invited to lunch at Lady Astor's.[13] When we arrived, we were shown into a spacious Georgian room, sparsely furnished but in excellent taste.

Left to right: Amy Johnson, aviatrix, Chaplin, Lady Nancy Astor, and George Bernard Shaw, London, February 25, 1931. (*Author's collection*)

Lady Astor is a dynamic personality. The moment she enters the room the air is electrically charged. One feels immediately a generous, warm-hearted soul. Ralph and I are introduced to the guests.

It is quite a large gathering. There is one tall gentleman with a white beard standing at the left of the fireplace. Of course I recognize him at once. It is Bernard Shaw.[14] I think I detect a slight shyness in his manner.

Lady Astor introduces me and I smile foolishly. "Oh yes, of course—Mr. Bernard Shaw," and then a nervous little "ha ha." I am so overwhelmed I am stumped for words.

Now Lady Astor has moved away, leaving Shaw and me alone. Everyone else in the room is talking except us.

I grin foolishly. If only I could think of something to say. We both keep changing from one foot to the other, but nothing seems to break the awful silence.

I'm about to remark on the weather. Thank God, Lady Astor comes up at that moment and announces luncheon.

During the meal she was most amusing. She has a gift for mimicry and gave us an imitation of a horsewoman of the Gay Nineties, going on and keeping the party in gales of laughter.

After lunch the ladies adjourned and the men drew their chairs together for a chat over the coffee. The general conversation was a little stilted and somehow couldn't get started. As for myself, I was completely hopeless and made up my mind to relax and listen. But Mr. Shaw kept the ball rolling and told a few anecdotes. This, I thought, was gracious and revealed an amiable side of him.

During conversation I had an opportunity to study him at close range. I was surprised at the freshness of his complexion. His eyes still have the clear blue twinkle of a much younger man and are keen and intense when conversing. I tried to imagine his features without the beard. I have an impression that the chin is long and the lower lip full, with a kindly expression. Shaw does not give you the impression of a satirist. His voice is pontifical.

As I sat listening to him, my mind was forming judgment. I like him and admire his intellect, but perhaps that's what disconcerts me. Wasn't he quoted as saying that all art should be propaganda?

To me, such a premise would restrict art. I prefer to think the object of art is to intensify feeling, color, or sound—if object it has—for this gives a fuller range to the artist in expressing life, in spite of the moral aspect of it. I would like to broach him on the subject, but I know that in such a controversy his intellect would win out.

Later we adjourned to the garden, where Lady Astor, Amy Johnson,[15] Mr. Shaw, and I had a picture taken.

"Turn this side, Mr. Shaw," said one of the cameramen.

"I'll do nothing of the kind," he replied good-naturedly. "This is the only side you'll get."

I'm always the last to leave any house. After the guests had gone, Lady

Astor, Ralph, and I sat around and talked things over. We got onto the subject of politics. We discussed the future prospects of the labor government, the crisis, and its causes. It was almost teatime before we left.

As we walked back to the Carlton, Ralph asked me what I thought of Shaw.

"He has wonderful charm, a great mind, and loves to play with ideas. But I don't see him in the Mephistophelean role depicted by the press. To me he is a benign gentleman who uses his intellect as a defensive mechanism to hide his sentimentality."

"Why do you think so?" Ralph inquired.

"His approach to art and his attachments to his friends partly disclose the fact. For example, those published letters to Frank Harris. In spite of their provoking frankness, they reveal a sentimental friendship."

London fascinates me! I shall never get enough of it. I find myself traversing the same ground I did ten years ago, steeping myself in its romantic tradition.

There is the world of affluence. Hyde Park, Lancaster Gate, Regent Street, Grosvenor Square. Each of these districts has a soul, a character.

Grosvenor Square, with its dignified houses uniformly arrayed in a circle with their respectable Greek columns like sentinels, elegant and austere. To me it represents the elegance of the Victorian era, an epoch of England's illustrious figures.

I can imagine four-in-hands with prancing thoroughbreds foaming at the mouth and proud flunkeys opening carriage doors, a Lord Palmerston or a Disraeli making a call. I see gentlemen of quality with black stock ties and fawn silk hats meticulously placed to bring out the elegance of their sideburns, and demure ladies with bustles and proud puffed sleeves and ivory-handled parasols, airing their poodle dogs in a morning stroll.

Then Parliament Street that leads up to Trafalgar Square. How many times I've walked along there and paused before that beautiful building, King Charles's Banqueting Hall.

It was through the hall that Charles the First walked to his execution and came out through the corner window onto the scaffold built in front of it. That very window still exists, the very same stone masonry around which the scaffold was built.

I have the soul of a tourist, for I love to visit the spots where the deed took place. I try to get an empathy, a feeling into things. I imagine myself as Charles the First coming through that window to be beheaded—where he might have looked. Then as a spectator, placing myself in a position where the citizens must have stood that day.

Then again there's the personal side. Lambeth, Kennington, Brook Street, West Square, and Westminster Bridge Road. How well I remember as a child the stores there.

The artificial limbs' shop, the depressing wax foot that demonstrated a fallen arch, and the horrible colored lithographs of the human anatomy, exposing a labyrinth of nerves like the design of some coral undersea growth.

The shabby corset shop and the indecent wax bust of a female with an elaborate headdress, smiling inanely over her shoulder. Among the shabbiness of these stores, one touch of respectability—the blue-painted door front of the dentist with polished brass fittings and a small showcase at the entrance.

As a child I would gaze at that showcase with its savage-looking teeth. How alive they looked, yet impotent. It was a habit of mine to look in the mirror of the case and after all these years, it is still there but impoverished. There is only one set of teeth, and I can no longer see myself in the mirror. It is tarnished and blistered with age.

Lambeth, the land of concertina music! As I walk along the darkened streets, I hum to myself some of the old familiar tunes again:

Why did I leave my little back room in Bloomsbury,
Where I could live on a pound a week in luxury—

These old songs have their associations and a flood of memories surges through my mind. The streets are deserted and there is a slight mist. The houses are just visible in outline. Here in these humble quarters I walk along as though I were visiting some fairyland. Another song has come to me:

For old time's sake, don't let old enmity live,
For old time's sake, say you'll forget and forgive,
Life's too short to struggle,

Heart are too precious to break,
Shake hands and let us be friends
For old time's sake

How often I have heard this waltz refrain on a Saturday night played on concertinas by Cockney lads as they strolled by the house, the music gradually diminishing in the distance, dying off into the night.

Now I make my way to a fried fish shop and pause outside. I'd love to buy a pennyworth, but I haven't the courage. One of the customers recognizes me, so I steal away in the darkness before they have a chance to follow.

I'd give anything if I could hear a concertina now. But that's gone. As I pass a house, someone has turned on a radio and a solemn symphony comes forth. How paradoxical! This pretentious music coming from such humble quarters. It is going on eleven o'clock. I must go over to West Square.

West Square! At the back of the Bedlam Lunatic Asylum. This is as far back as I can remember as a child. It was there somewhere around the age of three, we lived in a large house.

It was there I almost died through swallowing a halfpenny. I had taken my money box to bed with me. My brother had been impressing me with conjuring tricks, pretending to swallow the coin and bringing it back through his nose. Of course I did it realistically with the awful consequences.

What a rumpus it caused! I have a vague memory of being held upside down, shaken, slapped, and probed and brought into the glaring light of the sitting room. Then for some reason everything subsided and I slept.

Soon after my accident I remember causing great hilarity in the household. I was playing on the floor and suddenly made a discovery that was the bone of my mother's ankle.

Bones, like halfpennies, I associated with swallowing and when informed what it was, I exclaimed, "You must have swallowed a big one to have it stick out like that."

As I walk around West Square, I come upon a stationer's shop, where they sell toys, sweets, and tobacco. The store has an odor that awakens memories. It smells Christmasy. In the window I see a Noah's ark with painted wooden animals. I can't resist it. I go in and buy it just to get a whiff of the paint and the feel of the excelsior that" packed inside.

I have always wanted to see an English prison and to see it preferably of my own free will. Arrangements were made to visit the Old Bailey,[16] which is the central criminal court of London, and Wandsworth Gaol, the prison where Oscar Wilde was confined for a while.

The Sheriff of London kindly consented to conduct us through Old Bailey and scheduled the program. We were to hear two cases, then lunch with the judges.

I was present at the conclusion of a case where a woman was being tried for throwing vitriol in the face of her paramour. There were extenuating circumstances in the prisoner's favor. She had been ill treated by the man and was driven to desperation. Fortunately, the man escaped the vitriol and the victim himself would not prosecute. The point in question was whether or not the act was premeditated.

The judge in summing up said, "Vitriol-throwing is a horrible and cruel crime, but if the act was done on the impulse of the moment, I will be lenient. If premeditated, I will impose the extreme penalty of the law—ten years."

It was for the jury to decide. The woman had a good character and every favorable fact was taken into consideration. The jury returned with a verdict of guilty, but recommended mercy as the act was not premeditated. She was given six months with hard labor. This, I thought, was a very fair and just trial. The case took no longer than twenty minutes. Afterward we adjourned for lunch.

We sat down to a T-shaped table, about twenty in all, the sheriff presiding with the dignitaries of the law on either side of him. It is a tradition that the sheriff of London pays the cost of the luncheon daily out of his own pocket.

The scene has a look of the theatrical. It could be the Green Room of the Drury Lane Theater. The judges now are a little less dignified than before, having removed their wigs and gowns. The only remnant left of their legal splendor is the Samuel Johnson neckwear known, I believe, as cleats.

For dessert we were served the traditional red apple and currant cake. The sheriff made a speech and several of the judges also. I got up and responded as well as I could.

From there we were conducted to Wandsworth Gaol, where we were shown through the departments by the prison governor. England still has the system of enforced silence among her prisoners. I cannot understand why this is continued. To deprive a man of that most civilizing factor in human society—speech—seems to me unscientific.

We were finally shown the condemned cell and execution room. I noticed chalk marks left upon the trap doors, evidently where the last unfortunate man had stood. The lighting was weird and dramatic. It came from a high small window and threw us into silhouette. Not like the American sentimental method of cutting strings to release the trap, the English frankly pull a lever, which is done by the legal executioner. It was very depressing, but thank heaven nobody was awaiting execution.

We ended our visit by having tea with the governor and his wife, who were very charming and cordial to us.

Alistair MacDonald, whom I met in California, had kindly invited me to meet his father, the Right Honorable Ramsay MacDonald,[17] the British Prime Minister, at his official country house, Chequers,[18] situated among the glorious hills of Buckinghamshire, the battlefields of Oliver Cromwell.

Upon arriving with his son, Alistair, we were met by the Prime Minister and his daughter Ishbel, who were taking a quiet stroll. I was given a cordial welcome and we left the car and joined them in their walk.

The Prime Minister has a handsome face with the eyes of a dreamer, and speaks with a slight Scotch accent. He loves to walk and he took me for a climb to the top of a hill, where we got a view of the magnificent scenery of Buckinghamshire, but the bitter cold winds soon drove us into the house, where tea was served in the main hall and I was shown Cromwellian relics.

Eventually we got comfortably settled around a warm fire. Now is an opportunity, I thought, to discuss a little politics. The conversation had veered around to my visit to England.

"Do you know," I said, "I find a great difference in England since I was here ten years ago? Then there were gray-haired old ladies sleeping on the Thames embankment and shops looked poorly stocked and the children poorly clad.

"But today there is a difference. Those old ladies have gone, the shops look well stocked, and the children well clad. And," I continued, "they can say what they like about the dole, but I think it's been the saving grace of England. It has kept the wheels of industry going and money in circulation is necessary, no matter where it comes from."

But the Prime Minister would have none of it. He just nodded with an "Is that so?" expression. To draw him into politics was quite hopeless.

That evening Princess Bibesco[19] was a guest for dinner. The affair was delightful. The Prime Minister was in excellent form and told many anecdotes.

I was shown through the kitchen and had a long visit with the house staff. I made a special hit with the cook. She was from Manchester and had heard that I'd lived there. Since she had met me, she said, I was to be given a place of honor over the mantelpiece in her sitting room.

"There are my favorites," she said, pointing to a mirror upon which were stuck printed news pictures of all the royal family. "Of course I can't put you with them, but I'll place you at the side."

"I don't care where you put me so long as it's at your left side," I said coyly.

Alistair MacDonald and I left for London after dinner. We were met outside by the press and as usual I was bombarded with all sorts of questions. But I have a technique now for such interviews. I usually answer in monosyllables and to foolish questions just smile.

And so the interview went something like this:

""Did you find the Prime Minister interesting?""

"Yes."

"Did you discuss politics?"

"No."

"Did you do your funny walk for him?"

Smile.

"Are you going to put it in a funny picture?"

Another smile.

And so I would "yes" and "no" and smile my way through the interview.

Monday morning was devoted to shopping. There is nothing more delightful than doing this in London.

I made several purchases, including some gaudy pajamas and dressing gowns. I think my appetite for these dates back to the time I was a small boy. How longingly I would look at the beautiful garments in the Burlington Arcade. I would often declare that if I ever got rich, I would buy out a whole stock of them.

Afterward we lunched at Quaglino's[20] with Randolph Churchill[21] and several friends, among whom was Lord Birkenhead,[22] the son of the famous statesman. At that time he was writing a biography of his father. This was quite a task, I thought, and wondered if a son, in doing such a biography, could sufficiently detach himself from the subject so as to see the deep shadows as well as the highlights that are necessary to a true portrait of a great man.

After luncheon I got away early. I had a desire to visit Tower Bridge. I had had recurring dreams of walking over it and the scenery was so vivid and always the same. Now I wanted to find out whether the background of my dreams was a reality or not.

Ralph thinks I am crazy, but I insist. I am tired of seeing London through taxis and motorcars, so I mount the top of a bus. Of course in the mad scurry up the steps, I slip and tear my trousers. This little accident caused me to be recognized by everyone inside the bus who immediately crowded outside. It was no use. I had to set off after signing several post-cards and pocketbooks.

However, I hail another one. Ralph remonstrates, but I am insistent. This time I catch a running one, hoping to elude the crowd, but they follow and pile in after us. Ralph, who is extremely nervous and loathes crowds, is beside himself.

"Look here, Charlie, you're going to create a riot."

I eventually relent and hail a taxi, and to my disappointment discover that Tower Bridge is nothing like my dreams. I shall never again trust the authenticity of locales in the realms of Morpheus.

The following day I had luncheon at the House of Commons with Sir Philip Sassoon and later took tea with Lloyd George[23] in his private chambers there. I was immediately struck by the charm and easy manner of this great statesman.

He has that faculty of putting you instantly at your ease. I found myself discussing all sorts of projects and enterprises for the relief of the unemployed. He was very patient and even assumed an air of enthusiasm when I suggested rebuilding the southwest side of London and turning it into a modern business center, doing away with the slum district.

"London is too narrow and the streets are too congested," I said. "The advent of the automobile has made them inadequate for rapid transportation and is a handicap to British commerce."

In spite of his interest I could not help noticing a stifled yawn and then I saw Sir Philip look at his watch. So I suggested I would not take up any more of his time with my nonsense.

"Not at all," he said kindly. "I understand you are dining with Lady Astor next Wednesday here at the House of Commons, and I have been invited, so we shall have the pleasure of continuing our conversation."

And with that we shook hands and I took my departure.

Lady Astor's dinner was a glorious affair. She had arranged for a representative of each political party to be present that evening and they all met on neutral ground.

There were conservative, liberal, and labor members—even communists—all sitting at the same table, about twenty in number. Lloyd George sat on Lady Astor's right and I on her left. Facing "L.G.," as everyone calls him, sat Kirkwood,[24] the communist, a brawny Scotsman whom Lloyd George had put in prison during the war. And now they were dining together.

After dinner we all made speeches, the subject being what we would do if we had the power of a Mussolini to help England in her present crisis. I was the first to speak. For some unknown reason I wasn't nervous. Fools shout where angels fear to whisper, and so I started.

"The first thing I would do is reduce the government. The world is suffering from too much government and the expense of it. I would have government ownership of banks and revise many of their laws and those of the Stock Exchange. I would create a government Bureau of Economics, which would control prices, interests, and profits.

"I would endeavor to bring about an amalgamation of England's colonies into an economic unity. I would issue scrip to alleviate the expense of the budget, to use internally for those commodities which England can produce, such as the purchasing of coal, the payments of rents, and so on, the scrip to cease as soon as economic order could be arranged.

"My policy would stand for internationalism, world cooperation of trade, the abolition of the gold standard, and world inflation of money.

"The limited amount of gold is not sufficient to serve an increasing population as a medium of exchange, especially with the rapidly decreasing man power in labor. Gold scales are too small. They have ceased to weigh man's output. Larger ones are necessary. Gold, as a medium of exchange, is as inefficient as trying to deliver a ton of coal in a child's toy cart. The coal may eventually be delivered piece by piece, but in the meantime the household is freezing to death. Enlarge those scales to silver ones or something else. Broaden your trucks and let's make adequate deliveries, for there's plenty of coal and plenty of fire grates to consume it.

"I would endeavor to raise the standard of living, preferably internationally, otherwise throughout the British Domain.

"My policy would stand for the reduction of the hours of labor and for a minimum wage of no less than a comfortable amount to all men and women over the age of twenty-one. I would stand for private enterprise so far as it would not deter the progress or well-being of the majority."

The speech was taken good-naturedly and many edifying and serious ones followed, although some were pessimistic, one saying he didn't think anything could be done unless it was the discovery of more gold or the creation of new enterprises which would stimulate industry.

Lloyd George, in summing up, took the facts of everyone's speech in consideration and examined them, agreeing in part with many. He was, however, adamant in his principles of free trade.

That evening Lloyd George showed evidence of his power of leadership. He was an interested listener, sympathetic and encouraging, imparting constructive criticism with discretion, with a force and conviction native to his genius.

Ralph and I would occasionally ramble over London at midnight. We would poke around the back of Fleet Street into the land of Samuel Johnson. One can step into the fifteenth and sixteenth centuries there.

One night we were passing through Trafalgar Square, where several derelicts were standing around. I was recognized. "Good old Charlie!" and one of them approached and was about to make a touch.

But another shouted, "Hey, leave him alone! Don't you know who that is?"

The deference shown me was pathetic and complimentary. I wasn't a touch—I was a friend, and I was deeply moved by it. The Cockneys are wonderful people.

Another compliment was from a respectable old gentleman, well clad and muffled up, who was walking briskly down Pall Mall on a winter's day. Upon recognizing me, he stepped aside and politely doffed his hat.

The gesture was so simple. There was no familiarity, no handshakes.

It was the beaming look on his face and the simple raising of his hat that stirred me so.

Today I am going to visit the workhouse school,[25] where I spent two years as a child—from the age of five to seven. More than anything else this school has been the object of my visit to Europe. I suppose I spent the unhappiest time of my life there. To me it was a prison and a house of shame. We had gone through extreme poverty, and poverty was a crime. Even at the early age of seven I realized this.

And now I am to turn back the years and look into the past. I am almost afraid to tell the driver where to go. The name of the school is my only source of information. I haven't the faintest idea as to the direction. The chauffeur looks puzzled when I inquire. The suspense is awful.

"Let me see—that must be Highgate way."

Thank heavens he is at least cognizant of its existence. Throughout the journey I am trying to recognize the familiar spots. I only know in my childhood the school seemed far out in the country, but now everything is built up. We stop at a crossroad and the chauffeur inquires from a policeman:

"Which is the way to S—?"

"That must be the booby hutch," says the constable.

The chauffeur turns to me. "Is it the booby hutch you want?"

"The booby hutch? What's the booby hutch?" I answer weakly.

"The madhouse—where they're a little—you know," said the policeman pointing to the top of his helmet. My spirits are getting lower.

"Oh, no," I said, "this is a school for children—an orphanage."

"Oh, the orphanage," said the officer. "That's about two miles from here, then turn to the left."

Once again I'm relieved, yet we pass nothing but buildings. As we turn to the left, however, there are vacant lots and fields ahead of us. My spirit rises. We now turn into a lane and come suddenly upon a building with Roman pillars, the first recognition of my infant days. I am so thrilled and excited I can hardly wait to get out of the car.

We have no letters or permits. We have come purely on speculation as to whether we shall get in or not. Upon inquiry, we are shown into a room and meet the head of the school.

"Oh, yes, we were expecting you in a way," he said. :There was a rumor you were coming. As a matter of fact," he went on, "I have been looking up

Chaplin among the boys at Hanwell School, just outside London, where he attended for a short time as a boy, February 20, 1931. (*Charlie Chaplin Archive*)

some old files and discovered the record of your entry and discharge dated 1896. It read, 'Sydney Chaplin handed back to mother March 10, 1896. Charles, ditto.'"

Ralph and I giggled. "There, you see? You're just a 'ditto,'" Ralph commented.

The head official is very courteous. Would we like a cup of tea before going around? But I am too anxious to see the interior of the school. I can't wait for anything, so I politely decline. He has told off an attendant to show us around and we start on our way.

There is the yard, just as it was when I was a child. Contrary to some ideas about objects or locations appearing smaller after one grows up, it looks just as big as it ever did. There are the tailor's shop, the school steps; the punishment room; the blacking hole where we would shine our boots on a frosty morning; the dormitories and the depressing slate wash sinks.

I went in and up the stairs that used to seem so close to me as I climbed them, the walls pressing in on me, the tread of the stairs so near my face. It was the same now. These stairs, enclosed, steep, narrow, pressed in on me just as they had then. I felt those walls. I felt the steepness of the steps. I felt myself going up them with the same sensation of oppression and confinement that I had then.

Yes, it was all there, and the children were all there. The same types, only more smiling and happier. I went into the dining room—a large hall—and there was my place, the third seat at the fourth table. I wonder who occupies it now!

How well I remember one Christmas Day sitting on that same seat, weeping copious tears. The day before I had committed some breach of the rules. As we came into the dining room for Christmas dinner, we were to be given two oranges and a bag of sweets.

I remember how excited I was awaiting my turn. How joyous and bright the oranges looked in contrast to the gray surroundings. We never saw oranges but once a year and that was at Christmas.

I am speculating what I shall do with mine. I shall save the peel and the sweets I shall eat one a day. Each child is presented with his treasure as he enters the dining-room. At last it is my turn. But the man puts me aside.

"Oh, no—you'll go without for what you did yesterday."

And there, on that seat at the fourth table, I wept bitterly. The children were more humane than the attendants were and so the little ones at our table contributed one candy apiece and made up my loss.

As I stand in the dining room there are hundreds of smiling faces looking up at me. The children seem happy and light-hearted—so different from the days when I was there.

Then the attendant, as though reading my mind, remarks, "The school has a different policy since the days when you were here, sir. Then it was very military with strict discipline, but today the children have more freedom and get better treatment."

And it's quite obvious, for the children are smiling and playing around in front of the head master without any restraint. It is apparent that he is adored by them all.

He calls them to attention and makes an announcement: "Children, you're to be presented with a motion picture machine. We are to have a gala night with motion pictures, and sweets and oranges will be served."

Part II

I am looking forward to a visit with my friend, the Right Honorable Winston Churchill. Ralph and I are invited to his beautiful country residence in Westerham, Kent. The first time I met Mr. Churchill was in California while he was lecturing there.

I was charmed by his direct, unassuming manner. He has a slight lisp when he talks and a stoop in his carriage like Napoleon. You feel immediately a dynamic force—a man with a thirst for accomplishment. He is a wonderful talker and will rattle off brilliant epigrams. Besides being a statesman, he is a great writer and an excellent painter.

He told me he had read that I was considering making a picture of the life of Napoleon. "You must do it," he said. "Apart from the drama, think of its possibilities for humor. Napoleon in his bathtub arguing with his imperious brother, who's all dressed up, bedecked in gold braid, and using this opportunity to place Napoleon in a position of inferiority.

"But Napoleon, in his rage, deliberately splashes the water over his brother's fine uniform and he has to exit ignominiously from him. This is not alone clever psychology," said Mr. Churchill. "It is action and fun."

When Ralph and I arrived at his home in Westerham, it was quite dark. We motored down and took our dress clothes with us. It was a bitter cold evening and I was thankful for the nice warm bath that awaited me.

I changed in Mr. Churchill's bedroom. Desks were piled with papers and stacks of books were everywhere. I noticed hurriedly a set of Plutarch's *Lives* and many volumes on Napoleon.

At dinner there were several young Members of Parliament present who added much to a dialectic evening. Mr. Churchill loves to talk shop. He loves his profession. During dinner he humorously heckled and harangued some of the young Members and much wit sallied forth.

Chaplin and Winston Churchill at Chartwell in England, February 26, 1931. (*Charlie Chaplin Archive*)

Someone referred to Gandhi as being a menace to the peace of the Far East.

I ventured a remark—that Gandhis or Lenins do not start revolutions. They are forced up by the masses and usually voice the want of a people.

Mr. Churchill laughed. "You should go into Parliament."

"No, sir," I replied. "I prefer to be a motion picture actor these days. However, I believe we should go with evolution to avoid revolution, and there's every evidence that the world needs a drastic change."

Nevertheless we were one and for progressive government. Mr. Churchill said much has to be done to preserve civilization and guide it safely back to normal.

One of his hobbies is laying bricks. He has built several beautiful walls around his estate. In his dining room I noticed several paintings—still lifes and landscapes—signed "Churchill." Ralph Barton and I had an opportunity to examine them. Ralph, who was an expert on these things, said they were masterful.

He is surrounded by a charming family. His wife and children are a source of inspiration and delight to him. He is a real family man and a sincere patriot, and, I might say, a healthy reactionist in the House of Commons, which is most necessary today.

Tomorrow is the opening of my picture. It is arranged that I should dress at the theater so as to avoid the crowds. I am to have a meal in the dressing room. All this is irritating. To think I can't dine somewhere like an ordinary normal person.

About five o'clock Ralph and I left for the theater and dined quietly in the dressing room, and waited for the opening, which was to take place at nine o'clock.[1]

Dear old London! True to tradition it always rains at the wrong moment, and a regular cloudburst happened around eight. This did not dampen the spirits of the people, however. They were out in thousands. I would occasionally go to the window of the theater and wave to them. But whatever I did, I could never compensate them for their devotion and good will.

The evening went off with a bang. Mr. Gillespie, the impresario, and the man who was to exploit my picture in London did exceedingly well and produced it in excellent style.

Chaplin taking a bow at the Dominion Theatre premiere of *City Lights*, London, February 27, 1931. (*Charlie Chaplin Archive*)

I sat next to Bernard Shaw throughout the performance. I was anxious to hear what he had to say about it. He made several favorable comments.

I was called upon to make a speech, but I was so thrilled and excited that nothing seemed to come out. However, the audience was most appreciative.

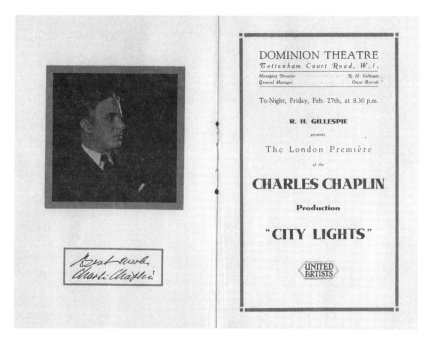

Premiere night program for *City Lights* at the Dominion Theatre, London, February 27, 1931. (*Author's collection*)

I had arranged a party afterward at the Carlton Hotel, inviting everyone I knew—about two hundred people in number.

The Right Honorable Winston Churchill made a speech and started as follows: "My lords, ladies and gentlemen—" and ended by paying me a charming tribute.

In responding, I took the cue from Mr. Churchill and began: "My lords, ladies and gentlemen—" Then realizing the eminence of the occasion, it behooved me to become more grandiloquent and I continued, "—my friend, the late Chancellor of the Exchequer—"

Then I heard the voice of Mr. Churchill boom forth, "I like that—'the late, the late,'" he repeated laughingly.

"Pardon me," I said nervously, "I mean the Ex—the Ex-Chancellor of the Exchequer—"

After this I was gone. However, I started again. "My friend, Mr. Winston Churchill—."[2]

This caused more merriment, and so the speech went on. Later there was entertainment and dancing.

Incidentally, I meet a lady with whom I dance the tango several times,[3] but my secretary is a little concerned.

"Let up awhile," he whispers, "and dance with someone else or the press will have you reported engaged."

But tonight they can say what they like. I'm going to be myself and enjoy the evening.

And so we went on into the morning until five o'clock, at which time I got to bed.

The following day, we were busy scrutinizing the papers for the reviews of the picture. Nearly all were enthusiastic, but it was obvious that a certain section of the press was deliberately otherwise. However, these adverse criticisms had little effect on me. I had made up my mind to enjoy my holiday.

My friend Ralph Barton is leaving tomorrow for America.[4] His behavior has been strange lately. A few days ago he told me that he hated the ticking of clocks and if he got the chance, would stop them. Strangely enough, I found the clock in our room, which was electrically wired, had been cut. Ralph confessed he had done it because it got on his nerves. I never placed much importance on his action at the time, but since his death, I realize its psychological significance.

All the next day was spent preparing for his departure. He was feeling much better and was anxious to get back to work. This was the last I heard from him.

Although he promised to write, never a word came and about two months later, during my stay in the south of France, I read of his suicide.

Poor Ralph! It was an awful shock to me. He had such a quiet pensive manner I little realized he was capable of such violence. He was one of the most charming cultured men I have ever known and in the circle of my few intimate friends, he has left a vacuum.

I have been besieged by all sorts of invitations and requests, and letters are piling up. I must change my location, otherwise my social affairs will become complicated. One cannot find time to see all one's friends, and I cannot make too many plans ahead. So there is only one thing left. If I do not wish to offend them, I must pack up and leave. I suddenly make up my mind to visit Germany.

We have arrived in Holland and I am journeying on my way to Berlin. Holland has a distinct character different from any other country, with its canals and windmills and stubby trees, all uniformly pruned with their branches turned upward.

At various stations there are for sale wooden Dutch shoes filled with chocolates and prettily tied with blue ribbons. These I purchase to send to friends.

The Dutch countryside is neat and tidy. Nothing looks out of place. And what a tremendous number of cyclists along the road! Bicycles are everywhere.

The Dutch press board the train en route. They are very courteous and most of them speak English so I have no difficulty in giving an interview.

One informs me there is a bridge in Rotterdam in construction that will have a statue of myself placed on it. My comment is somewhat banal. "Oh, really? How wonderful!" I exclaim, endeavoring to cover up my excitement, but at the next station I have to get out and walk.

My manager came up to me all excited and impressively exclaimed, "Do you know they're building a statue of you on one of the bridges in Rotterdam?"

"So I understand," I remarked lightly. Then assuming an air of equanimity, I continued to walk up and down the platform. However, I darted into the telegraph office and wired my brother the news.

On my first visit to Berlin in 1921 I was little known, as very few of my pictures had been shown there during the war.[5]

But this time it is different. I had been told that in Germany I had become a favorite and that I must expect quite a reception. I can assure you I'm not disappointed. Thousands cover the station and throngs are outside. I hear in English such phrases as "Gold Rush Charlie! . . . Circus Charlie!" Everybody is excited. Pressmen and officials are all mixed up and swept aside by the multitudes.

Throngs were along the roads. That, I think, was the most exciting reception of all—even greater than London.

At the Hotel Adlon[6] we are met by more crowds, so I am shot up into the elevator and into my room, where I immediately go out onto the balcony and wave to them below. There is a "Hoorah!" in response and I leave the window. Eventually we are left to ourselves for a refreshing cup of coffee.

With German dignitaries and admirers in the lobby of Hotel Adlon, Berlin. (*Charlie Chaplin Archive*)

Again there are letters and invitations from friends, one from the British Embassy. I am to have dinner with the Right Honorable Sir Horace Rumbold,[7] the British ambassador and his family, and go to the opera afterward.

Then there is my friend von Vollmueller,[8] poet and author of Max Reinhardt's great production, *The Miracle*. He has arranged a Bohemian party for me at his flat.

I have engaged Countess York as my secretary. She is most interesting, being a modern young German who knows her Berlin thoroughly.

That evening we visited a *rathskeller*, a place of amusement, where we saw Garro,[9] a popular favorite of Berlin. He is a comedian of the slapstick type—very unctuous and full of rough and tumble, and an artist.

During the performance he heard that I was in front and so made an announcement. I was brought onto the stage. He said something in German. Suddenly he turned and embraced me, and before I knew it, I was kissed. Then he waxed eloquent. I heard "circus" and "gold rush" mentioned.

Then he mimicked some gesture of mine and the audience went into gales of laughter. Then again he became dramatic, punctuating his remarks with effective pauses and with modulated voice. Tears came to his eyes. Then with a dramatic gesture, he pointed to me. The house went into rounds of applause. Then with rapid transition he spoke an aside and again embraced me with a kiss, which brought another roar of laughter. We then left the stage amidst tremendous applause.

I haven't the faintest idea what he said. I only know that he played upon the emotions of the audience at will.

The program for the following day was to take tea with the officials of the government and afterward to visit the prisons and police museum.[10] For dinner I was to be the guest of von Vollmueller.

In the afternoon I had tea with several members of the Reichstag. They were all worried about the economic future of Germany.

"It is impossible to go on for another year," they said. Every member seemed pessimistic of the future.

"What would actually happen if you did not go on?" I inquired.

"Bankruptcy," was the answer.

Government officials and men in civil service would not be paid. There would be a general disintegration of all the government departments. In other words, it would mean anarchy and Bolshevism. Their plight seemed pretty awful and their future dark.

"Even if we get through this year," they said, "we shall have trouble. Just think of the conditions of our universities. We have young men graduating in qualified professions and passing their examinations, only to leave college and stand in the bread line with the rest of the unemployed. These things are bound to create trouble and it does not look as though conditions will improve."

When I returned to the hotel, von Vollmueller had left a note saying dinner would be early on account of going to the theater. Later there was to be a supper at his flat with a few friends.

The entertainment was a musical comedy and the production and cast were excellent, as well as the music. I should say that the German theater excels above all others in Europe for ensemble and stagecraft.

I saw a production of *Liliom* in the Workmen's Theater. This is a wonderful institution built by the workmen and supported by them. It is reputed they produce the best plays in Berlin. I know the one I saw was magnificently put on.

They have a revolving stage and scenes are produced by magic lantern slides thrown on a blank background. Such a method facilitates rapid change of scenery and wonderful effects are achieved. The admission is all one price. No seats can be reserved. They are obtained by lottery.

After the entertainment we finished at von Vollmueller's apartment for supper.

There were several interesting people there, Friedrich Hollander,[11] the composer of "Falling in Love Again" and other melodies, who gave us a few little sketches at the piano. Also a beautiful German girl, "G,"[12] a well-known dancer; and as the evening progressed, we each performed. "G" danced beautifully for us, I gave an imitation of a bullfight, and several others contributed to a charming Bohemian night.

Tomorrow we are to visit Potsdam.[13] Prince Henry of Prussia, nephew of the Kaiser, is to conduct us over the palace. Sir Philip Sassoon has arrived in Berlin for a couple of days and is coming with us.

We lunch at Potsdam. The town seems deserted and there is little left of the brilliancy of bygone days. The exterior of the palace would be beautiful but for the ridiculous figures that stand upon the edge of the roof. They are for all the world like balancing acrobats.

The approach is beautiful, but I find that all palaces are alike. They all have that same candy-colored interior, one baroque room after another. Before we were halfway through, I was exhausted and depressed. As far as comfort is concerned, it is nil. One room was especially awful, done in shells, and gave me the feeling of the interior of an oyster bar or the entrance to some Coney Island concession. Every known shell in the world was supposed to be in it. I never saw such a conglomerate mass of barnacles. It looked like the bottom of a pier painted for a carnival. However, the gardens were lovely. Here the pretentiousness of man cannot offend.

On our return we had tea with Marlene Dietrich. She was in Berlin at the time, enjoying a well-earned rest.

I heard much of the Berlin nightlife and thought it would be interesting to do the rounds. There are all sorts of wild rumors as to what goes on in these cafés; men dressed as women and women as men. So we arranged to go to a certain café where we would see things unprintable.

I must say I was very disappointed. It was a most feeble entertainment and very self-conscious of its naughtiness. As we entered, the band struck up and two effeminate youths danced together. This was the big noise of the evening, the something unspeakable we were privileged to see. Each time fresh customers would enter, the same youths would hurry to their feet again.

We were too horrified to enjoy this form of vice for long, so hurriedly drank our ginger ale and fled out into the night and as Oscar Wilde said, "down the long and silent street, the dawn with silver sandaled feet, crept like a frightened girl."

Professor Einstein telephoned this morning. He has returned from Hollywood and I am invited for tea. He has given me instructions how to reach his flat, but the directions go askew and I have difficulty in finding the street. We pull up the car and inquire the way from a passer-by. No one seems to know the street or the number. At last I have an idea.

"Could you tell me where Professor Einstein lives?"

"*Ach, ja,*" and I am immediately given the directions.

I could not imagine the kind of surroundings that Professor Einstein would live in, for his personality does not fit into any background. He seems detached from everything.

It is a small modest flat, the comfortable home of any workingman. The sitting room I recognize from pictures I have seen in magazines.

I will try and give you an impression of this great man. The eyes have a look as though they see clearly the simplicity of all things. The brow wears no furrows. One feels that all the superficial entanglements of thought that obscure our vision have been swept aside by him, and that he sees only the fundamentals. His voice in conversation seems like inspired whispers. There's a warmth in his personality.

I remember in Los Angeles when he came to my house I was nervous and concerned and prepared to be awed, but the moment he entered, I was put at my ease. I felt immediately someone human and kindly. His simplicity is disarming. You forget the professor, the illustrious man of science. You welcome a congenial friend, a man with a twinkle in his eye and a sense of humor, and a quiet, subtle one at that.

After dinner I arranged an entertainment—some little Japanese children to dance for him. One of them presented her autograph book for me to sign, and I drew a comic sketch of my big shoes. Then the little girl whispered, "Will the professor sign it?"

He smiled and took the autograph book, and with a chuckle drew one of his famous geometric equations.

"But yours is more interesting," he said humorously, comparing the two sketches.

"More comprehensible to the little girl perhaps," I laughed, "and to me and many others."

Arriving at his flat I was introduced to his family. He has a son and daughter, the latter a very good sculptress, and I was shown some specimens of her work. But one doesn't dare admire anything in Einstein's house.

"That is beautiful," I commented, pointing to one of her pieces.

"Do you want it? You may have it."

And I have to vigorously decline. I see I must have more restraint in my admiration.

We sat down to delicious home-baked tarts made by Mrs. Einstein. During the course of conversation, his son remarked on the psychology of the popularity of Einstein and myself.

"You are popular," he said, "because you are understood by the masses. On the other hand, the professor's popularity with the masses is because he is not understood."

Mrs. Einstein told many anecdotes about the professor and gave interesting sidelights on his character. When he is not working, he is extremely lazy and indulges himself puttering around in his sailboat, which is his hobby.

One interesting story went back a few years. He had been working assiduously for several days alone in his study. One morning he came into the drawing room and sat down at the piano, running his fingers nervously over the keys. Suddenly he turned to his wife.

"Do you know, I've got a wonderful idea!" he said with all the enthusiasm of a novelist who has discovered the plot of his next book.

He then got up and returned to his study whence he emerged two days later with papers and data that shook the world of science with his theory of relativity.

All conversation eventually converges to that one topic—the world's crisis.

"These are dangerous times," he said, "with depression and growing unemployment.

"But most of the wise men," I remarked, "when discussing the depression, will invariably answer that it all happened before and that history is only repeating itself.

"Only the other day I was speaking to a prominent business man who said England never thought she could pay her national debt after the Battle of Waterloo because of the lack of trade. But steam came along and started new industries. Then electricity developed and put men back to work. Depressions come periodically he insisted, but new enterprises crop up like the automobile industry or radio and solve the problem."

Professor Einstein listened attentively and I was encouraged to hold forth.

"History today is not repeating itself," I said. "The recovery of past economic depressions may have been due to inventions and new enterprises, but since those days the necessity of man power has been rapidly decreasing because of modern machinery, and whatever new enterprises crop up in the future, they will not require the man power that was necessary in the past. Therefore as man's only means of consuming what machinery produces is by work, our problem becomes a different one."

"Whatever the problem may be," said the professor, "a change of some kind is necessary to keep men from starving."

"The business world," I continued, "has acquiesced and welcomed the fundamental industrial change from man power to machine power, which has cheapened the cost of all our commodities. But it stands resolute against any fundamental change in the capitalistic system that might cheapen money and facilitate the means of buying those cheap goods.

"They insist on maintaining the gold standard, at the same time doing business with credit, using both as a medium of exchange. They use credit for business expansion to improve values, only to knock them down again by restricting credit and reducing values to the gold standard.

"These two mediums of exchange—credit and gold—will never stabilize prices, for credit is more elastic than gold. Therefore, the value of all our enterprises built up by credit will always be at the mercy of the gold standard, which can reduce those values at will."

Professor Einstein smiled.

"You're not a comedian," he said. "You're an economist. However, how could you cure all this?"

"Three things," I said. "Reduce the hours of labor, print more money, and control prices."

"I'm not especially interested in the business mathematics of it," he said smilingly, "but I think that every man living should be clothed and fed, with a roof over his head, for there is enough for all."

Before leaving, we exchanged photographs. One had been taken of the professor and myself in California that he signed as follows: "To Charlie, the Economist."[14]

I autographed one in return and for the life of me, I couldn't think what to say. The professor came to my rescue.

"Why not '*Et tu, Brute*'?" he smiled.

"Modesty forbids," I said jokingly and signed it as he suggested. "To Professor Einstein—'*Et tu, Brute*.'"

It was my last and wonderful evening in Berlin, for tomorrow I was to leave for Vienna.[15] When I returned that evening to the hotel, Sir Philip Sassoon was waiting for me.

"G" was to dine with us, so I quickly scrambled into evening clothes. We had dinner at the Adlon and danced to the strains of a tango.

"G" is very lovely. When I first saw her dance, I was struck by her extraordinary charm, the rhythmic motion of her body, and her volatile expression. She knew I appreciated the nuances and subtleties of her dance.

That evening after Sir Philip left, "G" and I sat and talked. I attempted to define the quality of her art.

"In your dance you seem to express an exotic loneliness—to be in pursuit of some strange beauty. This quality is part of your real personality."

"G" took my hand. Hesitating to find words, she replied, "Charlie, I love you—you're so appreciative. Although we may never see each other again, I will not regret it, for we have met in our pilgrimage. It is good to know that you are in life, and a living part of it."

That was "G"—that was her philosophy.

The following day I saw Sir Philip off to England and at midday we departed for Vienna.

I arrived to another big demonstration. Each crowd seems to get bigger and more demonstrative, God bless them! This time I am carried shoulder high out of the railroad station. It is impossible to retain one's personality in this fashion. One looks foolish and concerned.

As we progress, I am thrown more out of balance, but am eventually dumped into a touring car, with my secretary and Kono being pushed in after me. And so we sally forth, waving and honking our way out of the crowds.

Vienna is sad. One feels the spirit of gayety has left it. It is a city of yesterdays. As we pass through the wide avenues and broad cobblestone streets, I count many café bars as they are called. People buy their cup of coffee and sit for hours in these places, doing their correspondence and negotiating their business. It is an address for many people—where one can meet.

Upon arriving at the hotel, I am ushered into a palatial apartment. It is the royal suite. The rooms are large and lofty, painted white and decorated in rococo style. It is extremely impressive, but you get tired of it after a few days.

I attempt to go shopping. I do not take my entourage with me. When my secretary and Kono are along, they seem to do something to attract attention. They march each side of me as though I were under arrest. So I decide to go alone.

I meander through the city. Were I addicted to *cacoethes scribendi* I should go into pages of rhetorical rapture extolling the beauties of Vienna. Therefore, I shall spare you all too suffering readers any conscious pleonasms on my part.

I find myself on a bridge over the Danube River. I can understand the charm of Vienna. It must have been wonderful before the war. I seem to be walking along an endless avenue with shops and beer gardens. Occasionally I am recognized, but there are no demonstrations.

There is a psychology in the gathering of crowds. I can be walking along a thoroughfare with an occasional recognition. People just look and nudge one another, then go on their way. But occasionally an excitable wench will exclaim, "Oh, look—there's Charlie Chaplin!" and the crowd immediately takes on her excitement and gathers around until I have to make for a taxi. But this day I am lucky and so have a chance to enjoy myself.

I have an extensive program for this afternoon. I am to visit the Workmen's Apartments. These are flats built by the government with rents at a minimum cost and with little or no profit to the state. Then I am to take in the museum and the late emperor's palace, and later dine with two charming ladies and go to the theater.

After the theater we went to a cabaret. I danced several tangos and was having a wonderful time until we struck one of those excitable wenches. This time there were fireworks.

She was a Hungarian. "*Ach*, here is a great artist," she announced, eulogizing me with all the superlatives she could think of.

I am not a man of false modesty, but I actually squirmed. She suddenly fell to her knees and with a panache gesture, grabbed my hand and kissed it. In endeavoring to pull away, she yanked me off my balance and I toppled over on her.

I might mention I was perfectly sober, not having had a drink that evening, but the manner in which the proprietor picked me up convinced me that he suspected that I had.

"Everything is all right, Mr. Chaplin. It is quite all right." Feeling an explanation necessary, I endeavored to tell him I was perfectly sober, but he insisted. "Don't mention it, Mr. Chaplin."

The affair was exasperating and I left with a resolve never to enter a cabaret again.

The following day I met Oscar Straus,[16] the composer of *The Chocolate Soldier*, et cetera. He wanted to arrange a party for me, but there was no opportunity as I was leaving the next day, and that night I was dining at the British Legation.

There were over three hundred guests present, all bedecked in their finery and decorations, Vienna striving to recapture some of its bygone splendor, which only accentuated its sadness. There was an atmosphere of shabby gentility—impecunious old Austrian families making heroic efforts to keep up appearances. There were stories written on many faces.

During the evening I met members of the French Legation. They had a message from Paris stating that Monsieur Briand expressed a desire to meet me, and would arrange a luncheon when I went there.

I intended making an extensive tour through Italy before going to Paris,[17] but upon hearing this, I changed my plans and decided to go immediately after my visit to Venice, which was my next destination.

Everything is packed and we are leaving. There is politeness everywhere—the hotel manager, the waiters, the porters, even to the man in the street. They are a nice people and I am sad to leave them.

The northern part of Italy is a miniature California grown old. I am excited about Venice, wondering whether it will come up to my expectations. I have heard so much about the moonlight nights, the music, and the gondolas.

On crossing the border I was in slumber land. A note was left by an Italian custom officer: "Greetings, Charlie, here comes my address. Have it a signature on it and send it again to me. Did not want to wake up your sleep so good-bye."

At last we arrive in Venice. Latin temperament is at its height. Upon leaving the train, I am seized by an ardent admirer, a young man about twenty, who shoulders me high and proceeds out of the station. I am carried by four of them, but the weight is not evenly distributed.

The bulk of the burden is upon this young gentleman. I feel him trying to change the position a little, only to increase the burden upon himself. I endeavor to explain he should put me down and let me walk. But no! He insists upon carrying me on. Wherever we were going seemed interminable. I doubted whether he understood, and so I made signs to him, but he was resolute.

Poor lad! I can feel him sweat and grunt under a weary lot. I try to tell the others to distribute the weight more evenly, but they succeed in making it heavier for him. He has the sharpest collarbone I ever sat on. Give me Austrian collarbones to Italian ones! They're plumper.

The journey from the station to the canal is a half mile, so I am resigned to let the lad die of his own insistent will. There is hope, however. Now he has stopped hooraying and his breathing becomes more difficult. Again I will plead with him. This time I am more successful. He throws me down in disgust, and without saying good-bye moves on into the crowd, rubbing his paralyzed neck. Poor lad! I feel I've lost an ardent admirer.

One's first view of the canal is overwhelming. The color and beauty of its architecture are beyond description. One can only sit in silence, awed by its splendor.

Crowds are along the canal,[18] shouting and applauding as we pass. One hears on all sides, "Chow." It is their greeting, and so I am "chowing" from then on.

At last we are settled in the hotel. My secretary and Kono have gone to the station to arrange about my baggage and other things and I am alone.

For some reason the holiday takes on an aspect of utter futility. Perhaps it's the condition of my nerves. I am exhausted. I am in a new city and asking myself, "What am I here for?"

I wish I were home in California at work again. What an abject animal man is. It seems he is never happy unless he has the burden of some task.

My room is on the first floor. As I move about the apartment, the crowd can see me from the outside. I ring for the waiter to pull the curtains. There is a murmur of disappointment—"aw"—like one hears at a motion picture when the film breaks, so I make one final appearance on the balcony, hoping they'll leave.

My nerves are on edge. I know these demonstrations are a great compliment, but there are moments when one wants to feel alone. I've often thought of my popularity. I've never been impressed by the magnitude of it. I happen to have the good fortune to work in a medium that has a large circulation. But I am impressed with the quality of it, which inspires affection more than admiration.

Someone once remarked, "How does it feel, Charlie, to meet so many smiling faces? You rarely see sad ones."

The streets of Venice are just as beautiful as the canals. As we wandered through the labyrinth of winding thoroughfares, some so narrow permitting only three to walk abreast, we would come upon medieval plazas and squares, in the center of which was usually some ancient church.

The hour is midnight and in the dim light of street lamps, one sees the outline of cloaked figures passing through shadows. A street is occasionally broken by a flood of light coming from a doorway or restaurant. Groups of young men are standing on corners in animated conversation. Italians love to talk.

I ask my friend to translate the nature of their conversation, and this was a phrase he heard: "Art is the treatment applied to work, and has nothing to do with the subject matter."

That night I went to bed encouraged with life and a passionate belief in the Italian people.

The following day I had tea with the British consul and his charming wife, later visiting the prisons and dungeons under water. The horrors were not as bad as I expected. In ancient times the cells had been paneled in wood, not half as grim as our good old dungeons in the Tower of London.

That evening we were the guests of a touring company which was playing the local theater. As a special privilege, we were permitted to use the dining room for a supper dance. Venice is very strict about her music permits, and no music is allowed in any public place after a certain hour, which is rather early.

On this night we were devilish and played the phonograph until twelve-thirty. I was a little surprised to discover such conditions in Italy. They are bad enough in England and in some parts of America, but I am shocked at the Latin temperament permitting such restrictions.

Leaving Venice en route for Paris, the Duke and Duchess of Westminster boarded the train. Later we were introduced. The duke is a tall, handsome, powerful-looking man with a congenial manner. The duchess is grace and beauty personified.

They have invited me to their place in Normandy to go boar hunting and I am to let them know when I am free to leave Paris.

I have a letter from Cami, the humorist-writer, stating he will be at the station in Paris to meet me. I haven't seen Cami in ten years. In the meantime, he writes he has learned a little English.

Paris![19] Crowds showing, gendarmes pushing, Cami hugging, ropes breaking, crowds oncoming, rushing for limousine, slamming of doors, photographers remonstrating, police demonstrating, horns honking, gears shifting, and we're off!

I sit back with a sigh of relief. Cami is talking, but I am too tired to listen. My nerves are all upset. I have discovered his English is as good as my French, and that's saying a small mouthful. However, we get along famously in pantomime.

Mr. Guy Croswell Smith, my Paris representative, is to accompany me to lunch with M. Briand. It is for one o'clock and as we have a little time to spare, we go for a drive and visit Napoleon's tomb.

One can hardly realize that in that marble casket lies the most dramatic mortal that has ever lived. I think for sheer drama, Napoleon comes first. As I glance over the balcony, I am reminded of the line in Gray's "Elegy"—"The paths of glory lead but to the grave."

Lunch was at the French Ministry Building. Upon arriving, I was intro-

Waving to fans from the balcony of the Hotel Crillon, Paris. (*Author's collection*)

duced to many celebrities. The celebrated poetess, Countess de Noailles,[20] was present. She is an alert, active little lady with birdlike movements and a scintillating mind.

M. Berthelot, the Permanent Secretary of the French Cabinet, was there also. He was the gentleman who afterward decorated me. M. Bailby, then the editor of *L'Intransigeant*, Princess Murat, Prince and Princess de Bourbon, M. Rothschild, and many others were present.

M. Briand arrived a few moments later—a small, delicate man, round-shouldered, whose face bore lines of responsibility. There was a hidden humor in his expression and a look of weary resignation. He lacked the twinkle of Lloyd George. Briand has a tragic face. Unfortunately, he did not speak English. In giving a toast, he turned to the countess and said:

"I drink to your future, and to Monsieur Chaplin, I drink to the present."

He was in excellent form, and during luncheon remarked to the count-

Chaplin about to receive the Légion d'Honneur from Aristide Briand (not shown), March 23, 1931. (*Charlie Chaplin Archive*)

ess, "I see so little of you these days. Your presence is as rare as one's discarded mistress."

Afterward we sat around and talked. "Mr. Chaplin, you are a poet," said the countess.

"A poet without verse," I replied smilingly.

"On the contrary, your verses are moving," she said quietly.

Someone asks, "Why are the themes of your pictures so sad? I suppose like all comedians, you like the tragic."

"Not actually," I answer. "As a matter of fact, I dislike tragedy. Life is sad enough. I only use pathos as a means of effecting beauty, for so much of the tragic is in all beauty."

On my return to the hotel, I received the following an anonymous letter, which a friend translated for me:

Dear Sir: Allow me to thank you for all the happiness you have given this sad old world. I have read an announcement that you are to be decorated. During the war I myself was given the Legion of Honor, and now I give it to you, having no further use for it, as I've only a little while to live. By the time you receive this, I shall probably have passed on. It is my express desire that you keep it as a token of my appreciation for all the good you have done humanity. There is no one more worthy to wear it than yourself.[21]

I was deeply impressed. Unfortunately, there was no way of finding out the name or address of the sender.

That evening Count LeMuir and I dined quietly, going later to witness a rehearsal of a revue at the Folies Bergère.

I had heard that Alfred Jackson, an old associate of mine, was working there with his troupe of dancers. Jackson and I were kids together in his father's troupe called The Eight Lancashire Lads.

Upon arriving at the Folies Bergère, I met his father also, and after a warm greeting, we started to reminisce.

"My lad," said Jackson's father, "I remember the very first laugh you got from an audience."

And then he recalled an incident that occurred at the London Hippodrome. I was about eight at the time. The troupe was engaged to play cats and dogs in the pantomime, *Puss in Boots*. I was dressed as a dog. It was the first performance and on we came.

Wanting to give a little touch of nature to my portrayal of the canine species, I ran lambent over to the corner of the scenery and proceeded to go through the motions of absolute realism that my childish impressionable mind had seen other little dogs do.

The house came down in an uproar. With the laughter and appreciation of the audience, I was inspired to go further, and so I started to take a sniffing interest in the other little dogs on the stage. This also was most realistic and brought forth another burst of laughter. I would sniff, then look suddenly at the audience. This action was most successful.

It appears that my dog's mask wore a startled expression. At each sniff, the audience would laugh and I would look at them. There was a sort of tempo to it, the laughter, the look, and the sniff. This seemed to work the audience into a state of hysteria. I was feeling very happy and encouraged until my attention was drawn to the side of the wings. There were Mr. Jackson and several gentlemen in white shirtfronts, all protesting violently, shaking their heads and making motions for me to exit. This left me bewildered and somewhat discouraged, so I put my tail between my legs and slunk off the stage to the tune of laughter and applause.

"What on earth are you doing?" they all said. "You'll have the police close up the theater if you carry on like that."

I thought everybody ungrateful after giving such a splendid characterization.

"Ah," concluded Mr. Jackson, "you were a whimsical little fellow in those days. I always knew you had something in you."

"I must have been a pretty bad lot," I laughed.

"Not at all," said Jackson, "you were gentle as a little girl."

Mr. Jackson is a grand old man. He is well into the seventies, but he is just as bright and vigorous as he ever was. I see little change in him in all these years and he is still actively running troupes of dancers and finding new talent. It was his schooling that laid the foundation for my career. He was a good teacher—a just and kind man.

The King of the Belgians[22] was in Paris and expressed a desire to meet me. It was arranged that I should go to the Belgian Embassy. The appointment was for three o'clock.

When we arrived, the King had evidently just returned from some official affair. We were kept waiting in the dark recesses of the reception hall. Suddenly a door opened from one of the chambers, and a tall stooped figure appeared with no coat and braces dangling, and with his back toward us, went ambling down the corridor in a preoccupied manner. He turned to enter another chamber and as he did so, he caught sight of us, then exited rapidly.

I had my suspicions as to the identity of the gentlemen and I think everybody else did, but we pretended not to notice it. One of the emissaries, however, remarked that the King might be changing his uniform as he usually does four or five times a day should official occasions warrant it.

After a minute or so the Belgian ambassador appeared, and after signing the visitors' book, I was ushered into the presence of His Majesty. The ambassador, having introduced me, made his exit and we were left alone.

His Majesty pointed to a chair and commanded me to be seated, at the same time drawing one up for himself. The King is an extremely tall man with a benevolent face and quiet manner. His imposing height accentuates his royal dignity.

Unfortunately, my seat was extremely low and the King, drawing his chair—a high one—in close proximity to mine, added greatly to the contrast in our height. My nose was somewhere up to His Majesty's knee when we were finally seated. His Majesty was quiet, so I felt I should start the conversation. "It is a great honor and pleasure, Your Majesty, to be given this opportunity to meet you."

The King nodded. After this I was at a loss.

"I suppose you're not staying here long," I said.

"No," he answered quietly.

And I proceeded, "I understand you flew here."

"Yes," the King replied.

With my voice becoming weaker and my confidence gradually ebbing away, I continued, "Well, that's wonderful—quite wonderful. I enjoy flying myself. Yes, I enjoy flying," I repeated. "It is so thrilling and exciting." Somehow I can't get off the topic. "Yes," I said with my hands in the attitude of prayer and looking toward the window thoughtfully, "it has come to stay—the airplane is here to stay." The last phrase somehow confused me. Was I discussing airplanes or talking pictures?

I saw His Majesty looking strangely at me. I smiled somewhat sickly. "I suppose you are a busy man these days." Now I feel I have said something too familiar. Should I have said "man"? Yet one could hardly say, "I suppose you are a busy king these days."

His Majesty, as though not having heard anything I'd said, asked, "Do you make all your pictures in California?"

"Yes, sir," I answered quickly.

"Isn't it possible—since the advent of artificial lights and all the new appliances that you have developed in photography—that you could make them anywhere now?"

"Oh, yes," I replied.

This seemed to break the ice and from then on, the conversation was easier. It wasn't confined to pictures, but to art, literature, and science, and the King was most stimulating on these subjects.

When leaving, again I became a little confused as to the etiquette of my departure. I had been told as a child one must back out of a room before royalty, but being alone with His Majesty, I felt this preposterous. However, I compromised and went out like a crab, sidling myself to the door and groping for the handle as I bade farewell to His Majesty.

Part III[1]

Lady Deterding[2] was staying at the Crillon. She had arranged to give a party one evening. We were to have Russian music, caviar, vodka, and champagne. It was a very grand affair. The whole of Paris society was there, including princes, barons, counts, dukes, lords, earls, and misters.

The dinner was a grand success. As it progressed, the Russian musicians would sing a toast to each guest, who, with a full glass of champagne, would drink it down to the chorus.

I might mention I am not a sincere drinker, but I was told that two gentlemen of the party had conspired to get me drunk. They had bribed the musicians to repeatedly toast me during dinner. This meant that I would have to empty a full tumbler of champagne each time. Before dinner I found the waiter who would be serving me and so I bribed him to substitute ginger ale for champagne.

Nobody was aware of the deception and so I drank about nine large glasses of ginger ale. The conspirators were greatly impressed with my capacity, but I also conspired. I insisted that if I drink to all these toasts, they—the conspirators—must drink with me. So after the ninth glass, the conspirators were no more.

This is Wednesday evening and I am to leave with the Duke of Westminster for Normandy to hunt wild boar. I go to his hotel to arrange about the journey. I meet Sem,[3] the renowned caricaturist, there. He is a friend of the duke's. It is unfortunate that he cannot speak English. So I have to be contented with translation.

He is very small in stature being several inches shorter than myself. I learned he had already been on one of these hunting expeditions and when I inquired if he were coming with us this time, he quickly shook his head and positively affirmed the negative. I did not get the significance of his

An example of photographer Lee Miller's photos of Chaplin, taken in Paris, as they appeared in *Pour Vous*, April 14, 1932. (*Author's collection*)

refusal at the time. Only after my own harrowing experience did I appreciate his resolute stand.

We left Paris that evening and dined on the train, arriving that night in Normandy. From the station we had about two hours' drive to the duke's chateau, a house of about sixteen rooms, simply furnished, old-fashioned but comfortable. It was a bitter cold drive there, but we were shown into a nice warm room with a cheery fire burning and a table spread invitingly with all sorts of victuals. There were appetizing cold cuts and long-necked bottles and so we supped.

Afterward we sat around the fire with our whiskies and sodas and discussed the prospects of the morrow.

"I have never been on an expedition of this nature before," I said.

"Of course you can ride," said the duke.

"In a way," I replied hesitatingly. "But I haven't ridden in ten years. In fact, I've done practically no riding at all."

I thought I detected concern in the glance of His Grace. "But," I continued reassuringly, "I have never fallen off—yet." And I laughed, perhaps a little too heartily.

The duke explained to me the method of hunting. "We first send out men who find the tracks of the boar. Usually they lead to a forest where he's hiding, and from there the hunt begins. The hounds are put upon the scent and we proceed to track him down. You will have a knife—a sort of spear— which you will use to thrust at the animal if it's your luck to corner him."

"Quite so," I said feebly.

"You get off your horse for this purpose. But be careful not to dismount until the boar is securely pinned down by the dogs."

"I understand," I muttered.

"The boar is very ferocious—in fact, most dangerous. If the dogs haven't a secure hold on him, he's liable to get up and attack you."

"Oh, yeah?" I gulped.

"I've known them to attack a horse," he said. "But there, I'm talking too much. Tomorrow we may not see one and then you'll be disappointed."

"Oh, not at all," I said airily.

"However, let's find the tracks of the boar and do the talking after."

"Quite right," I put in. "Don't let's spear our boars before they're tracked."

And so we retired, agreeing to be up at six the following morning.

In spite of the comfort of my bed, I didn't sleep a wink all night. Many problems were running through my mind—what would happen if I were confronted with the boar? However, my greatest concern was whether I could stay on the horse. The more I thought of this, the less I liked the animal. I could never understand man's sentimental attachment to the beast. I'd remember every accident I" ever had with him.

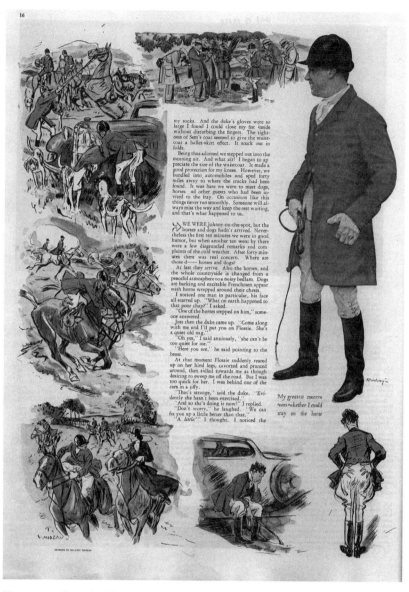

My greatest concern
was whether I could
stay on the horse

Illustrations from the November 1933 installment of "A Comedian Sees the World,"
Woman's Home Companion, of the boar hunt. (*Author's collection*)

The Duke of Westminster and Chaplin on the boar hunt. (*Charlie Chaplin archive*)

I had hired a horse in Oldham where the roads were paved in cobble-stones. I remember galloping down the main street until he slipped and I went sprawling, and how the horse regained himself and I was left dangling by the stirrup, his hind hoofs just missing my head. How the streetcars stopped and the women screamed until I was eventually rescued. These thoughts kept me tossing throughout the night.

By morning I was a complete wreck. My bones ached and my eyes smarted from lack of sleep. My brain felt like a piece of lead in a vacuum, a sort of top-heavy feeling. However, I was thankful to be over the torture of that restless night. On coming downstairs, I was informed that the boar's tracks had been found.

The duke was dressed in huntsman style, a red coat and a hard, plush jockey cap. I felt a little *de trop*, not having the correct costume. I had hurriedly bought riding breeches and boots, but no coat or helmet. However, the duke provided me with a rig-out. I wore Sem's little red coat, which made my breathing difficult, and one of the duke's helmets, also his waistcoat.

I might mention the duke is a man about six feet three and thickset in proportion, and so his waistcoat hung to the level of my knees. In reaching for a match from the pocket, I looked as though I were pulling up my socks. And the duke's gloves were so large I found I could close my fist inside without disturbing the fingers. The tightness of Sem's coat seemed to give the waistcoat a ballet-skirt effect. It stuck out in folds.

Being thus adorned we stepped out into the morning air. And what air! I began to appreciate the size of the waistcoat. It made a good protection for my knees. However, we bundled into automobiles and sped forty miles away[4] to where the tracks had been found. It was here we were to meet dogs, horses, and other guests who had been invited to the fray. On occasions like this, things never run smoothly. Someone will always miss the way and keep the rest waiting, and that's what happened to us.

We were johnny-on-the-spot, but the horses and dogs hadn't arrived. Nevertheless, the first ten minutes we were in good humor, but when another ten went by, there were a few disgruntled remarks and complaints of the cold weather. After forty minutes there was real concern. Where are those d——horses and dogs?

At last they arrive. Also, the horses and the whole countryside changed from a peaceful atmosphere to a noisy bedlam. Dogs are barking and excitable Frenchmen appear with horns wrapped around their chests.

I noticed one man in particular, his face all scarred up. "What on earth happened to that poor chap?" I asked.

"One of the horses stepped on him," someone answered.

Just then the duke came up. "Come along with me and I'll put you on Flossie. She's a quiet old nag."

"Oh yes," I said anxiously, "she can't be too quiet for me."

"Here you are," he said pointing to the beast.

At that moment, Flossie suddenly reared up on her hind legs, cavorted and pranced around, then sidled towards me as though desiring to sweep me off the road. But I was too quick for her. I was behind one of the cars in a jiffy.

"That's strange," said the duke. "Evidently she hasn't been exercised."

"And so she's doing it now!" I replied.

"Don't worry," he laughed. "We can fix you up a little better than that."

"A '*little!*'" I thought. I noticed the qualifying adjective. Thereupon another horse was produced. I must say he was better mannered than Flossie. After being bunked up or bundled up, as it were, I proceeded to adjust my trappings. I had never ridden before with so much paraphernalia—spears; whips, gloves, reins had to be managed. I had quite a problem fixing the reins between the duke's gloves.

Reporters and cameramen have also arrived and I am photographed. Now that I am in the saddle, I feel agreeably confident. I see the reporters eying me admiringly—at least I think so. I feel very debonair. I have a desire to impress them that I've done this thing before. I glance discreetly at my waistcoat. Even that falls gracefully about the horse. If I can only make a good start, says I to myself, everything will be "jake."

The animal, not having moved since I mounted, was busy nibbling the tops of some bushes, so with a jerk and a "giddap," I attempted to move him. But he paid no attention.

Knowing the eyes of the reporters were on me, I affected an air of indifference as though I'd changed my mind. The duke's secretary pranced up to my side.

"Now this is the idea," he said. "Follow the hounds or the direction of the bugle call. Then you won't go wrong. Stick close to me and you'll be all right."

"I shall do my level best," I said sincerely.

And so we were ready, the duke leading the way. We started quietly down the lane in lazy fashion. I was really beginning to enjoy it all. The glory of the morning sun and the aromatic smell of the earth made me feel attune with nature, man, and beast. I turned to the secretary. "Of course," I said, jokingly, "we go faster than this."

"Oh, yes, when the bugle sounds," he laughed.

His remark left me with a tinge of suspense—in fact a growing anxiety. At that moment we were coming to a shady part of the lane with gorgeous oaks on all sides when something went, "Tata ta tah, tata ta tah."

The next I remember was swallowing the horse's ear. He had been quick on the uptake at the sound of the bugle call and was off to a flying start. I found I had suddenly embraced him around the neck. I could hear someone yell, "Hey, stop! You've dropped your hat and whip!"

But that didn't worry me. I was concerned with what would drop next. We swung around the trees and ducked branches. Oh, yes, we were off the road and galloping through a forest. In the blur of it all, I saw a fence ahead of me. Fortunately, the horse must have seen it too, for he stopped, but not abruptly enough to extricate him from my caressing arms. So I hung on. But we didn't stop long. Before I could say "Jack Robinson," he turned and was off again.

In that short time I discovered I was an expert rider. By some miracle I managed to get back into the saddle, doing many things at once—controlling my balance, ducking branches, and at the same time trying to catch the stirrups with my feet, and I succeeded in doing all three of them.

Eventually we came upon the secretary, with a dash and a pivot pulling up crosswise in front of him. "I wouldn't ride too hard if I were you," he said.

"Tell that to the horse," I replied.

I was handed my hat and whip, and arranging my cravat, went off in hot pursuit again; or at least the horse did. We went bouncing and jolting in one direction and then another. By now I was able to follow the secretary. We would bound up a hill, then stop, look, and listen. How I would love those pauses. How sweet and restful they were, just looking and listening. It was the one moment I could gather myself together.

"Did you hear anything?" the secretary would ask earnestly.

Feigning deep concern and striving to look intelligent, I would answer, "I don't think so."

But the infernal horn would blow or the dogs would bark and with great enthusiasm we were off again.

This sort of thing kept up for hours.

At the beginning of the meet I met a charming French lady. She had evidently followed the hounds all her life. She had that bronzed complexion—a regular daughter of the outdoors. She rode sidesaddle and exceedingly well, and for the last two hours of the hunt we kept, somewhat together. At first I thought it considerate of her, but after an hour it became irritating.

She was always behind and I never had an opportunity to rest. Every time I looked back, she would remark, "Il est très gentil, n'est-ce pas?"

"Oh, oui, absolutely," I would smile sickly.

Now I cannot sit upright. I half-slide over to one side of the saddle, embracing it with the calf of my leg, thus relieving my spine. At intervals I change to the other side.

At this juncture the duke came riding up. "It looks pretty bad," he said. "I'm afraid we're out of luck today."

I must have looked sick or something, for he exclaimed, "Look here, old man, you look tired. Don't overdo it. You'd better take my car and go home."

I needed no further encouragement, so went down to the road to find it. When I arrived, a reporter was there with his camera. I must put on a front, I thought.

So, affecting a jaunty air, I threw my leg over the saddle and jumped to the ground. My knees gave way immediately and refused to regain themselves. Eventually I staggered onto my feet. Through riding, the muscles of my back had stretched so that I had no control over them. I would straighten up only to flop over again. Good heavens! I thought, I must have curvature of the spine! By superhuman effort I staggered to the limousine in time to sit on the running board and there I was interviewed.

"Did you enjoy the hunt, Mr. Chaplin?" was the first remark.

"And how!" I answered.

"Did you see a boar?" was the next question.

I could have made a wisecrack as I looked at him, but I wearily shook my head. However, the chauffeur came to the rescue and drove me home.

That evening we stood around the fire—at least I did—discussing the happenings of the day.

"We were just unlucky," they said, "but it's all a part of the game."

"If it's a game," I thought, "I prefer tiddledywinks."

My one concern was Paris and a Turkish bath, so after dinner I left for the city, and I might mention it was four in the morning before I emerged from the manipulations of a masseur.

On reflection, it seems I'm a little unappreciative to my host for his kind and generous hospitality. Perhaps there is caricature in my narrative. If so, it is only in a spirit of fun.

I am not going to bore you with all the minor happenings and social affairs that occurred during my stay in Paris. There were dinner dances, theaters, cabarets, and excursions of all kinds.

My next move was to the south of France to visit my brother, who had been living there for the last six months. I was to be the guest of Frank J. Gould in Nice,[5] so after nine days in Paris, I arrived in the south of France, the playground of the fashionable world.

Chaplin at a private party in Nice, France (Syd Chaplin pictured far left holding glass). (*Charlie Chaplin Archive*)

Nice is a night's journey from Paris, and you arrive on the Côte d'Azur, "the blue coast," about noon, getting your first glimpse of the Mediterranean. It is a pity the railroads are so near the sea. They spoil the coastline. I am a little disappointed with my first glimpse of the country. It seems so congested with its houses on top of one another, so different from the open spaces of the coastline of California.

My friend Frank Gould and his wife[6] met me at the station, along with my brother Syd[7] and his family. I shall not go into the details of the welcome I received from the crowd. Nevertheless, Frank Gould was considerably moved by the demonstration.

"It must make you very happy to be so admired," he remarked.

But after lunch he went with me to buy some tennis rackets, and as we walked along, crowds started gathering until we stopped the traffic. People were pushing and shouting, "Hooray, Charlie!" They became so dense and demonstrative that we could hardly move on our way.

I could see Frank getting quite worried and when we eventually arrived home, he declared, "I wouldn't be you for ten million dollars."

In the afternoon we went to the Municipal Casino for tea. This is a magnificent building decorated in very good style with large dance floors and baccarat rooms. It is reputed to be the largest in the world. Hundreds of people gather there for tea dances and excellent music is provided.

Quite a number of Americans live on the Riviera. I was surprised to hear how bitterly they renounced the States.

"No place to live," they went on, "with their prohibition and Blue Laws and all the don'ts of organized puritanisms. Give us France. There is no humbug. Politics have to suit the people here, but in America the people have to suit politics."

This kind of vitriolic criticism I would hear on all sides and in most cases from Americans. Europeans admit to the genius of the American people, their contributions to science, and their enterprise, but as a country to live in, they shake their heads.

It took me some time before I began to like the south of France. The casino life I found dull and silly, but one could meet nice people who had very attractive homes, and they would entertain in a delightful way. I later discovered there were many lives to live there—the social, the intellectual, and the Bohemian, and, of course, the "casinian."[8]

I am beginning to like Nice. Each morning I get a nice workout at tennis and in the evenings there are friends and parties to keep me happy and well amused. One day I was present at a delightful luncheon, and met many of my friends. Elsa Maxwell,[9] Sir Philip Sassoon, Sir Oswald Mosley,[10] one of the most promising young men in English politics in spite of his momentary defeat.

Dear Elsa! I haven't seen her in years. She is delightful company. With songs of her own composition, she can amuse for hours. She has a special genius. She has taken society as her mode of expression and made an art of it.

That afternoon Sir Philip Sassoon and I went to the house of His Highness, the Duke of Connaught,[11] for tea. The duke is a grand old gentleman past eighty, with a pleasant genial manner. His house is a small simple one surrounded by beautiful flowers and situated in Cap-Ferrat. The duke carries a marked resemblance to his ancestors, the Georges of England. There is no mistaking his lineage. We sat down to a simple cup of tea, about six of us in number. His innate politeness and marked consideration for his guests revealed the charm of his personality. He spoke of going to the opening of my picture. So after a pleasant chat, we made our departure.

At the presentation of my picture in Monte Carlo, I was to be a guest of the Prince of Monaco,[12] the prince and his government having a financial interest in the theater where the picture was to be shown. It was arranged that I would dine with the prince and later be his guest at the theater. But on arriving that evening, I was informed by the Monacan government that the prince was not dining with us as several urgent affairs had arisen and he would be detained, but that he would join us later at the theater, and to compensate me for my disappointment, I would have the pleasure of dining with the whole of his ministry instead. Outside of the British consul, not one of them spoke any English, so I struggled through dinner, looking sweetly idiotic at everybody.

We finished dinner early, but were informed that we were to wait and not go to the theater until ten o'clock as my picture would not go on until then. I suggested to the British consul that we might go earlier, but he remarked that we could hardly take the matter out of their hands as we were their guests and they had charge of the whole affair.

At last word came through that we could leave for the theater. When we arrived, the Prince of Monaco and his daughter were already in the box. It was apparent there had been some sort of misunderstanding. However, after the performance I had the pleasure of being congratulated by the Duke of Connaught, who expressed himself as having enjoyed the picture.

But later I learned that a section of the British press had printed a story imputing that I had kept the Duke of Connaught waiting for hours at the theater, and that I had aroused the indignation of the audience by not showing up until ten o'clock. As I have explained, I was the guest of the Monacan government both for dinner and the theater, they having scheduled the whole program for the evening.

Another story which emanated from that section of the British press declared that I had refused a royal command to perform before the King of England. This also is untrue, I having received only a telegram from a "Mr. Black," who requested me to appear at a vaudeville benefit which was termed "a command performance" because Their Majesties would be present. This was not a royal command. It was the "command" of Mr. Black, who has no official position with the royal household whatsoever.

Mrs. Gould has arranged a most thrilling lunch at the Municipal Casino and some of the most famous names in art and literature will be present—Maeterlinck, Marchand, Domergue, and many others. There was something incongruous about the lunch and these illustrious gentlemen and the background of the casino. Nevertheless, after a cocktail they loosened up and adjusted themselves to the environment.

Maeterlinck's manner is quiet and reserved. He has beautiful silver hair and well-defined features. He is a combination of philosopher and child. On first meeting him I got the impression that he was sullen and moody, but as lunch went on he became jocose. It was very difficult to converse because neither of us could speak the other's language. Conversation is impossible when it has to be repeated and so we all developed into a light and frivolous mood.

Maeterlinck is drawing funny pictures on the bill of fare, which I've asked him to sign, and making humorous comments with a sobriety of manner as though quoting some beautiful passage from his work. I am fascinated as I watch him. In this casino—Maeterlinck, the disciple of beauty, the essayist, and philosopher, who wrote those beautiful words, "There comes a moment in life when moral beauty seems more urgent, more penetrating, than intellectual beauty; when all that the mind has treasured must be bathed in the greatness of soul, lest it perish in the sandy desert, forlorn as the river that seeks in vain for the sea."

He has finished drawing on the bill of fare and smilingly hands it to me.

I have received a telegram from Emil Ludwig.[13] He is on his way to America and will be in the south of France for a day only. I've arranged a program for his stay. We are to lunch at the Palm Beach Casino, a beautiful location opposite the island of Sainte Marguerite upon which stands the historical prison reputed to be the place where The Man in the Iron Mask was incarcerated.

Ludwig has a likeness to Byron—the same high, lofty brow and well-formed chin, with a full, sensitive mouth almost feminine—a man in his early forties. Upon meeting him, I was impressed by his eager, youthful spirit.

During lunch he produced a bay leaf and presented me with it, saying, "It was a custom of the ancient Greeks to bestow a laurel leaf upon those whom they admired, and so I want you to keep this as a token of my esteem."

We also discussed what we considered some of the most beautiful things we had seen in life. I related the action of Helen Wills playing tennis, also a moving picture from a news weekly of a man plowing the fields of Flanders after the war. The tragic stoop of his back, the determination and courage as he furrowed into the soil, the indomitable spirit and will to build up over the wreckage.

Ludwig gave a beautiful description of the glow of a red sun setting on the beach in Florida, an automobile rolling along at twelve miles an hour, and a girl in a bathing suit reclining on the running board, her toe lightly trailing over the smooth surface of the sand, leaving a thin line as she rode along.

In speaking of his little boy, he said, "I have a great deal to live up to. I am looked upon as God in his eyes. The little chap has heard that his father is an author and writes books, and he is bewildered to think they are written in so many languages. He therefore believes that nothing is impossible for Father to do."

Speaking of books, I told him that in my life I had read very little compared to the average man of intelligence. One reason- I was a very slow reader, and therefore very choosy in my selection of literature. I suppose the foundation of my literary education would take in the Bible, Shakespeare, Plutarch's *Lives of the Great*, Burton's *Anatomy of Melancholy,* and Boswell's *Life of Johnson*, with a few philosophers thrown in such as Nietzsche, Emerson, Schopenhauer, and Robert Ingersoll, the latter the first to arouse my interest in philosophy. Emerson and Nietzsche followed.[14] Ingersoll happened around the age of seventeen, quite late in life, I thought. I have but a superficial knowledge of the other classics. Ludwig, on the other hand, has read everything from the early Greeks to the most modern writers of our day.

We agreed that one has very little time to read nowadays and that the novel will eventually pass out, due to the demands of modern life. I asked if the rumor were correct that he was going to do a biography of Edison, Ford, and Rockefeller. He denied this, saying that he was tired of biographies and that he had reverted back to his old love, writing for the theater. He told me he had been an actor before he became an author.

In discussing Jesus and the different conceptions various authors had written of him, he asked me which story I liked best.

"The one that was the most beautiful to me," I replied, "was The Last Thirty Days of Christ written by Sadakichi Hartmann.[15] In his conception, Christ was both the mystic and philosopher, a lone figure, misunderstood even by his disciples."

Ludwig went on to say, "There are many interpretations, but the key to His nature was not in His genius, but in His human heart. This, more than His philosophy, is important."

In the evening we dined at a quiet restaurant. We got onto the subject of luck, how a little accident will change the course of your whole life.

"If it hadn't been for Mack Sennett missing a date with a friend one night, I might have been raising hogs in Arkansas now," I told him. "Sennett has often told of the incident. He had missed an appointment with a friend of his, and so wandered into the American Music Hall, where I was playing. He afterward remarked that if ever he had a company of his own, he would engage me.

"It was only two or three years later that he was part owner of the famous Keystone Film Company. I was a member of a pantomimic troupe working the vaudeville theaters throughout America. I had had indifferent success, and was so discouraged that I made up my mind to become a farmer. A member of the company and I were going into partnership in this enterprise. We were saving our money to buy land in Arkansas and raise pigs. I bought books and studied hogs' diseases, when a telegram came and threw a monkey wrench into the whole works.

"We were playing somewhere in the 'smalls' of Philadelphia. The wire read: 'Are you the man who played the drunk at the American Music Hall three years ago? If so, will you get in touch with Kessel and Bauman, Longacre Building, New York?'

"I hadn't the faintest idea who Kessel and Bauman were. Perhaps it was a firm of lawyers and some rich relative of mine had died and left me a fortune. I was a little let down when I discovered it was a motion picture concern; nevertheless, I was elated.

"Mr. Kessel informed me that Mack Sennett had instructed him to get in touch with me. I remember how well I played my cards at that interview with Charlie Kessel; how I boosted my salary. I was getting seventy-five dollars a week at that time. I assured Kessel that my only interest in motion pictures was the consideration of my health. The work would be in the open air and the outdoor life appealed to me. It was for this reason only that I would consider pictures. Of course, I went on, I got two hundred and fifty dollars a week in vaudeville, but on account of the nature of the work, I would make a sacrifice. We eventually compromised for one hundred and fifty dollars, and I left the office firm in the belief that I was an embezzler.

"My one anxiety now was to justify my salary. On my arrival in Los Angeles to fill my contract, I went to a theater, and seated in front of me was Mack Sennett, and I made myself known to him. He was quite shocked that I looked so young, for it was the first time he'd seen me without my make-up.

"'Are you sure you're the man I saw play in the American Music Hall?'

"'Of course,' I replied, but he seemed to doubt me.

"However, he told me to come to the studio in the morning.

"When I arrived there, I was so nervous and shy I stood outside contemplating whether or not to go in, but my courage failed me and I returned to the hotel. For three mornings I did this. On the fourth, Mr. Sennett telephoned me asking what had happened, so that day I steeled myself for the ordeal.

"For a week I wandered around the studio watching the companies at work. Mabel Normand and Ford Sterling were the stars and they were very kind to me. Occasionally I would meet Mack Sennett crossing the lot in a preoccupied manner. Sometimes he would notice me and I would smile weakly. Somehow I had a feeling that now I'd arrived, I wasn't wanted. Perhaps he was disappointed in my youthful appearance. I was convinced he felt he'd made a bad bargain.

"The most frightening thing of all was the fact that the great Ford Sterling was only getting fifty dollars a week more than I, and other members of the company three dollars a day who I thought were very good actors. All this gave me a great deal of anxiety.

"At last I was put to work. The picture was called *Making a Living* and I played the part of a reporter, but for this I didn't dress in my familiar screen make-up. The set was the interior of a newspaper office where I was to apply for a job. In those days, nobody worked by script, but made it up as they went along. When I started, the whole studio came over to our set to watch the new comedian.

"The director stood musing, thinking of business which would get a laugh. I offered a suggestion which was accepted. I remember the awful moment when the cameras were prepared and I stood in back of the scenery, ready to make an entrance.

"The piece of business I suggested got a laugh from the onlookers. This encouraged me and I made other suggestions, but in doing so I aroused the ire of the director. In my anxiety I suppose I wanted to do too much.

"Comedy stories in those days were only an excuse for a chase, but I wanted to stand still and be funny. They argued, 'That takes up too much footage.'

"I had many set-tos with the director on the subject. I would argue that anyone could chase or push over an apple cart, and that it wasn't necessary to pay a man my salary for doing such things. I was reported to Mack Sennett as being difficult to handle. After that picture I was laid off for a week and I became anxious about my job.

"But again I was put to work. A hotel set was built for Mabel Normand's picture and I was hurriedly told to put on a funny make-up. This time I went to the wardrobe and got a pair of baggy pants, a tight coat, a small derby flat, and a large pair of shoes. I wanted the clothes to be a mass of contradictions, knowing pictorially the figure would be vividly outlined on the screen. To add a comic touch, I wore a small mustache which would not hide my expression.

"My appearance got an enthusiastic response from everyone, including Mr. Sennett. The clothes seemed to imbue me with the spirit of the character. He actually became a man with a soul—a point of view.

"I defined to Mr. Sennett the type of person he was. 'He wears an air of romantic hunger, forever seeking romance, but his feet won't let him.'

"He was quite a success with the members of the studio, but the public hadn't seen him yet. After that bit in Mabel's picture, I was given another director. But they all went to Mr. Sennett complaining I was difficult to handle. Four pictures were made in that character when the matter was brought to a head.

"'You'd better do what you're told or quit,' said Mr. Sennett.

"I little realized how close I came to being cashiered. I afterward found out that he intended dismissing me that day, but later that evening the atmosphere changed for some mysterious reason. Mr. Sennett came into my dressing room.

"'Look here, Charlie,' he said, 'you don't want to raise the antagonism of all the directors. They like your work, and they like you personally, and whatever they tell you is for your own good.'

"I couldn't understand this sudden change of attitude, but Mack told me later that that evening he had received a telegram from the New York office of Kessel and Bauman telling him to hurry and make more pictures with 'the fellow with the big feet and baggy pants' as there was an increased demand for them.

"That evening I asked him to let me direct myself in a picture.

"'Yes, but who's going to pay for the negative if you spoil it?'

"'I will,' I said and pleaded with him to give me a chance.

"He eventually acquiesced, so I immediately corralled a few Keystone cops, a nursemaid, and a soldier, and with a few bricks and comedy ammunition, went off into the park to make my first picture.

"When it was finished, Mack saw it run off in the projection room. Occasionally he would laugh and when it was over, he said, 'When are you going to start another one?'

"From then on I was established as my own director."

I was encouraged by Mr. Ludwig to relate many anecdotes of my early career and it was his fault that I monopolized so much of the time. It was two o'clock in the morning before we left the restaurant and said good-bye, he having to leave the Riviera for Cherbourg, where he was to embark for America.

H. G. Wells[16] was staying near Grasse and invited me to spend a few days with him. He was just completing his book, *The Work, Wealth, and Happiness of Mankind*—a colossal undertaking upon which he had been working three years.

"What are you going to do after it's finished?" I asked.

"Start on another one."

"Good heavens! I should imagine you'd want to get away from work for a while and do something else."

H. G. laughed mischievously. "What else is there to do?"

Discussing my pictures, he said he would like to see me return to the

Left to right: Chaplin, Mrs. Goldwyn, H. G. Wells, Paulette Goddard, and Sam Goldwyn in Los Angeles, California, December 4, 1935. (*Charlie Chaplin Archive*)

shorter comedy subjects. "You set yourself a difficult task, adhering to plot and theme so much. Who remembers the plots of Dickens's books—*Pickwick Papers,* for instance? It was their incidents and characterizations that made the appeal. Personally I would like to see you oftener on the screen in those two-reel pictures, which had so much spontaneity."

We arranged to visit Grasse, the beautiful city with the atmosphere of the twelfth century. It is picturesquely situated on the hills sixteen hundred feet above the Mediterranean.

Grasse is celebrated for the manufacture of perfumery, and H. G. and I planned to go over some of the factories. I've heard somewhere that the preparation of attar of roses requires the crushing of four million flowers to obtain a pound of essence, which costs approximately five hundred dollars.

We intended viewing the monuments of the city and the cathedral. However, as we were climbing the narrow streets, my garter broke. This made it necessary for us to go to the shopping center to buy a new pair.

As we wended our way, H. G. extolling the beauties of the city, he was unconscious of the people who began to crowd in the doorways of the stores. They seemed to come from nowhere, and before we knew it, we were like the Pied Piper of Hamelin.

It was no use. Normal conversation was impossible. H. G. became alarmed. "I think you'd better walk by yourself," he suggested, "and I'll meet you at the car later."

"Oh, no," I insisted. "You're going to see it through."

We took refuge in the shop for a while, but eventually had to brave the storm, marching through alleys with the throngs at the back of us.

To visit the perfume factories or the cathedral now was impossible. "I'm sorry, but you'll have to put it off until you've grown a beard," he said and so we made our way back to the automobile and escaped.

Not all our excursions were like this. We made several others and had charming times.

I suppose it is bromidic to say that H. G. Wells is a vitally interesting companion. During my visit to Europe, I had occasion to enjoy many wonderful evenings with him, and whatever subject was discussed, he was most entertaining. He has that gift of making clear the most abstract of sciences. I remember one evening discussing the fourth dimension—how lucidly he defined the principles of relativity.

He told an amusing story of how, as a young man before he ever had any fame as an author, he wrote a paper that touched on that subject and submitted it to several editors. His only response came from Frank Harris, the famous editor of *The Fortnightly Review*, who told him that he'd read his paper and wished to see him.

H. G. said he procured a silk hat, which he carefully brushed for the occasion. When he was shown into the office, he placed it on the editor's desk. He said Frank Harris's brusque manner almost petrified him.

"'Your article interests me,' said Frank, 'but how on earth do you expect the public to understand it? Go and write something we can publish.'

"During the interview," H. G. went on, "Frank would occasionally pound the desk and the silk hat would jump nearer to the edge of it. I reached to save it as discreetly as I could when Frank remarked, 'Where on earth did you get that hat?' I left the office humiliated, resolved never to wear the thing again."

Chaplin sunbathing on the French Riviera (May Reeves lying down far left). (*Charlie Chaplin Archive*)

During the rest of my sojourn in the south of France, I met many celebrities, men of both national and international reputation. M. Bailby, then publisher of *L'Intransigeant,* gave a lunch at his beautiful house in Biot. Among the guests were Princess Murat, Baron and Baroness de Rothschild, and Madame and M. Berthelot. The house is exquisitely done in modern style.

Before leaving for Algiers, I had the pleasure of dining with Paul Morand,[17] the author of that delightful book, *New York,* and many other works. He too has a charming modern house near Monte Carlo.

If my vocation were that of a writer and space would permit, I should like to elaborate on the great personalities I met during my holiday. Owing to the blur and excitement of meeting so many eminent people all at once, it was difficult to absorb much of their personalities. For more than their impressions affecting me, I can modestly—or immodestly—say I was more concerned in effecting the right impression on them. 'Twas ever thus—the creed of an actor. Nevertheless, in reading over this manuscript I find it most revealing—the eternal "I, I, I"—and what happened to me.

There is something romantic about the name Algeria. It stimulates my imagination. I can visualize wild Saracenic tribes adorned in flowing colored togas.

I have a profound respect for their mode of living. They have the true meaning of life—these children of Omar Khayyam—with their camels and dates, so different from us victims of industry.

Owing to the mildness of the climate, Algiers has become a favorite resort for those seeking to escape the rigors of a European winter. As we approach its port, the city with its dazzling white terraces, its myriads of windows reflecting the glow of the African sun against a green hilly background gives one the impression of a cluster of pearls set in an emerald frame.

With all his Omar Khayyam philosophy, the Arab is an enthusiastic film fan, for when we arrived, thousands were lined along the road all the way to the hotel.

The modern part of the city is little different from any town in France. But for a great number of natives in their Arab costumes, one could as well be in Spain or any French town along the Mediterranean coast. The Arab part, however, is more colorful.

I made an excursion through that section. You leave your automobile at the bottom of a hill and take an Arab guide, who conducts you through the narrow winding streets. Here life is picturesque. You will see artisans working at their trades in the same primitive way they did centuries ago. As we passed through the streets, peering into strange hovels and dark alcoves, we would occasionally turn into an open square—a sort of rampart—overlooking the city and the sea.

Algeria has many points of historical interest, among which is the tomb, Kubr-er-Rumia, reputed to be the burial place of Cleopatra Selene, the daughter of the famous Cleopatra and Mark Antony. Unfortunately, I didn't go there. It was bad enough walking the streets with the throngs that followed. On one occasion while shopping, the crowd became so riotous they smashed in the window of a store and the police had to be called.

During my stay in Algeria I intended to make several trips through North Africa, but, unfortunately, the season was at an end and the hotels were closed for the summer months.

On my return from Algeria[18] I stayed in the south of France for a while and visited the late Frank Harris,[19] who was then living in Nice.

I have been an admirer of Frank's for many years and read almost every book he has written. To my mind, his biography of Oscar Wilde is one of the greatest in English and will rate on a par with Boswell's *Life of Johnson.* It is a chronicle of the Gay Nineties—the period of Whistler, Beardsley, Rossetti, Meredith, Swinburne, Browning, Ruskin, Pacer, and hosts of others who were the center of arts and letters of that time.

Poor Frank has been so criticized for his recently published autobiography, *My Life and Loves,* bur nevertheless one will always remember him for his masterpieces such as *The Man Shakespeare, Unpath'd Waters, The Bomb,* and *Montes the Matador.*

The first time I met Frank was in 1920. I went with a friend of mine, Haldemann Julius, to hear him lecture. I remember my surprise on hearing his resonant voice. In appearance he looked somewhat like the Kaiser did before the war. He had tremendous magnetism and assurance on the platform.

We afterward went to his house for supper where I met his beautiful Titian-haired wife. We sat talking into the small hours. Frank was a wonderful conversationalist. He told a story of Bismarck, who had been verbally attacked in the Reichstag by a member of his own party. Frank imitated the great statesman addressing the assembly.

"I respect an enemy," said Bismarck, pointing to a socialist, then turning to his attacker, "but I despise a traitor."

All this Frank acted in German.

At his house in Nice we dined quietly. He told me he was touched by the courtesy of the American immigration officials during his last trip to America. He was given the freedom of the port and treated with every civility.

"This was a surprise after the way they treated me during the war. Nevertheless, I am at that age when courtesies of this nature move me deeply."

Talking of personal experiences, I said, "Do you realize that a public man or celebrity seldom gets a normal reaction from people? They are either over-interested or will assume an attitude toward you."

I told him the following story, which happened to me a few years ago and which illustrated what I meant:

One evening during the preparation of a picture, I was walking the streets of Los Angeles. The day had been disappointing. Ideas were not coming, and feeling depressed, I decided to go downtown and lose myself in the atmosphere of some small lunch counter and dine alone. On this particular evening I had on an old suit of clothes and a week's growth of beard and in appearance looked like a bill poster out of a job.

As I walked along Main Street, I noticed a young girl, modestly attired, evidently a factory worker, with rather a wistful face. She was not pretty, but there was something in her manner—a whimsy, a sadness—that intrigued me.

Being depressed and disappointed with the events of the day, how refreshing, I thought, to get away from my work and to talk to someone who had no notion of it. How nice if I could make the acquaintance of this girl. Yet I daren't. It would be misunderstood.

As we walked along, I noticed she was eating some candies. Accidentally she dropped the bag but, as luck would have it, she picked it up before I had a chance to do so. She noticed my attempt and smiled.

"Too late," she said.

"That's always my luck," I answered and that started the conversation.

"Where are you going?" I inquired and she told me she was waiting to pick up her girlfriend whom she was to meet outside the Owl Drug Store at seven-thirty.

"Then do you mind if I keep you company till she arrives?" I asked.

"Not at all," she said.

I could tell that she didn't know me. Here was an adventure. Her indifference was a little disturbing. But it was so natural and honest that it challenged my vanity. I found myself wanting to make an impression, not as Charlie Chaplin, but as a personality for my actual self.

"Do you live in Los Angeles?" I asked as we strolled along.

"Yes, but my real home is in the east."

"What part?"

"New York."

"Oh, I've been there," I said boastfully. "As a matter of fact, I've just returned from a trip around the world."

"Oh, yes?" she said mechanically.

"Yes, I've traveled everywhere."

She dismissed my attempts to impress her by announcing it must be seven-thirty and she must meet her friend.

"Tell me," I said as we made our way to the drugstore, "why did you pick me up?"

"I don't know. I had nothing to do for half an hour."

"But why especially me?" I insisted. "You could have picked someone else."

"Oh, I don't know—I thought you looked nice."

"How can I look nice? I need a shave."

"Do you? I never noticed it."

"Tell me," I insisted, "do you really think I'm nice?"

"Why of course. Otherwise I wouldn't have spoken to you."

This was the first time she really showed interest. Then after a pause, she exclaimed, "Say, you're funny. Who are you anyway, and where do you work?"

For some unknown reason, I told her my name was Gale and that I was a professor of English in Hollywood High School. A cloud came over her face and I felt that my occupation had not met with her approval.

We arrived at the corner of the drug store where she was to meet her friend. A thin, poorly dressed girl with aquiline features approached us and I was introduced in a perfunctory way.

"This is Mr. Gale," said my companion. The newcomer merely nodded a quick "How do you do," then dismissed me abruptly and became engrossed in her friend.

For two blocks they were absorbed in conversation and I felt like an unnecessary appendage. Eventually they became conscious of my presence and turning to me politely, my companion remarked to her friend, "Mr. Gale is a professor of English."

The friend looked bewildered.

Now I thought I'd have fun. I'd surround myself with an air of mystery. So I talked of my travels and bragged of the famous people I knew—my friend Charlie Schwab, the Vanderbilts and Astors whose names I flipped off in a most casual way.

I told them I had several cars, including a Rolls Royce, but I rarely used them as I preferred to walk for the exercise. The effect was amusing. They would occasionally glance at each other with a look of bored resignation. It was evident that I was tolerated as a hopeless liar.

Later I announced that I was hungry and would like dinner. I told them that in spite of all the big hotels, I occasionally went to Childs' as I enjoyed the buckwheat cakes there.

My friends smiled superciliously. "Very well, then we shall leave you."

"But won't you dine with me?"

"I should like to, but there are two of us."

"I should be charmed to have you both."

She turned to her companion inquiringly, then to me and said, "Look here, we'll walk with you as far as the restaurant. Then we'll leave. You can't take two of us to dinner. It isn't fair."

I was touched by her consideration. We stood for a moment outside Childs'.

"Please won't you both dine with me?" I implored.

"Well of course if you feel that way about it, we'd like to."

As we were about to enter, I hesitated.

"If I'm taking two ladies to dinner, I'm not going to Childs'. I think the Biltmore would be much nicer," I said, referring to one of the best hotels in the city.

My companions winked at each other. "That's quite all right. We're not going to call your bluff. Childs' is good enough for us."

But I was resolute. "Oh, no," I insisted, "let's go to the Biltmore." And before they could remonstrate, I led them off by the arm.

From then on they were completely baffled. For the first time I had made an impression. But I still carried on my braggadocio. This time they listened politely.

My appearance was not prepossessing, but as we passed through the hotel lobby, several bellboys recognized me and bowed respectfully, the head waiter also, without mentioning my name.

I began to put on airs to impress my friends. I was most fastidious about the selection of my table and imperious with the waiters. I ordered all the expensive dishes I could think of from duck *á la presse* to crêpes Suzette and others that required cuisinal finishing touches at the table. Every culinary piece of machinery was in operation.

Now their attitude changed. The thin one lost her personality and sat dumb and frightened, but my companion made an effort at "literary" conversation.

"Do you know Percy Hammond, the dramatic critic of *The Tribune?*" she asked.

I answered in the negative. Eventually the conversation got around to motion pictures and the friend suddenly awakened from her stupor and scrutinizing me, remarked, "Do you know your face is familiar, but I can't think where I've seen it. It's been worrying me all evening and now I know who you look like. It's Charlie Chaplin!"

"I hope not!" I answered quickly. "He's not a very imposing figure."

"Oh, I don't mean on the screen, but just around the eyes."

"As long as it isn't around the feet," I rejoined. "What do you think of him anyway?"

"Not much," she answered. "I don't care for comedy. I prefer the serious things."

At that moment a waiter came up. "I'm sorry, Mr. Chaplin, but we have no fresh asparagus."

"You—Charlie Chaplin!" said the thin girl, astonished.

I nodded mischievously and she started to giggle.

"I'm so tickled to death you aren't an English professor."

And I'm proud to say that their manner changed immediately to warm friendliness.

Afterward I asked them what they thought of my bragging. My friend said of course she didn't believe a word of it, but that when we came to the hotel, she was baffled. All sorts of ideas were running through her mind.

"I thought you might be a spy or a detective, and then I gave up and accepted the fact that you might be what you said you were—an English professor."

After dinner we went to a movie and I saw them home.

"Mr. Chaplin," said my friend, "this has been the most wonderful evening of my life and I shall always remember it."

There was something wistful about it all when we said good-bye.

"You should write," was Frank's comment after I finished the story.

I was flattered by his remark, especially coming from one I admired so much. He little realized what an insidious seed he had planted in the soil of my literary desire.

"You're touching a vulnerable spot that's everybody's weakness," I said. "I'd like to write, but grammar would cramp my style."

"Grammar nonsense," said Frank. "Who has the authority to say what's grammatically correct? Colloquialisms come into usage and are accepted. Ambiguity is the only fault in a sentence."

"Quite true," I said. "There are many grammatical phrases ambiguous as far as I'm concerned. For example, in Tennyson's *Idylls of the King*—'His honor rooted in dishonor stood, And faith unfaithful kept him falsely true.' That and some of the phraseology of our congressional records are beyond me.

"So many people are snobbish about grammar," I continued. "They think it's a sign of good breeding. Shakespeare and others had no qualms about using ungrammatical sentences, and many of them are vividly expressive and euphonious, such as Shelley's 'Ode to the West Wind'—'Be thou me, impetuous one.' How unmusical 'I' would sound in that sentence. Then in Julius Caesar—'The clock hath stricken three.' Also the line from *As You Like It*—'Rosalind lacks then the love which teacheth thee that thou and I am one.' The last line may not be grammatical, but I like it. 'Thou and I am one' vividly expresses the oneness of two persons."

"You carrying on like this and you tell me you haven't a flair for writing!" exclaimed Frank.

"I'm just doing my stuff to see if I could get away with it," I said jokingly.

That evening was the last I saw of him, for six months later he died. He was a great man in the literary world, although very much maligned. He made enemies, but also many friends. He championed the cause of the underdog and fought for those principles he believed in. He may have written frankly, but he wrote well and I feel sure his works will live after him.

Part IV

After my visit to the south of France, I motored to Paris with my friend, Harry D'Arrast.[1] This gave me an opportunity to see the beauties of the countryside, the richness of Burgundy, and the fecund province of Oise with its rich green fields and cattle with their noses steeped in buttercups.

He told me that I must visit Biarritz, the fashionable seaside resort situated near the border of Spain. We motored down, spending the night at Château Brissac, the present home of Duke de Brissac, a magnificent old house built in the twelfth century. That evening we visited the wine cellars, sampling many of the vintages. They were most insidious. Before the evening was over, I was a connoisseur, retiring that night feeling mellow, but arising with a sharp edge.

Biarritz, at one time a fishing village, was made popular by the patronage of Emperor Napoleon III and the Empress Eugenie and is now one of the most famous resorts in Europe. The season is continuous.

In spite of the depression, life is gay and amusing. Before dinner everybody gathers at Bar Basque. The atmosphere is festive and congenial. You sit outside at one of the many tables and talk over the affairs of the day. This lasts from about five to seven. All nations are represented, with a predominance of Spanish, English, and Americans.

Later one clamors for a seat at the Café de Paris, a most popular restaurant with excellent cuisine. Princes, earls, and millionaires all wait in line. The place is small and their business big, and prices are quite reasonable.

Then there were the delightful parties given by Jean Patou[2] at his beautiful house, a little way out of Biarritz.

Also the Marquis de Sorreana, a Spanish nobleman, has a remarkable house in Biarritz, where he keeps pet polar bears. As you look through one of the windows of the sitting-room, you gaze directly into the cage of these creatures.

Adjoining the house is his own private factory, where he builds racing motor boats for a hobby—not made for profit, but to sell to his friends at cost price. His factory consists of ten employees, engineers, and mechanics, whom he keeps working the year round.

A most beautiful yet revolting afternoon was spent at a bullfight in San Sebastian. For thrills and drama, it excels any sport I've seen. On the other hand, its sanguine brutality disgusts one. I had been told much about the technique of the bull fight—the beauty of the dance of death.

My friend, the Marquis de Sorreana, warned me that I would probably have several bulls dedicated to me, so I ordered four cigarette cases for the event.

The fight took place at four o'clock in the afternoon. The arena was crowded with men, women, and children. The band struck up a lively Spanish march and on came the procession of toreadors in their colored regalia, a symphony of blue, red, and gold. They saluted the president's box. Then all of them exited save the matador and his assistants, who were to fight the first bull.

The matador came to our box and, with a grandiose gesture, threw his gold-embroidered cape toward me, saying, "We who are about to die salute you!" Then turning, he threw his hat over his shoulder and I caught it. My friend told me to put the cigarette case inside and throw it back to him after the fight.

Everything is ready for action. The matador and his assistants stand waiting. All attention is directed to the opposite side of the arena. Everyone's watching the condemned's door. Suddenly it opens and out stalks the bull, magnificently powerful, full of life and courage, his head erect. A feeling of pity comes over me for I know he is doomed.

The toreadors attract his attention by waving a red cape, and the bull comes bounding over towards it with a joyous gait. But as he gallops, he seems to develop a mood for attack, and finishes plowing his head foremost into it. The toreadors are spread over the arena. Each in turn attracts the bull's attention with a cape, running him around. The matador, the killer, stands studying the bull, looking for bad habits. Then he takes him in hand for he is the artist, the expert with the cape.

This is the *pièce de résistance*. This is the ballet, the dance, in which the fury of the bull is controlled and merged into beautiful plastic design.

The bull is all fury, circling around the man, obeying the dictates of the cape. Both merge into a sculptural unit. The horn scrapes the man's chest, taking with it a piece of gold braid. Everyone holds his breath until the matador, with a flourish of his cape, dismisses the bull and saunters away, giving him over to the toreadors, who keep him occupied until the picadors arrive.

The popular resentment among foreigners witnessing bull-fighting is the cruelty to horses. As a matter of fact, these wretched animals are half-dead before they enter the ring. I asked a Spaniard why it was necessary to use the poor creatures. "A bull must have one triumph while he's in the arena," he said.

The horses are finally led or dragged out and the performance continues. Banderillas are plunged into the animal's back and again the matador takes him in hand until the bugle sounds, the signal for the bull to die. He then takes a sword and a small cape, which hangs over it. Again the bull makes several passes at it.

Now the beast is exhausted. He stands panting in front of the matador, who cautiously draws the sword from the cape, trailing it in front of him, moving the bull into position for the mortal stab. The head must be low and the legs a certain distance apart in order to thrust the sword between the shoulder blades in reaching the heart. At that moment, the chances are equal. Any miscalculations in timing as the bull charges would mean disaster to the matador.

That afternoon I saw a dramatic killing. Imagine a large arena, the silence of thirty thousand people, and standing in the bleak sunshine a man and a bull facing each other, the bull in the throes of death.

The beast had been courageous and had given a wonderful performance—perfect foil for the artistry of the matador. The man had made the fatal plunge and everyone held his breath. But the animal did not fall immediately. He stood motionless, looking into the eyes of his slayer. There seemed to be an exchange, a questioning.

The silence of those thirty thousand people was intense. An assistant attempted to go forward, but the matador stopped him with a gesture of authority, knowing his thrust was fatal. For almost a minute they stood motionless, facing each other. The attitude of the matador seemed one of triumph, yet regret—a pity for the dying animal.

In the silence of that arena one heard the rumbling of a wagon passing outside. As the sound died away, the beast crumpled to the ground and thirty thousand people broke spontaneously into wild enthusiasm and applause.

From Biarritz I returned to London, where I intended to stay for a couple of months and make several excursions to the north of England before returning home to Hollywood.

I arrived in London during those trying times[3] prior to England going off the gold standard, and had several lunches at the House of Commons.

The House of Commons[4] is a mass of traditions. In the cloakroom are little bits of red ribbon tied on each hanger. In former days members fastened their swords to them. In both the House of Commons and the House of Lords there are long mats about three feet wide before the Speaker's bench. To this day it is a strict rule that any member getting off the mat is, metaphorically, not in the House. In olden times, members facing their adversaries in debate would get excited and draw their swords, so a law was passed forbidding any member to step off the mat during a controversy.

I dined many times in the homes of members. Some of them have special bells in direct connection with the House of Parliament so that when in session, they can be signaled when voting is about to begin. Occasionally I have sat down to dine at a large party and on hearing a buzz, would be left flat—the only male sitting through the rest of the dinner.

When voting, the members walk through a gate by the entrance of the House of Commons. The ayes and nays go through different ones. I remember a Scottish member returning after a division, very concerned.

"Good heavens!" he said, "I voted for Sunday cinemas and didn't know it. Not realizing that a division was in progress, I left by the wrong gate. This will be most annoying to my constituency."

I might add that I argued to convince him that his constituency ought to be very pleased indeed of the fact.

Dinners at the House of Commons are most interesting.[5] You will meet kings and potentates from all parts of the world. I remember receiving word from the Honorable Mr. Thomas asking me to dine quietly with his family there. I was five minutes late and profuse with apologies.

Rotogravure of Chaplin and Mahatma Gandhi in London, *New York Herald Tribune*, October 4, 1931. (*Author's collection*)

"That's quite all right, Charlie. I want you to meet His Majesty, the King of Serbia. Also Mr. McKenna and my son and daughter. Now bring up your chair and sit down by the King."

A message from Mahatma Gandhi stated that he would like to meet me, either at the Carlton Hotel or elsewhere. We eventually decided on the home of his friend, Dr. C. L. Catial, in Beckton Road, Canning Town.

Frankly, I have not followed the ramifications of Hindu politics. My knowledge has come only through an occasional scanning of headlines in the daily press. Nevertheless, Mr. Gandhi is a figure of the twentieth century, a dissenter and reactionary of a new kind, who has utilized passive resistance, a modern method in warfare, which has proven a force almost equal to violence.

The house of Dr. Catial is situated in the East End of London. To get there, I journeyed through Clerkenwell, Whitechapel, and East India Dock Road on to Camden—the literary background of Thomas Burke. Endless lines of two-story hovels, all uniformly alike. They made me shudder. How hopeless they looked!

Eventually we turned into one of the byways onto Beckton Road. Dense throngs were gathered and countless automobiles were parked along this humble street. To quote from the *Daily Mail*: ". . . when Mr. Chaplin stepped out of his taxicab, the waiting crowd surged around him, cheering madly. Smiling broadly, he had almost to fight his way to the door of the house through the surging throng which the few police on duty were powerless to control. A bunch of flowers was thrust into his hand, and dozens of hands patted his back."

I had great difficulty in forcing my way up the narrow stairs. At last I was wedged or pushed into a small room about twelve feet square, packed by representatives of the press and followers of the Mahatma.

Dr. Catial introduced me to them, including Miss Slade, an Englishwoman, wearing white calico over her head in the style of a madonna. Mr. Gandhi had not arrived, so I was asked to sit and wait. I was plied with a hundred questions from the press. What was the object of my visit and so on. However, it was interrupted. A yell was heard outside.

The Mahatma is arriving. The whole street is in a cheer. I look out of the window. Below is a limousine. The police are endeavoring to make a way to the house. Someone struggles to open the car door. Smiling and serenely cool, Gandhi gathers his calico around him and steps out of the machine.

From the window a Hindu lady showers him with flowers. "Here, you throw some too."

"Oh, no," I answer. "I never make demonstrations."

The scene has a touch of humor—the crowd affectionately mauling Gandhi as he endeavors to hold his calico around his middle section. It looks so insecure the way it falls about him, I feel he might lose it. Nevertheless, when he came into the room, he was still intact.

Mr. Gandhi greeted me warmly, though somewhat bewildered. He was still holding on to his calico as he extended one hand to shake mine.

The crowd was still cheering, so he went to the window. One of the Hindu ladies pushed me also and the Mahatma and I stood smiling and waving. Afterwards a request was made for the press to leave, but before doing so, they insisted Mr. Gandhi and I pose for pictures. When the room was cleared, I finally found myself seated next to him. He was talking over personal matters with his followers.

An admirer of Gandhi's—a young English girl—sat down beside me.

"Don't you think Mr. Gandhi has a wonderful personality?" she asked. "After you've talked to him, I feel sure he'll win you over."

For some reason I find it difficult to make conversation, what with the milling crowds cheering outside and a gaping audience inside. I become self-conscious. It all seems like a revival meeting.

Now Mr. Gandhi is free and sits alone. Suddenly a voice breaks in: "Look here, young woman, Mr. Chaplin is here to talk to Mr. Gandhi, not you. So give them a chance."

Whereupon the young lady got up and excused herself, and Mr. Gandhi and I were left on the settee.

The woman's interrupting remark terrified me. I felt it was a challenge. I shifted uneasily, then giggled at Mr. Gandhi. They must be waiting for me to say something profound.

How on earth do you get into these situations? I thought. Here you are, a harmless actor on a vacation, striving to have a good time, and you get into this predicament. What do you know about India, politics, cabbages, and kings, and what do you want to know about them anyway?

However, I pulled myself together and started. "I was just telling a young lady that I couldn't quite agree with all your principles. I should like to know why you're opposed to machinery. After all, it's the natural outcome of man's genius and is part of his evolutionary progress. It is here to free him from the bondage of slavery, to help him to leisure and a higher culture. I grant that machinery with only the consideration of profit has thrown men out of work and created a great deal of misery, but to use it as a service to humanity, that consideration transcending everything else, should be a help and benefit to mankind."

"What you say is very true, but in India conditions are different," said the Mahatma. "We are a people who can live without machinery. Our climate, our mode of living, make this possible. I wish to make our people independent of industry, which weapon the western world holds over us. When they discover that there is no profit in exploiting India, they will leave it to us. Therefore, we must be independent of your industry. We must learn agriculture to grow our own rice and spin our own cotton. These are essentials necessary to the lives of our people. Their wants being modest and their demands few, they do not warrant the complexities of western machinery."

"But," I argued, "you cannot retrogress. You must progress like the western world. Sooner or later you will adopt machinery."

"When that time comes, we shall use it," he said. "But before doing so, we must make ourselves independent of it if we are to gain our freedom."

Later on prayers were offered. On one side of Mr. Gandhi sat Miss Slade; on the other, two Hindus. Throughout the ceremony the Mahatma bent his head, but never spoke. The prayers lasted about five minutes—a series of little singsong chants—concluding in a minute of silence.

It seemed strange and unrealistic, here in this small room in the East End of London with the milling crowds outside. As the bronze-diffused sun sank over the begrimed housetops, four figures sat cross-legged in silent prayer—three Hindus and one Englishwoman—while an audience of twenty or more of us looked on.

And I came away wondering whether this was the man destined to guide the lives of over three hundred million people.

The next day I had tea at Lady Ottoline Morrell's.[6] Lytton Strachey, Aldous Huxley, Augustus John, and others were there. I told them of my visit with Gandhi.

I have a phobia when introducing people. I cannot memorize names. I forget even my own brother's. To me the actual name of a person symbolizes nothing. After all, memory is the association of ideas, and what can you associate with a name like Peabody or Finkelbaum? Personally I should like introductions done away with—just your hostess to greet you. Then society would become an adventure. How nice to talk naturally to a celebrated man without being conscious of his trademark.

When Lady Ottoline Morrell, at whose house I was for tea, lightly tripped off names like Augustus John and Aldous Huxley, I lost all sense of hearing. Huxley I'd met before, but when she announced Augustus John, that name was still ringing in my ears so that I didn't pay much attention to the rest.

During tea I noticed a young gentleman sitting opposite me with a youthful, bespectacled face and a Biblical brown beard, and remembered that he was the subject of a large portrait I'd seen during a ramble through Tate's Gallery. It was a striking one, almost verging on caricature, yet vividly alive.

I was explaining my feeling for society in general, saying that my love for

Chaplin and the Prince of Wales at the Ice Carnival, a benefit for Northern Hospital, November 19, 1931. (*Charlie Chaplin Archive*)

humanity was different from my love of the crowd. My love for humanity is a fundamental, deep-seated instinct, but my love for the crowd depends on my mood. At times they are inspiring, at other times frightening, for I instinctively sense that they are capable of either loving or lynching.

"Mr. Strachey there," Lady Ottoline said smilingly, "is a selfish man who confines his love only to his friends."

Then it dawned on my inert brain—of course this was Lytton Strachey, author of *Queen Victoria*, *Eminent Victorians*, et cetera.

"I would go further and say that my love is confined solely to myself," Strachey said jokingly. "I have no altruistic conception about people in general other than writing about them."

Augustus John has a compelling personality. He is tall and handsome, with a Vandyke beard, and has that faculty of commanding attention without the slightest effort. You feel flattered by his interest in you. He is able to draw you out in conversation, and that afternoon I told him the story of my first taste of popularity and its psychological effect on me.

When the evidence of my popularity first manifested itself, I would walk the streets of Los Angeles. All around me seemed magic. The world was warm and friendly, so different from the apathetic days of obscurity. People were interested in what I said. I was surprised to see how seriously my views were taken. Popularity had suddenly endowed my opinions with importance.

I got the full significance of it on a trip I made to New York. It was two years after I'd worked in pictures. I had wired my brother there that I was coming on to look for a job, and a million-dollar-a-year one at that.

In a hurry, I had boarded the train with only a small suitcase, little realizing what would happen on the journey. The telegraph operators must have relayed the news ahead for when I arrived at Amarillo, Texas, the station was packed with children, with the mayor and city officials present.

I was in the washroom taking a shave, and as the train drew in, I heard rousing cheers. Voices were exclaiming, "Where is he?"

The passengers, including myself, were wondering what the commotion was about.

Then a shout went up, "Three cheers for Charlie Chaplin!" and I almost cut my throat.

A passenger remarked, "He must be on this train."

"Yes," I said weakly, my face covered in soap.

Several men came down the corridor. "Is Charlie Chaplin here?"

"That's me," I sputtered.

"I'm the Mayor of Amarillo, and on behalf of the children of our city, we invite you to be our guest at dinner during your half hour's stay."

I was escorted into the railroad depot, where tables were decorated and streamers hung from the ceiling with "Welcome, Charlie Chaplin."

What the mayor must have thought of me, I don't know. I was dumb throughout that meal. His Honor afterwards made a speech wishing me luck and a safe journey to New York.

When the train drew away from the cheering crowd, my reactions were strange. I was a little frightened. It made me thoughtful. I felt sad and alone—a feeling of being set apart from people, to be looked at and treated like a curiosity.

At each stop the crowds grew larger. Thousands lined the railroad depots and I would go to the back of the car and show myself. At first it was a pleasure, then it became a duty, but towards the end it was a task. I had yearned for success and popularity, but was not prepared for it on this scale, and the suddenness of it frightened me.

A telegram en route from my brother said that the New York newspapers were full of my arriving, that the police were concerned and had notified him that they thought it advisable for me to get off at One Hundred and Twenty-fifth Street instead of the main depot.

Like royalty I arrived incog, changing my name when I registered at the Hotel Plaza. The newspapers had headlines, "Charlie Chaplin has arrived and is in hiding," but it wasn't long before my identity was revealed.

Yet with all the glamour of success, I was depressed. Here was I walking the streets of New York alone. I felt all dressed up and no place to go. Everybody knew me, but I knew nobody. I would ask myself: how does one get to know people? Is this all success means, just a series of public demonstrations? How does one make interesting friends? I felt success had changed nothing of my personal life. I didn't realize that making friends was a slower process than making a success.

In the early days of my career, I spent much of my time touring the provinces of England. In those days I loathed traveling. It took me away from my little flat in London.

Now I have a yearning to visit the small towns of Lancashire, to sit by the glow of a Lancashire kitchen fireside with its clean blue hearthstone and smell the home-baked bread or pot roast in the oven. How nice to hear again the patter of wooden clogs of the lads and lassies on their way to work in the morning.

When a boy of fourteen, I was a member of Sherlock Holmes Touring Company. I lived alone, being too young to mix or room with the older members of the cast. So to alleviate my loneliness, I decided to purchase some companionship—a rabbit and a dog.[7]

I used to carry my grips to and from the station. And now I added my new friends to my paraphernalia. As the dog grew up, I trained her to follow me until we were nearing the depot. Then she would crawl into a grip and I would steal her past the station master. Later the dog had five pups and so I became a walking menagerie.

What a problem it was to get them by the landlady. I developed a technique for this. I would engage a combined sitting-room and bedroom and would say nothing about the family, which I kept hidden. Later when the landlady discovered her room had been turned into a zoo, I would smile disarmingly, picking up one of the puppies and exclaiming enthusiastically, "Isn't he sweet? When they're a little older I'll give you one."

This good will and generosity would usually dispel any objections she might have. But towards the end of the week, the odor of the animals would lessen the landlady's tolerance. But I managed to tour with them for over a year.

It was after the election and MacDonald's government had been returned that I decided to visit Manchester. I'd heard rumors concerning the destitute conditions there.

I wanted to go quietly and, if possible, to escape publicity. I hired a touring car and made my first stop at Stratford-upon-Avon, the birthplace of Shakespeare.

I arrived there on Sunday evening and put up at a charming old inn that had been built in the Bard's time. After dinner I took a ramble around the village. I wanted to find Shakespeare's cottage.

It was quite dark. I had never been there before and as I wandered through the streets, I instinctively paused before a house, which, strange to say, was the one.

The next morning, Sir Archibald Flower, the Mayor of Stratford, called and was gracious enough to take me through it, and also over the new Shakespeare theater by the river.

Leaving Stratford, I arrived in Manchester in the pouring rain. Unlike London, it was strange to me. Only the Midland Hotel was slightly familiar, and that had become begrimed with age.

I didn't stay long there, but made my way to Blackburn, the town where as a boy I had bought the pup and the rabbit. I had a general idea of the large market square, the Haymarket, and the Bull Hotel.

When we arrived, I was not so disappointed. Everything was familiar, including the Bull Hotel. In the old days I thought it was a grand place. How different it looks now—an inn with about a dozen rooms for guests. We reserved one for the night, and after a wash and brush up, partook of some bacon and eggs and later went to look over the town.

I stood in the market square and heard some political speeches. One group was listening to a lecture on the Douglas Plan,[8] a new economic system which is rapidly gaining many followers in England.

Another was listening to Communists who were decrying the fate of the Labor Party, calling the leaders traitors.

Later I returned to the Bull Hotel and sat in the taproom, listening over my hot toddy to the gossip concerning the new government.

During conversation I remarked, "How is it Lancashire went Conservative?"

An old coal miner spoke up, "For the past few years it has been a perfect Utopia here, living on the dole and taking life easy. That doesn't do the country any good."

What irony, I thought—"a perfect Utopia"—coming from a man who spends half his life underground.

But this is the spirit of the English—their loyalty, their sense of responsibility, their belief in what they think is right and just.

During the evening, in paying for some drinks, I happened to pull out a considerable sum of money. I noticed a suspicious-looking character eying me carefully. Later when I went upstairs to retire, I saw him lurking around at the bottom of the stairs.

I had been told that conditions were desperate in the north, and that it was hardly safe to be seen in an automobile. My chauffeur's room was at the other end of the building and my own was away from everyone. I also found my door wouldn't lock. I endeavored to dismiss that awful face from my mind and so read awhile.

About twenty minutes later, I dozed off. How long I'd slept I don't know, but I was suddenly awakened by the sound of someone moving outside in the corridor. I sat up with a start. Everything was deathly silent. I could hear the throbbing of my heart. Then I heard someone creeping and stop outside my door. Carefully the handle turned and the door creaked.

The room was in complete darkness. Frantically I groped for the electric bulb over the bed and quickly turned it on and behold!—the door was moving, but stopped.

All sorts of notions were running through my mind. I could imagine big headlines, "Charlie Chaplin Found Murdered in Blackburn Hotel."

I got up cautiously and gently closed the door again, placing a chair under the handle. A few moments later the footsteps crept away. That night I lay in a cold sweat, waiting for the dawn to break.

At last morning came and I ordered breakfast. A pretty little Lancashire girl came in with some orange juice. "Did you sleep well last night, Sir?"

"No. I had awful dreams of someone creeping outside my door."

She giggled mischievously and left without saying another word. Why did she laugh, I thought? And so mischievously? When she came in with the coffee, I asked her and she shyly confessed.

"Well, Sir, one of the maids asked me to go with her to your room so she could take a peek at you while you were asleep. It was her only chance of seeing you. We waited outside your door for half an hour and were about to peek in when suddenly the light went on. We got scared and left."

And to think how I'd suffered all night! Nevertheless, I expressed my regrets that I didn't see her, for I'm sure I'd have felt happier had I done so.

Nobody's consistent in life. Many of us take a stand on principles and make resolutions, but they are colored by moods and desires. Time and circumstances change them. That's why we seldom live up to our philosophy. I think it was Walt Whitman who said, "If I contradict myself, well, I contradict myself."

In the beginning of this manuscript I stated that I was tired of love and people. I should have said I'm tired of myself, especially now when writing this book. However, dear readers, you are partly responsible for this. You should not encourage a movie actor to take himself "literarily."

Nevertheless, since coming to England my object has been fulfilled. I have dwelt in the past and recaptured my youth. I have roamed in Kennington, dreamed in Brixton, and paused in every part of London. Through all these peregrinations I rarely met an old associate. It was not my intention to do so. My reverie I did not want to share with anyone.

Now I feel the urge to renew old acquaintances. Many of them have passed away. Others were killed in the war, and very few remain.

There is a great change in the vaudeville world. Many music halls that I worked in as a boy have been changed to motion-picture houses. The Canterbury and Paragon, the Tivoli and the Oxford have vanished, and only the Holborn Empire and a few others remain. While I was in London they started to revive vaudeville. At the Palace Victoria Charlie Austin was topping the bill. George Robey was also headlining at the Holborn.

Robey was my idol as a boy. I remember how I used to wait outside the stage door at the Tivoli and follow him along to Trafalgar Square, where he

Left to right: Unidentified, Chaplin, George Robey, music hall comedian. London, November 1, 1931. (*Charlie Chaplin Archive*)

caught his bus. Charlie Austin I haven't seen since the old days at Barnard's Theatre, Woolwich. How funny and delightful he was. So I've made up my mind to go to the Palace Theatre. I want the spirit of old-time vaudeville, to sit in the stalls in the cigarette smoke with a glass of beer and join in a popular chorus.

During the intermission I went backstage to see Charlie. We had a grand old reunion. His friend Rose, the greengrocer of Covent Garden, was there. We sat in the dressing-room and split a bottle of wine. We talked of the old favorites: Joe Elvin, Joe O'Gorman, the Egbert Brothers—"Those Happy Dustmen"—one of whom married Dainty Daisy Dormer, and Sanford and Lyons, "The Simultaneous Dancers."

"What has become of them?" I inquire.

Many are alive and going strong. Some of them are Water Rats, an exclusive club for vaudevillians, which has been in existence since the days of Dan Leno.

"Charlie," said Austin, "we want to make you a Water Rat. It'll be a wonderful thing to meet some of the old-timers again. After all, you were one of us and we all feel you belong."

I noticed his remark, "you were," and it affected me.

I'm not prone to ally myself to clubs or organizations. I'm not a good fraternizer, but if I am to join a club, it shall be the Water Rats.

The initiation was impressive[9]—a gathering of harlequins and pierrots in profound solemnity. There were Joe Elvin and Joe O'Gorman, fine old chaps in their seventies, the clowns of other days paying homage to a younger one. Will Hay, the comedian, was Grand Master, and Fred Russell, the ventriloquist, officiated.

When it was over, I came away with a feeling of gratification at the honor paid me by those whom I had honored and worshiped in other days.

Many of my American friends have expressed the opinion that the English are a most hospitable people, but they take a great deal of knowing. They are apparently diffident, with a reserve to a point of coldness, but when once you've gained their confidence, they are cool-eyed and warm-hearted.

I've never been intrigued by Switzerland. Personally, I dislike all mountainous country. I feel hemmed in and isolated from the rest of the world. The ominous presence of mountains towering above me gives me a feeling of futility. I suppose I am indigenous to the lowlands near the ocean, for my Romany instincts tell me that here I'm better suited to survive. Life opens out on a wider vista.

Nevertheless, having basked in the sunshine of the Riviera and enjoyed London's spring and survived its autumn fogs, I felt that a change of atmospheric diet would be beneficial. Besides, Douglas Fairbanks was in St. Moritz[10] enjoying the winter sports, and that was a good excuse to go there.

You leave London in the morning and arrive in St. Moritz the following afternoon. The air is bracing and the whole country is blanketed in snow. The sharp whiteness gives zest and life to your spirit.

But all this is knocked out of you on discovering the price of your rooms. But it's worth it. The answer is I intended to stay two weeks and remained two months.

Douglas Fairbanks insisted that I be initiated into the art of skiing. I always thought it was easy, but oh, boy! I never knew how many knots I could tie myself into!

Charlie and Sydney Chaplin in St. Moritz, Switzerland, 1932. (*Charlie Chaplin Archive*)

For the first two hours I suffered with impediment of the legs and was continually standing on my own foot. Turning was most difficult, but this I mastered in my own fashion, deliberately sitting down and pivoting in the direction I wished to go. Sometimes, however, the sitting was not deliberate.

To a beginner, skiing down a hill is very simple, especially if there are no obstacles in the way. But the problem is stopping. This is most difficult. You are instructed to assume a knock-kneed position, at the same time spread your feet apart and turn your ankles in, digging the sides of your skis into the snow. When I attempted it, I invariably went into the splits.

To give you an idea of the enjoyment of my first day's skiing, you must imagine yourself starting slowly down a hill, developing speed as you go, thrilled and exalted with a sense of your own motive power and the icy breezes blowing against your cheeks. As the speed increases, however, your exhilaration changes to a growing anxiety, especially when the hill becomes precipitous and the going increases to about fifty miles an hour. You go flying past rocks, trees, and other obstacles that miraculously escape you. After such gymnastic triumphs, you accumulate confidence and go whizzing on, resolved to see it through to the bitter end.

Then a sinister rock approaches and comes rushing at you menacingly. This time it is determined to get you. Your heart leaps up into your mouth. You become philosophic. You relish the sweet memories of life before skiing. Death is contemplated. You see your skull crashed against the rock and your body flung over it like a pair of empty pants. But you are not killed. You survive. You go on living, crippled for life.

Then a miracle happens. Some metaphysical force moves the rock to compassion and lets you skim by it, and you go shooting onward, relieved. Your mind gains control of your reflexes and you make a decision to sit down, not perhaps as gently as you'd wish. So plunk!

You extricate your head from the snow. You discover you're still conscious. You involuntarily sit up and look around for fear somebody has seen you. But a superior individual in slow tempo comes gliding up with the query, "Are you hurt?"

And you sally with a cheery, "No, not at all, thank you."

Then you endeavor to start off again. But when the stranger is out of sight, reason becomes the better part of valor, so you change your mind, take off your skis, and call it a day.

However, dear readers, 'twas not ever thus, for later I became—but there, modesty forbids, so I shall quote from the newspaper, the *South Wales Argus*: "People at St. Moritz were electrified to see a small man go tearing down a steep village street at a terrific speed, to pull up suddenly at the door of his hotel. He was Charles Chaplin, film clown, says Reuter's correspondent. Perhaps there were painful memories of misadventures with the hotel revolving door that made him stop so sharply. Skiing experts declare that this dash was a very fine achievement. Charlie, in fact, is becoming an adept on skis."

The above is one of my most treasured clippings.

The social life is a very gay one. The mornings are devoted to sports, skiing parties to Mt. Covilla, and excursions to Davos; then tobogganing on the Cresta Run and sports carnivals, including ski-jumping and horseracing on the frozen lake. One looks forward to the gay lunches on top of the mountain at the Covilla Club, where you bask in the sunshine with the snow all around you. Afterwards you ski down into the town below in time for afternoon tea at the hotel.

After changing, it isn't long before seven o'clock arrives, which is cocktail hour at the bar. Here festivities are at their height. You are reminded to "lay off" the olives and potato chips as you're dining at eight-thirty. Then someone is giving a supper party you must go to in the bar at ten, so you must "go light" on the dinner. From then on high life goes on till about three, four, or five, depending on your capacity or vitality.

During the season almost all one's friends show up at some time in St. Moritz. You will find both the elite and illustrious well represented from Hollywood, London, Paris, Berlin, and New York.

You will be surprised to hear, however, that there was one outstanding figure I did *not* meet. That was His Royal Highness, the ex-Crown Prince of Germany, and I'll tell you how this happened.

One day I was sitting in the hotel having my afternoon tea when somebody said, "Ooh, there's the ex-Crown Prince of Germany over there!"

And I said, "Ooh, is it?"

Then all sorts of things flashed through my mind. As I sat gazing at His Royal Highness sipping his English Ceylon, my memory took me back to a picture I made called *Shoulder Arms*, a comedy on the World War in which His Royal Highness played an important part. Then suddenly I remembered I had to make a telephone call, and I left the hotel immediately.

I'd arranged to return to California via the Orient, catching a boat at Naples[11] and going through the Suez Canal on to Japan, my brother accompanying me. So he was awaiting my arrival in Rome.

I left Switzerland with a friend of mine, M. Plesche, traveling by automobile to Rome, which would give me an opportunity of viewing the country. On crossing the border into Italy, I was impressed with its atmosphere. Discipline and order were omnipresent. Hope and desire seemed in the air. In the midst of these medieval surroundings, a new life has crept in. Every place we stopped we were given efficient service and treated with courtesy.

Upon arriving in Rome, a message awaited saying that arrangements could be made for an interview with Mussolini. But this did not materialize as I could only stay in Rome for two days, and that was too short a notice for Il Duce to give me any of his valuable time.

Meeting people formally is like viewing a house without going inside. I shall always remember the interview with the late President Wilson at the White House during the Third Liberty Loan Campaign. There were four of us—Mary Pickford, Marie Dressler, Douglas Fairbanks, and myself. We were ushered into the famous Green Room and told to ""please be seated." I'd rehearsed a speech for the occasion and intended telling the President several complimentary anecdotes about himself that I thought amusing.

Eventually an official came into the room. "Stand up in line, please." Then in came the President. "Will you all come a pace forward?" and we were formally introduced.

The President was gracious and felt it incumbent to tell a story as we stood lined abreast in front of him. Anxious to brighten the solemnity of the occasion, I laughed before he came to the point which caused the others to glance at me with concern. Then came that moment of embarrassing silence. However, Marie Dressler came to the rescue and also told a story. Not having heard either one at the time, I cannot record them now. I only know that I laughed politely.

Then Mary found herself and told the President the wonderful spirit and cooperation that was evident throughout the country. Now was my opportunity, so I piped in with, "There certainly is—or are." I remember the singular and plural worried me at the time. This was my only contribution to the interview and I left the White House pleasantly dazed and proud.

I should like to have stayed longer in Rome as there was so much to see

Chaplin viewing the Roman Forum, Rome, Italy, March 6, 1932. (*Author's collection*)

there, but one needs leisure for this. I was in a continual rush of excitement and expectation, which can better be described kaleidoscopically:

Arrive at midnight. The streets deserted. Impressed with lights of the Tiber. Receive warm welcome from friends and the press. At the hotel a message—arrangements can be made to meet Mussolini. After cold supper I take a long walk. Rome falls short of my imagination.

Retire at four in the morning. Up again at eleven. Expect news from Mussolini. In the meantime, visit St. Peter's, the Roman Forum, and Museum. Back to hotel. No news from Mussolini. Out again sightseeing. Return to hotel. This time news of Mussolini. Impossible to arrange meeting on such short notice. Decide to leave Rome for Naples the following morning to embark for the Orient.

The voyage was uneventful and the weather calm throughout. The only event was changing to shorts when we came into the Red Sea. Shorts are tropical trousers that show the knees, but I don't believe in them.

By the time we reached Colombo, the capital of Ceylon,[12] it was pretty warm and I began to envy my brother's shorts. The boat docked there for twenty-four hours, which gave us an opportunity to spend the night at the sacred city of Kandy, seventy miles from Colombo. Ceylon was the realization of all my exotic dreams. It has all the mysticism of the Orient and the charm of the tropics. As we motored to Kandy, we were thrilled viewing strange sights and drinking in perfumes that lay heavy on the air.

The night of a full moon is a ceremonial holiday for the Ceylonese. Suddenly we came upon a procession. Festoons of lamps and torches stood out against the light. Jugglers were twirling cans of fire attached to a rope, which they spun like a baton, making pinwheel designs, followed by men and women chanting to the beat of the tom-toms. Then two warriors appeared, their Hindu armor glistening in the torchlight. They were devil dancers, our chauffeur informed us.

We pulled up to watch them pass, and the devil dancers approached. I became a little scared as they looked quite fanatical. The rest of the procession surrounded us, still chanting to the tom-toms. Then the dancers suddenly jumped in the air, twirled and pivoted in a most weird and demoniacal manner. After they'd finished, they came over and bowed, and we understood. So we dipped in the exchequer and went on our way.

Throughout the journey I kept saying to my brother, "Did you ever realize there was such a place? We must settle down here in our old age and buy a tea plantation." This was my first reaction.

It was quite late when we arrived in Kandy, and after supper at the hotel, we hired a couple of rickshaws and went slowly around the sacred lake. I shall always remember that night, or morning rather; the warm, sultry air and the strange sound of insects as our rickshaw boys walked silently in the moonlight, pointing here and there to wild turtles along the edge of the lake.

Returning to the hotel we were met by one or two stragglers who recognized me. I threw them a coin. "Thank you, my lord and master," and all for a quarter, but everyone was "my lord and master" here.

The next day, we visited the temple. Professional beggars were lined up on its steps with handkerchiefs spread and hands extended. Buddhism teaches never to refuse the helpless. It is an impressive sight to see a poor native woman walk majestically down the temple steps without pausing, her arm extended with a handful of rice, permitting a few grains to trickle onto each beggar's handkerchief as she makes her way out of the temple—a "widow's mite."

Before departing, crowds of natives surrounded the hotel and gave us a rousing cheer. Strangely enough, in spite of the seductive atmosphere of the tropics, I was happy to get away. My enthusiasm to settle down there was not as keen as it was when I first arrived, for you quickly realize the opiate lure that excites your ardor also repels it, and I came away impressed with its beauty, but realizing that it was not a place for Nordics.

Our next port is Singapore, meaning in the Malay language, the City of Lions. Near Singapore the scenery is fantastically beautiful. Trees grow out of the ocean like the designs on blue-willow China plates. My first view of the city surprised me. Perhaps my imagination was influenced by the lurid scenic portrayals of Hollywood's conception of it, with its narrow evil streets and sinister droves on every corner. But on coming into the harbor, I found green open spaces and gardens before palatial granite buildings. Myriads of sailboats listed in the bay, and white ocean liners lay dormant, waiting to be fed with cargo, and the harbor sang with color and tropical life.

The crowds were not as demonstrative here as they were in Ceylon, but then Singapore is two degrees off the equator and I don't blame them. Nevertheless, there was a medium crowd and I was cheered, photographed, and interviewed.

When we arrived at the hotel, we were in time for a *reistafel* lunch. This culinary concoction is native to the Straits Settlements and takes about twenty waiters to serve it. First you help yourself to rice. Then other waiters follow with curried meats, spices, vegetables, bananas, nuts, and so on—

Chaplin (*left*) and Syd Chaplin (*right*) among fans and admirers in Jakarta, Java. (*Charlie Chaplin Archive*)

all of which you dump on one plate. Then you do a bit of exploring, being shocked at this and liking that, finally leaving the table with gastronomical qualms.

From Singapore we sailed on the *Van Lansberge* for Batavia, the capital of Java in the Dutch East Indies. Upon arriving, we were greeted by a large crowd at the dock and presented with a wreath of welcome. We arranged to motor through Java to Soerabaja, and take a boat there for Bali.

I will not lucubrate on the details of our journey. However, from Batavia to Bandoeng took six hours by motor along fine roads. We put up at the Preanger Hotel[13] and indulged in a hot bath in European fashion, the only hotel in Java where you can do so, as all the rest of them use the dipper system, where in place of a bath there is a well-like structure filled with water, which you pour over yourself from a dipper.

After dinner we motored to Garoet and stayed there for the night. It was here that I encountered my first experience with a "Dutch wife" whom after you've lived in the tropics for any length of time you find indispensable.

A Dutch wife is a bolster-shaped pillow, which you place between your knees to keep cool during the sweltering nights, and which acts as a soothing comforter to your nerves. When first informed of their function, I laughed, but after my initiation, when retiring I always insisted on my "conjugal rights."

However, during the night there is more to keep you company than a Dutch wife. Flying bugs and tropical insects will hover around your mosquito netting, serenading you with strange noises. Whisks are kept in every room to shoo them away. My first night's adventure gave me many comedy ideas for a picture.

From our room we have a beautiful view of the mountains and valley below. Everything is green, effulgent with tropical growth, and we are refreshed and revived, ready to journey to Tjipanas Hot Springs for lunch. There we visited the lakes where native families go bathing and who, for a few coins you throw them, will come scrambling up the banks, unconscious of their nudity.

From there we journeyed to Djockjakarta and saw the famous Borobudur Temple, which was covered up by the jungle for many years, and from there on to the thriving city of Soerabaja,[14] where we were greeted by a large crowd at the hotel. This is the port where we embarked for Bali.

Part V[1]

Holiday Travel*s* Wind to an End

The first time I heard of Bali was during conversation with my brother. We were discussing the general unrest of the world.

"If it comes to the worst," he said, "I'll go to Bali. That is an island untouched by civilization, where you can sit under the sweltering palms and pick the fruit off the trees and live as nature intended. There one doesn't worry about depression. The problem of living is easy. And the women are beautiful."

At the time his description didn't arouse my interest. But when we were finally *en voyage* to Japan, the subject came up again. We were in the Mediterranean nearing Port Said when my brother brought me a book on travel.

"Here is an interesting article on Bali," he said and added, "There are two young American boys[2] on the boat who are going there."

During the day I browsed through the book and after reading a chapter, I was "sold."

The following day we had a talk with the boys. They were two young American artists who had been studying in Italy.

"It's no use going back to the States now," they said. "We'd only join the ranks of the unemployed. So we thought we'd save what little money we had left and go to Bali. You can live there for five dollars a week," they remarked, "and that's what appeals to us.

The captain of the boat which took us from Java to Bali showed us a map. The area of the island is about 2,241 square miles. It is separated from Java on the west side by the narrow Straits of Bali; on the east lies its neighbor island, Lombok. The capital is Singaradja. The island is densely populated with over a million inhabitants, or five hundred to the square mile. Little is known of its early history and there is very little trace of the influence of Java.

Religion plays an important role in Balinese life. The temple and society form an inseparable whole. The modern Balinese is a mixture of many different religions, partly pre-Hinduism and Polynesian with a superimposition of Buddhism.

My first glimpse of Bali was in the morning. We were cruising along its beautiful shores on the way to Buleleng, our landing place. Silvery downy clouds encircled the green mountains, leaving their peaks looking like floating fairy islands. Majestic landscapes and smiling inlets passed until we reached our destination. How different this port looks from those of civilized countries; no chimney stacks to mar the horizon, no begrimed dry docks nursing rusty ships, no iron foundries, stockyards, or tanneries. Only a small wooden wharf, a few picturesque boats, and houses with red-tiled roofs.

This was northern Bali, where the governor and the Dutch officials resided—a commercial center with a street of about thirty shops run by Chinese and Hindus.

The governor was courteous and invited us to his residence, where we met several of the officials.

To my horror, I discovered that the natives of Bali had seen one or two of my pictures. "Good heavens," I thought, "have I come all this way for another Rotary Club welcome?"

After tea at the governor's house, we got into our automobile and sped along the road to south Bali, our final destination.

Where were the beautiful women? I had been told that the natives went bare-shouldered, but I found they were all respectably covered up.

As we traveled, the country became progressively beautiful. Green rice shoots were growing in silver-mirrored fields, and wide green steps terraced down the mountainside. We passed through villages with beautifully built walls and imposing entrances along the roadsides. They were like the enclosures of some fine old estate. They looked like the remnant of some western influence. But no. They were the walls that surrounded the native compounds and built to keep out evil spirits. They were paradoxical—these magnificent walls and the primitive buildings they surrounded.

We had been riding about fifteen minutes when my brother Syd nudged me. "Look there, quick!"

I turned and saw a line of stately creatures walking along the road, dressed only in batiks wrapped around their waists and their chests bare. How picturesque they looked carrying curved shaped pottery upon their heads, with one arm akimbo and the other swinging in rhythmic motion as they filed by. The male of the species was just as admirable with the sheen on their lithe bodies and the play of muscles as they carried across their shoulders bamboo poles laden with bundles of golden rice.

The roads are good. There are no commercial signboards. The countryside is teeming with life. Men and women are working in the rice fields, others are driving their cattle to market. There is a ceremonial grace in everything they do, whether at work or play.

The hotel in south Bali has only recently been built. It is in modern style. I must say the Dutch do things well. The sitting rooms are open like a veranda, and partitioned off with sleeping quarters at the back.

How nice to be away from civilization, relieved of stiff shirtfronts and starched collars. I had made up my mind to go around native-like with just a loose shirt, a pair of trousers, and sandals. You can imagine my disgust when I found a notice posted in the room that read that all guests must be fully dressed when entering the dining room. I was most indignant. Nevertheless, I dined deliberately without changing my clothes or shaving.

Hirshfeld,[3] the watercolor artist, and his wife called that evening. They had been living on the island for a couple of months and invited us to their little house rented from one of the natives where Miguel Covarrubias, the Mexican caricaturist, had stayed before them.

After dinner the Hirshfelds, my brother, and I walked toward there. The night was warm and sultry. Eerie shapes loomed on all sides as we strolled along. Giant banyan trees and tall palms stood silent against the starlit sky. Not a breath of wind stirred. About three hundred yards away a flood of light came from a recess off the roadside.

Suddenly from that direction came the sounds of jingling tambourines and the clashing of gongs. Then out of the jangled confusion evolved a rhythmic tonal pattern—slow, deep notes like a treble mosaic counterpart.

The high tones were like pebbles dropped rapidly into a silent pool, the deeper ones like red wine in crystal bowls.

Upon arriving there we discovered groups of natives standing and squatting around. Maidens sat with baskets and small flares, selling dainty edibles. We edged our way through the crowd and beneath a patio were seated musicians in square formation with instruments like xylophones in front of them.

In the center were two girls not more than ten years old, posed in kneeling fashion, wrapped in gold-embroidered sarongs with yellow tinsel headdresses that flickered in the lamplight. They were dancing, their arms extended, weaving like serpents, swaying and undulating on their knees to the droning music.

It must have lasted half an hour, yet the girls were in perfect unison, each deviating occasionally with a solo part and continuing again in perfect unity. Their necks swayed and their eyes turned and flickered back. Their fingers quivered. There was something devilish about it, the click of the neck, the dart of the eye, the quivering fingers, all dancing in neurotic joy. At one time the tempo would quicken, developing a crescendo like a raging torrent, then calming down again like a placid river wending its way to the sea. The finish seemed an anticlimax fading into nothingness. The dancers sank back into the crowd and were lost to view. There was no applause and no compliments. Although they had performed beautifully, it was appreciated without comment.

Two words I've discovered are unknown in the Balinese language—"love" and "thank you." Those dancers had practiced assiduously, striving for perfection without any consideration for personal gain. Not one person gets paid for entertainment. It is all given free. A village will entertain another and walk miles to do so, and for their services will be given only a meal.

After the performance we strolled over to Hirshfeld's house and sat out on the veranda underneath myriads of stars. That was my first night in Bali.

How different, I thought, from anything I'd ever seen. How far removed I felt from the rest of the world. Europe and America seemed unreal—as though they'd never existed. Although I was in Bali only a few hours, it seemed I had always lived there.

How easy man falls into his natural state. What does a career, a civilization matter in this natural way of living? From these facile people one gleans the true meaning of life—to work and play—play being as important as work to man's existence. That's why they're happy. The whole time I was on the island I rarely saw a sad face.

All their standards are different. The Hirshfelds' landlord had two wives. The husband was indifferent to the older one. When Mrs. Hirshfeld broached him about it, he only shrugged his shoulders and remarked, "She is not beautiful anymore."

This may be cruel from our western viewpoint, yet his household worked in peace and harmony and both wives were well provided for. The older wife had a son whom the younger one cared more for than the mother.

They may have no love as we understand it, yet they live happily compared to our western world, that stands for all the virtues of love and romance with its moral insignia, "faith, hope, and charity." Look into the faces of the masses in our large cities and you will see harassed, defeated souls and in the eyes of most of them weary despair. Yet in the eyes of the Balinese is tranquillity.

Later in the evening we strolled down to the village for a cup of coffee at a store kept by an old Chinaman, who sold everything from ladies' garters to canned asparagus.

Returning home to the hotel, I noticed a pretty native girl walking ahead of us. She would occasionally look over her shoulder, giving furtive glances in our direction. She wore a little cotton jacket. I was told that in the south of Bali, only women of the streets covered their breasts.

In the morning breakfast was served on the veranda, where we reclined in our pajamas and took our pineapple and mangosteens and enjoyed the morning sun. Doves were flying around and curious humming sounds were coming from them. A boy told us that the natives put little wind instruments around the doves' necks to make music when they fly. They devise all sorts of strange toys.

Walter Spies[4] is lunching with us today. He is a young Russian painter and musician who has lived on the island for five years making a study of Balinese music. He is a handsome man between twenty-eight and thirty, and is adored by the natives, who treat him like a father confessor. He has made a penetrating study of their arts and is well versed on Balinese life.

After lunch he took us into the interior of the jungle to a remote village, where we witnessed a strange rite that was a special offering to the gods of the temple. Leaving our automobiles we walked for an hour to get there.

The priest was a gaunt figure wrapped in a toga, with hair that fell about his shoulders like a dervish's. The maidens turned up in their beautiful sarongs and bare shoulders, each presenting her offering before the altar and then taking her place in the large circle formed by the crowd. The priest went through a great deal of abracadabra. The offerings were placed on a bier and later taken outside the temple, where the youths of the village rushed upon them, pillaging and grabbing what they could, while the priest stood by with a large whip and slashed them unmercifully. This was done to beat out the evil spirits that prompted their uncontrolled desire to rob. The natives were quite good-natured about it and seemed to enjoy the fun, but the priest was most determined and thrashed them most vigorously.

Later we dined at Walter Spies's house. It is a beautiful bungalow with a thatched roof situated on the brink of a ravine with a rushing river below. He told many strange stories about the Balinese, the mystic side of them, and how cultured and refined they were.

Their taste for music is discriminating. When playing the piano to several natives, they listened indifferently to Chopin, Liszt, and Schubert, but only in Bach did they show any interest. The rest they dismissed as sentimental.

Spies said in the five years he had studied their music, he was unable to master their time. The tempo seems to defy all mathematical laws, it is so involved, yet the natives can play it identically over and over again. He said he has made a score of some of their simpler music, but it takes three virtuosos at one piano to play it.

Ghosts and spirits are just as real to Balinese as radio is to us. Spies told a weird story which happened prior to a cremation, which is their customary form of disposing of the dead. A deceased woman was placed on a bier in the center of a field. It had been her express wish to be cremated on a certain day, but there had been a delay. One night a native came rushing into the village, trembling with fright, saying he had seen a ball of light circling over the body. Spies and several villagers went immediately to the spot and to their amazement, the apparition was still there. He thought it might be the joke of natives reflecting a light in some way. But after seeing it, he was convinced it was a phenomenon. He described it as a ball of mercurial light about three feet in diameter and that it hovered over the bier where the deceased lay. It would rise and descend in spiral motion, and when they attempted to go near it, it would fade, appearing again when they moved away, eventually vanishing into the body.

Our routine for the day would start after breakfast, taking automobile excursions to various parts of the island. These excursions we usually took in the morning, returning before lunch, and in the afternoon we would take our siesta. In the evening, thanks to our friend Spies, there was always some form of entertainment, which would complete our day.

One festival lasted all night. It was given by a rajah who was celebrating because he had paid his debt to the government and was now free from the threat of imprisonment. An appropriate reason to celebrate, I thought.

It took place at night on the outskirts of the forest and hundreds came from all parts of the island. There were to be fireworks, a barong play, and a kris dance.[5] Most elaborate preparations were made, the cost of which I'm sure would again endanger our friend with threats of imprisonment.

The crowds sat around an egg-shaped ring, where the performance took place. First came the gamelan music and the dancers, then the barong play. The story dealt with an episode from the history of the popular ancient Javanese king, Erlangga, in whose reign a wicked witch, a widow, with her pupils brought all manner of ill luck to the flourishing kingdom. The witch was represented by a man with a terrifying mask, wild tangled hair, and long nails who never fails to fill the public with horror and fear. The play ended with her death, her magical power being taken away from her by the knightly son of the court priest. Eventually she was destroyed by fire.

The witch is a dangerous role to enact for the actor believes when playing the part, he is actually imbued with the evil spirit of the character.

As we sat that night, the glare of the fireworks lit up the jungle in the background. The sight was strange and dramatic. In the play the witch is supposed to recoil from the fire and run into a small proscenium built at the end of the ring, but this night the fear of the witch was so great that the actor lost control and rushed madly through the crowd and into the jungle, shrieking in a state of hysteria. We all followed, running into the darkness to see what had happened to him. Suddenly there was a scream and the natives came running back, trembling and frightened. The priest had rescued the actor and was bringing him back in a state of collapse. The witch's mask was taken off and holy water administered. It was almost ten minutes before he came to himself. Later we waited to see the final sacrificial ceremony, which was an offering to the witch's mask. A pig was killed and his blood mixed with leaves, and prayers were offered by the priest. The mask was then placed in a box and carried off by the natives. This was the end of the celebration.

I took motion pictures of many of the Balinese ceremonies. I had Walter Spies arrange an elaborate dance that included a full orchestra of thirty musicians and thirty others who performed and danced. When it was over, I asked Spies how much I should pay them.

"Five or ten dollars will be ample."

I suggested twenty-five dollars, but he remonstrated, saying it would spoil them. However, I insisted.

When the chief took the money, he looked puzzled and mumbled something to Spies. I thought he was dissatisfied. We had given him two tens and one five, which Spies thought generous.

"If you have twenty-five one-dollar bills," he said, "I think he can understand it better."

When these were produced, the chief was perfectly satisfied.

One evening Spies and I wandered into a village, where a small boy was being taught dancing by a youngish-looking man. We were cordially invited to squat and make ourselves at home. The boy was eventually taken in hand by an Amazon-looking woman, who danced beautifully while the little boy copied her.

As we sat under the flare of the oil lamp drinking the man's health in coconut milk, he pointed to the lady and told us that she was his daughter-in-law. We were greatly surprised and asked him his age.

"When was the earthquake?" he inquired.

"Twelve years ago," replied Spies.

"Well, I had three marriageable children then." Seemingly not satisfied with his sense of accuracy, he thought again, then exclaimed, "I'm about two thousand dollars old," clarifying the ambiguity by explaining that in his lifetime, he had spent about two thousand dollars, therefore we could figure it out for ourselves.

During my tour through the different villages, I was surprised to see a large number of automobiles lying idle in many of the natives' back yards, most of them recent models rusting from exposure. A few were polished and had lace curtains and were used for living quarters. The explanation is interesting.

A number of natives had purchased these cars. The initial cost, however, exhausted their life savings, but they were happy to ride around in them until they discovered to their bewilderment that the cost of gasoline to run a car for a day was as much as they earned in a month. So they were left discarded in the back yards of the villages.

I was eighteen days in Bali and every moment was interesting. Returning to Singapore we flew over Java, taking the plane at Surabaya for Batavia, a distance of six hundred miles. There were several days to wait before we could get a boat to Japan, so in the meantime, we merged ourselves into the life of Singapore.

Of course anything after Bali is a letdown. But Singapore has its charm. Every evening we would ramble through the native quarters in rickshaws. Occasionally we would go to the New World—the native Coney Island of Singapore—where every known variety of entertainment is given, from Malay opera to prizefighting.

The Chinese drama listed several nights. My brother and I would sit of an evening trying to guess the different symbols that the actors used during the play. One was a stick with a fringe of wool around the top and center, which the actors would shake majestically. I guessed correctly. It was a horse.

Japan, the adopted land of Lafcadio Hearn, has always stirred my imagination—the land of cherry blossoms, the chrysanthemum, and its people in silk kimonos living among porcelains and lacquer furnishings. I've often thought of the Japanese who work in our dank western cities, attired in our drab western clothes. How intensely they must feel the pangs of nostalgia. But today the western mode of living has invaded the Orient.

The city of Kobe was our landing place. When we arrived there, thousands were waiting on the docks to greet us. Airplanes were flying, dropping pamphlets of welcome.

While in Japan, the government graciously made me their guest while traveling by rail. On our way to Tokyo, at every stop we were greeted by cheering crowds. Geisha girls were lined up and I was presented with gifts of all kinds. The Japanese are generous and hospitable.

Syd Chaplin (*left*), Charlie, and Toraichi Kono (Chaplin's butler directly behind him) with the sumo wrestlers, Kobe, Japan. (*Charlie Chaplin Archive*)

Upon arriving in Tokyo, the throngs were so dense that four hundred policemen were helpless in keeping them from raiding the railroad depot. We eventually got on our way to the hotel, but stopped en route at the Emperor's palace, where we conformed to the Japanese custom and paused before the gates to pay our respects, then on again to the hotel. After the usual preliminaries of the press, I went straight to bed, exhausted but happy.

It is a thrilling sensation to wake up in a foreign country and realize that the adventure of the day is before you. My brother informs me, "There's a cartload of presents arrived and stacks of mail keep coming in, so I've arranged for a Japanese secretary to attend to them. The police have detailed a detective to look after us during our stay."

The program so far is the Sumo wrestling matches for this afternoon and the Kabuki-za Theater for this evening. Then tomorrow night we are dining with Mr. Tsuyoshi Inukai, the prime minister of Japan. Mr. Ken Inukai, his son, sent us tickets for the wrestling.

It is entirely different from jiujitsu or any other known wrestling and is one of the oldest forms in Japan. It is amusing to watch and if you don't understand the technique, the whole procedure looks comic. Nevertheless, the effect is hypnotic and thrilling.

As we were leaving, a courier rushed into our box and told us the awful news—that the prime minister, Mr. Tsuyoshi Inukai, had been assassinated in his home.[6] This was a dreadful shock to everyone and put a damper on the whole nation.

The prime minister's son told us later that we were responsible for saving his life, because the tragedy occurred while he was at the wrestling arena making arrangements for our tickets. Had he been home, the assassins would have murdered him with his father.

The tragedy is well known—how the murderers, dressed as soldiers, shot and killed several guards, then broke into the prime minister's sitting room and with the points of their guns confronted the old gentleman and his family; how he led them to another room, remarking that if they intended to kill him, to spare his wife and children the scene of such violence. The heroic courage of the Prime Minister was worthy of his exalted position. Not one word passed the assassins' lips as they were led by the august gentleman down a long corridor into a little room, where he calmly told them to state their grievances. Without a word, however, these murderers cruelly poured fire into their defenseless victim and left.

Some few years ago a company of Japanese players came to Los Angeles. They arrived without any publicity. But for the chance remark of one of my Japanese employees, I would have known nothing of their arrival.

I will not go into the detail of that evening's performance, but in a small theater situated over some stores, I sat enthralled. The singing, at first discordant to my unaccustomed ears, gradually revealed itself into meaning and beauty. It was like the lament of a poet desolate at twilight, and was accompanied by an ironic plucking of a metallic stringed instrument that seemed to answer the lament with a ruthless wisdom. The dance was like the capturing of designs, an expression of the loveliness of line—like merging of life into sculpture, the converse of Pygmalion and Galatea.

I was impressed by the superb acting of the players and their subtle technique. It was after this performance that I decided to go to Japan.

Luckily when we arrived in Tokyo, the kabuki season was in full swing, so we got tickets for all the performances.

The Kabuki-za Theater has a seating capacity of about two thousand. Instead of the curtain rising, it is drawn aside to the sound of clicking wood that is a signal that the performance is commencing. The actors sometimes enter and exit from a runway that extends on out through the audience to the back of the theater. A revolving stage facilitates the rapid change of scenery. These devices they have used for hundreds of years.

The performance starts at three and ends at eleven, and the program is diversified. There is a long play consisting of six acts. In the middle of the play, a one-act music posture drama is interposed. This is a story interpreted by dance. Female parts are acted by men who convey all the subtleties and nuances of a woman without giving any offense.

When a player makes his first entrance, instead of the customary European applause the audience shouts his name in a most fervent manner and the effect is stirring.

The tourist's opinions of countries he visits are usually in error, especially a celebrity's, who sees things through a glamor of excitement. Yet invariably, the first question the press will ask you on your arrival is what you think of their country. Nevertheless, external impressions are related to the soul of things.

Should you ask me offhand my opinion of Japan, I should say it is a nation of inconsistencies. A simple illustration is a man attired in a kimono wearing a derby hat, also the adoption of western dress at the cost of their own silk industry.

Even their art has been undermined by western influence. The beautiful school of some of the old masters—Harunobu, Hokusai, Uramaro, Hiroshige—is entirely neglected, and in place of it are hybrid entrepreneurs whose work is neither Japanese nor European.

Mr. Otani,[7] the president of the Shochiku Cinema, gave an interesting party at his house. Upon arriving, we took off our boots and were given felt slippers. After being introduced to his family, I was presented to members of the stage and screen, also several geisha girls. Each course through dinner was served in different rooms. Entertainment followed.

Another interesting episode was a tea ceremony at the house of Mrs. Horikoshi. This charming lady has a school that she supports herself for the daughters of her friends where she teaches the gentle art of the tea ceremony. More than anything I saw in Japan, the tea ceremony revealed to

Charlie and Sydney Chaplin enjoying a traditional Japanese tea ceremony, May 1932. Toraichi Kono, Chaplin's butler, is visible at the second table in front. (*Charlie Chaplin Archive*)

me the character and soul of the nation—perhaps not of modern Japan, but the Japan of yesterday. It exemplifies the philosophy of life, beautifying the simple action of preparing tea to please the senses, utilizing an everyday fact to express the art of living.

Its history is an ancient one dating back many hundreds of years. We hear of members of the samurai watching the lady of the house quietly prepare their green tea with modest grace. It had the effect of calming their nerves after a battle. Each movement is studied to create tranquillity. Not a sound is made during the preparation. Not a gesture is unnecessary. You watch in silence the beautiful preparation. In the sanctity of peace you refresh your troubled mind in liquid jade.

To the practical western world, the tea ceremony might seem quaint and trivial. Yet if we consider the highest object of life is the pursuit of the beautiful, what is more rational than applying it to the commonplace?

The trail is nearly over and I am returning to Hollywood. Looking back on my holidays leaves me with an outstanding impression. Europe and the different countries I visited, embroiled in unrest, seem brewing a new epoch—theistic, sociological, and economical—unprecedented in the history of civilization. It animates me with a desire for accomplishment—not in the old way but in something new; perhaps in another field of endeavor.

Seattle at last! I am interviewed by the press. Everyone seems warm and friendly. Something has happened to America since I've been away. That youthful spirit born of prosperity and success has worn off and in its place there are a maturity and sobriety.

As I journey from Seattle to Hollywood, passing through the rich farmlands of Washington, the dense pine forests of Oregon, and on into the vineyards and orchards of California, it seems impossible to believe ten million people wanting when so much real wealth is evident.

Nevertheless, I am glad to be back in America. I'm glad to be home in Hollywood. Somehow I feel that in America lies the hope of the whole world. For whatever takes place in the transition of this epoch-making time, America will be equal to it.

Appendix A
Tour Itinerary

1931

February

13   Left New York on the *Mauretania*

19   Arrives Plymouth; boat train to Paddington Station

20   Visits Kennington and Hanwell School

21   Old Bailey/Wandsworth Gaol

22   Chequers

23   Shopping at Burlington Arcade; lunch at Qualino's with Ran
      dolph Churchill and Lord Birkenhead; driving in the country
      with Philip Sassoon and then dinner in Park Lane

24   Lunch at House of Commons with Philip Sassoon and Lloyd
      George

25   Luncheon at Lady Astor's Cliveden; meets Bernard Shaw

26   Dinner and overnight at Churchill's Chartwell

27   *City Lights* premiere at Dominion Theatre; after party at Carlton
      Hotel

March

1   Visits Thomas Burke; visits Convent of the Notre Dame de Sion,
      north London with Ralph Barton (to visit Barton's daughter
      there)

3   Luncheon at House of Commons with Lady Astor, Lloyd
      George, and Kirkwood; first economic speech; sees George
      Robey at Holborn Theatre

5	Visit to Eton; entertained by the Eton Society
8	Leaves London via Liverpool Street Station
9	Arrives Berlin, Germany; checks into Hotel Adlon; greets Marlene Dietrich; sees performance of Erich Carow
10	Visits old Berlin; attends Metropole theater with Sir Horace Rumbold; attends party at Karl Vollmueller's Palais
11	Visits police museum; visits La Scala
12	Snowstorm; Chaplin sick
13	Meets ministers of the Reichstag, Dr. Joseph Wirth among them
14	Tours Potsdam with Price Henry; sees Hans Albers in *Liliom*
15	Tea with Einstein at his home; leaves for Vienna, where he will speak first words for a sound-film camera
16	Arrives Vienna; visits workmen's apartments; attends theatre and cabaret
17	Meets Oscar Straus; dines with British Legation
19	Leaves Vienna for Venice
20	Arrives Venice, Italy
21	Attends tea with British consul; visits prisons and dungeons underwater; supper dance
22	Departs Venice
23	Arrives back in Paris; checks into Hotel Crillon; cancels trip to Budapest due to scandal; lunch with Countess Noailles and Aristide Briand at French Ministry building; dinner with Count LeMuir; evening at rehearsal of Folies Bergère with Alfred Jackson
24	Attends boar hunt at Duke of Westminster's in Saint-Saens, France
26	Meets King Albert of the Belgians at Elysée Palace
27	Receives Légion d'Honneur back in Paris from Aristide Briand
31	Signs *Woman's Home Companion* contract with Willa Roberts; departs Paris

April

1	Arrives in Nice, France; greeted by Frank J. Gould and brother Syd Chaplin Elsa Maxwell luncheon; Duke of Connaught for tea

City Lights premiere hosted by Prince of Monaco
Attends Mrs. Gould's lunch at Casino, meets Maeterlinck

14 Leaves Nice for Marseilles with intention of visiting Algiers
15 Algiers
26 Back in Marseilles
28 Meets Aimee Semple McPherson in Marseilles and boards same train to Juan-les-Pins

May

French Riviera, mostly Juan-les-Pins

9   Refuses "command performance" from Juan-les-Pins
30 Lunch with Emil Ludwig, Cannes

June

French Riviera, mostly Juan-les-Pins
Stays with H. G. Wells in Grasse
Lunch with Frank Harris in Nice

July

French Riviera, mostly Juan-les-Pins

15 Attends actress Grace Moore's wedding at Cannes

August

6   Visits Maurice Chevalier at his Cannes villa; drives toward Biarritz with Harry d'Arrast; spends night at Château Brissac at Poitiers
8   Chaplin in auto accident (d'Arrast at the wheel) near Burgal
9   Attends bullfight in San Sebastian, Spain
14 Dines with Winston Churchill at Biarritz

September

1   Biarritz; flies looped-the-loop with Henri Cochet and pilot Michael de Trovat
2   Plays in benefit tennis match in Guethary, Spain
7   Meets Prince of Wales for the first time at a benefit for the war wounded

18	Back in London; mobbed after midnight leaving Café de Paris
19-21	Weekend with Churchill at Chartwell
22	Meets Gandhi at home of C. L. Catial in Beckton-road, Canning Town
23	Attends tea at Lady Ottoline Morrell's
30	Visits Paddington Green Hospital for Children

October

9	Meeting with Ramsay MacDonald outside House of Commons
23	Attends Conservative election meeting at Plumstead in disguise; meets Dando on the street
24	Sees performance music hall star Charlie Austin at the Victoria Palace
27	Attends election night party at Selfridge's

November

1	Initiation into the Grand Order of the Water Rats
8	Travels to Manchester and then Stratford-upon-Avon and overnights there
9	Visits Blackburn; stays overnight in White Bull Hotel
10	Brief stop in Chester
13	Attended Edgar Wallace play *The Case of the Frightened Lady* at the Wyndham Theatre
14-16	Spends weekend with Viscount and Viscountess Astor at the Eliot Terrace, Plymouth-on-Hoe
14	Attends whist drive and dance of the East End Conservative Association; attends fishermen's service in Plymouth, where he gives a speech
15	Attends opening of new cinema house by the mayor of Plymouth
16	Visits Ballard Institute (boys' school)
19	Attends Ice Carnival for Northern Hospital—Prince of Wales in attendance
20	Visits the House of Commons with Lady Astor
26	Visits Madame Tussaud's Chamber of Horrors

December

1   Attends court in London, settling suit of secretary May Shepherd

21   In St. Moritz, Switzerland, mastering the art of skiing with Syd Chaplin and Douglas Fairbanks

1932

January

24   Carlyle Robinson resigns

27   Serves as dancing judge for the Palace Hotel contest; auctioneer of wines for the Bobsled club

February

       St. Moritz

March

5   In Rome at the Hotel Excelsior after triumphal Progress from Milan by car

7   Departs for Kobe, Japan, today from Naples on *Suwa Maru*

20   In Cairo, after having traveled through Port Said; visits the Sphinx and Great Pyramids of Giza; stays at Shepheard's Hotel

21   Leaves Port Said for Ceylon

23   Arrives Colombo, motors to Kandy and overnights there

24   Returns to Colombo via motor, tours tea and rubber factories, departs Ceylon

25   Arrives in Singapore, rushed to hospital with dengue fever

28   Departs Singapore for Java

30   Mobbed by children in Batavia, Java

31   Motors to Garoet, overnights at Ngamplang Hotel there

April

1   Motors to Tjipanas Hot Springs, Lake Leles, and Bagentit, take train to Djockja, overnights at Grand Hotel there

2   Visits Borobudur Temple, motors to Soerabaja and overnights at the Orange Hotel

3   Sail for Bali on a K.P.M streamer

19   Comes down with dengue fever

22   Arrives at Singapore, rushed to hospital; recuperating in Singapore; waiting for boat to Japan

May

14   Arrives in Kobe, Japan; arrives twelve hours later in Tokyo

15   Views sumo wrestling in afternoon; Kabuki-za Theater at night; Inuka assassinated

25   Visits Kasuage Prison near Tokyo

28-29   Spends weekend at Miyanoshita, a mountain resort forty-five miles southwest of Tokyo

30   Attends supper in his honor hosted by Ken Inukai (father recently assassinated)

June

2   Lunches with Ken Inukai at popular restaurant Hamacho; calls upon Premier Saito; departs Tokyo on *Hikawa Maru*

13   Arrives Vancouver, B.C.

16   Arrives Los Angeles

27   "Economic Policy" released to the press

1933

January

7   First half of "A Comedian Sees the World" mailed to Willa Roberts

February

25   Second half of "A Comedian Sees the World" mailed to Willa Roberts

September

First installment of "A Comedian Sees the World" appears in *Women's Home Companion*

1934

January

Final installment of "A Comedian Sees the World" appears in *Women's Home Companion*

Appendix B

From the Archive Pressbooks

Receiving the Légion d'Honneur Medal

The controversy Chaplin endured in order to be decorated by the French government is not recounted in this memoir. His goal was always to receive the highly regarded *Légion d'Honneur* medal, equivalent to an English knighthood, but his acquisition of this medal and its attendant respect and honor took nearly ten years and probably ten times the difficulty it needed to. The story begins with Chaplin's first trip back to Europe in September-October 1921. While most of his focus on this trip was on London and his first homecoming there since moving to America to work in films, Chaplin and his party made three trips to Paris as part of the itinerary. Certainly, meeting the French public who greeted him as "Charlot" for the first time was an important part of these visits, but also there seemed to be a sort of promise to Chaplin that he would be "decorated," whatever that term happened to mean at the time. On the third trip to Paris, ostensibly to attend the French premiere of *The Kid* at the Trocadero, "it" happened, but the decoration was for something called "Officier de l'Instruction Publique," an award given to public school teachers in France. After all this effort, Chaplin still didn't receive the award he was after and returned to the

States empty-handed, although his account of it in *My Trip Abroad* reveals none of this disappointment:

> Mary [Pickford] and Doug [Fairbanks] are very kind in congratulating me, and I tell them of my terrible conduct during the presentation of the decoration. I knew I was wholly inadequate for the occasion. [. . .] Then they wanted to see the decoration, which reminded me that I had not looked at it myself. So I unrolled the parchment and Doug read aloud the magic words from the Minister of Instruction of the Public and Beaux Arts, which made Charles Chaplin, dramatist artist, an *Officier de l'Instruction Publique*.

The award he was after—the Cross of the Legion of Honor—is still in existence. Its official Web site offers this account of the award and its order's history:

> Le nouvel ordre, dû à l'initiative du Premier Consul Bonaparte, se voulait un corps d'élite destiné à réunir le courage des militaires aux talents des civils, formant ainsi la base d'une nouvelle société au service de la Nation.
>
> Le 14 floréal an X (4 mai 1802), Bonaparte déclarait au Conseil d'Etat : "Si l'on distinguait les hommes en militaires ou en civils, on établirait deux Ordres tandis qu'il n'y a qu'une Nation. Si l'on ne décernait des honneurs qu'aux militaires, cette préférence serait encore pire car, alors, la Nation ne serait plus rien.[1]

Fast forward ten years to Chaplin's next tour of Europe, 1931/32. Charlie and his entourage cut short his trip to Venice in order to be decorated in Paris on 27 March. This time the event had been secured by the devoted French caricaturist Cami and his friends. The press, unlike Chaplin in "A Comedian Sees the World," were less hesitant to discuss the event. On the next few pages, two articles transcribed from the pressbooks in the Chaplin archives give extensive details of the event, its context, and surrounding controversy. The second of these articles, penned by James Abbe, the gifted photographer of celebrities (his wonderful publicity stills for *The Pilgrim* are perhaps his most famous Chaplin images), offers us an important glimpse into this aspect of the story.

Seattle [WA] Post-Intel

26 July 1931

"Charlie Chaplin's Troublesome Legion of Honor Medal"
Kissed on Both Cheeks when Given the Historic Order, Then Scolded and Insulted for Taking It, and Now the Thorough Reform or Even Abolishment of the Decoration Is Being Urged in France

The conferring of the rank of Chevalier of the Legion of Honor upon Charlie Chaplin threatens to put an end to all similar honors by the wiping out of this order, which was founded by Napoleon Bonaparte. And it has been a troublesome decoration, indeed, to the famous comedian.

True comedy should have always in it something of the tragic or the sorrowful, and Mr. Chaplin is famous for situations on the film in which on kissing the hand of the fair lady, or while engaged in some other pleasant occupation, a brick falls on his head or a mule kicks him. This is precisely this situation in which he has found himself in the matter of his induction into the Legion of Honor, and while it is amusing on the films, Mr. Chaplin has found it far from that when it occurs in real life.

The glittering cross and the resplendent ribbon of the Legion of Honor were hung on his breast, and as if to prove that France not only honored and loved him and that there was no fooling about it, M. Philippe Berthelot, Secretary General of the French Ministry of Foreign Affairs, kissed him on both cheeks.

But he had hardly stepped from the Secretary General's office when the French press raised its collective foot and presented him with not one stout kick but several. And he read with astonishment that many members of the order that he had just joined were protesting to the Grand Chancellor of the Legion about it.

"Why should the red ribbon tinged with the blood of heroes be bestowed on a clown?" read the protest of one group. Mr. Chaplin was actually the victim of circumstances. Far from being in any manner unworthy, he is probably the most worthy to receive the decoration in a long time, but he received it just as France was boiling with indignation for what had gone before and what was expected to come.

It was his misfortune that hardly more than a few hours before he had received the medal, Josephine Baker, the young colored lady, or, as they laughingly call her, "the Vierge Noire," who comes from Harlem, New York, and who dances and delights the French by doing so in not even practically nothing, had announced that M. Berthelot had promised to give her the Legion of Honor. And not long before that, a lady inventor of a French cheese, which has nothing of the perfumes of Araby about it, was proposed for the same decoration. The latter broke no precedent, however, because the distinguished cook, M. Escoffier, had been given the ribbon and medal for the invention of "peach Melba" and similar triumphs of French cuisine.

The net result, however, is that for the third time in history the matter of abolishing the Legion of Honor, or at least its lower ranks, is now being discussed in Paris and will shortly be brought up before the Chamber of Deputies. The second time was when the medal was given to Mme. Cecile Sorel, ostensibly for her high qualifications as an actress, but those who had received the decoration for risking their lives in war for France, or for achievements more in line with those which Napoleon had in mind when he founded the Order, quite openly charged that there were other less creditable reasons.

And the papers printed cartoons much more insulting than those they have just been printing about Mr. Chaplin.

Picking up the well-known French newspaper, *L'Humanité*, Mr. Chaplin saw a caricature of himself wearing the Legion of Honor rosette in his buttonhole—the little red rosette taking the place for street wear of the medal—and a caricature of himself pointing a cane at it. Mr. Chaplin in his film character is known as "Charlot" in France. Beneath was the following caption in French:

"Charlot—What's this! Mr. Chaplin, have you been to the hardware market?"

A Frenchman had to explain to Mr. Chaplin that "hardware market" meant the same thing as junk shop. This was bad enough, but when he turned to the *Ciné-Journal* ("The Journal of the Film") he saw another caricature of himself standing on the Arc de Triomphe, the Legion cross on his chest, and saying in French:

"My proper place? Here it is! On the ground? Tush! That is good enough for the unknown."

When one realizes that the French Unknown Soldier is buried in the ground under the arch, it becomes apparent that the allusion to an "unknown" makes it about as insulting a caption as could have been devised.

On the same page was a sarcastic editorial in which the matter was discussed as if the Legion emblem had been given to "Charlot" and not Mr. Chaplin:

"All the members of the great League of Nations, who have applauded Charlot on the screen, will applaud with joy the action of France in raising him to the rank of knight of the Legion of Honor," says one of our colleagues.

"Should we laugh at this, or should we weep? Neither one nor the other. We should simply shrug our shoulders. We should dishonor the Red Ribbon instituted by Napoleon I if we acted otherwise.

"Charlot is a great artist. I do not contest that. But all the same, what has he done for humanity in general, and for France in particular?"

Still another cartoon showed a concierge, that is a caretaker, talking to a friend while the man passed down the stairs behind him. The concierge says: "I think there must be something wrong with the new tenant. He has no Legion of Honor like everybody else."

There is still a great deal of adverse talk because the picturesque poetess, the Countess Anna de Noailles, was given the grand cordon of the Legion of Honor, while it has not yet been given to Mme. Curie, who discovered radium and opened a new path in the world of science. The Countess was made a commander of the Legion. In this case, the resentment took the form of polite ridicule and a sarcastic controversy in Paris newspapers and magazines as to the proper way for her to wear her ribbon.

Not long ago, while complimenting some brave sailors who had saved the lives of a boatload of fishermen, an Under-Secretary of State expressed regret that he had only two Legion of Honor decorations to give.

What distressed so many Frenchmen is that, while there always seems to be a ribbon and cross ready for someone of dubious credit to the nation, the delays for real heroes and heroines are often outrageous.

Mme. Victorine Bessodes, a heroic nun, who devoted fifty years to nursing the fever-stricken in Senegal, did not get her cross till she was 79 years old. But Mme. Jeanne Lanvin, a dressmaker, got hers while she was young and able to show it off.

A midshipman, who died gloriously on the French ironclad *Iena* in

1897, was named a Chevalier de la Légion d'Honneur, as was fitting, but his family had to wait nineteen years for that recognition. Meanwhile, M. Cornuche, the well-known proprietor of gambling casinos, only had to wait a few months, after his friends suggested him to receive his "cross of the brave."

Mathurin Le Guilloux, an officer in the French navy and hero of twenty engagements, saved the cruiser *Jeanne d'Arc* from explosion. Was he admitted to the Legion? No, his name was merely "proposed." But a certain M. Duval, who watched over the interests of the Paris Omnibus Company at the Hotel de Ville, received a rosette, as did the man who piloted the engine of a train that conducted M. Gaston Doumergue, former president of France, to Cherbourg.

Another who did not have to wait was Dr. Voronoff, who got into the Legion of Heroes in recognition of his famous monkey gland transplantation operation, which has since become discredited. Had the glittering cross been pinned on Georges Carpentier, the prizefighter, some people would not have minded so much, for at least he fought bravely in the ring. But why, they ask, was he ignored in favor of Mr. Jeff Dickson, an American boxing promoter who has become a sort of Parisian Tex Rickard?

Other recipients who have made the French nation groan were Mlle. Carlotta Zambelli, a dancing girl; M. Dranem, a comedian by no means as well known as Charles Chaplin; Baroncelli and Roudes, two moving-picture directors, and M. Georges Marquet, a hotel proprietor at Nice.

But the last straw was when Josephine Baker, colored song-and-dance artist, announced that the same M. Berthelot had promised her the same honor for introducing the "Charleston" and "black bottom" to Paris. Cartoons have been printed in the Paris papers showing both Miss Baker and Cecile Sorel clothed only in their Legion of Honor cross and ribbon.

The sale of the Legion of Honor crosses to Frenchmen has been exposed over and over in the French press, but from patriotic motives little is printed about reasons for which they are given to many foreigners.

While such bribery does not make the best class of Frenchmen proud, at the same time, he realizes that it is done in the general interest of his country and says little about it. However, La Ligue des Droits de l'Homme (League of the Rights of Man) recently protested so vigorously at the way Legion crosses were passed out to bandits of Morocco, Syria, and Annam as a reward for betraying their brothers-in-arms, their race, and religion in the interests of French imperialism that it actually did get into the papers.

Though Charlie Chaplin was called a "clown," he is fortunate in that nobody thinks that he either paid cash for his decoration or sold out his country or business organization for the bauble. Why, then, did he get it? He deserved it quite as much and more so than many others, but also, once in a while, it must be presented to some foreigner of world-wide eminence, otherwise it would soon have no great value as a bribe for obscure persons in a position to secretly fix something up for France on the back stairs that would cost millions if done openly and legitimately in the front office.

The honor can be withdrawn, and that power has caused almost as much scandal as its bestowal. The Grand Chancery of the Legion is notorious for attempting to protect and to keep in its ranks members condemned for fraud and other offenses in the courts, such as M. Eiffel, convicted of stealing 20,000,000 francs of public funds.

In 1879 the Grand Chancery had to prohibit grocers, haberdashers, and makers of lingerie, perfumes, and liquors, whose "civil merit" had won the decoration, from using it as an advertisement and window display to sell their goods. Like British titles, the crosses were for sale to the highest bidder.

In 1927 M. Marcel Ruotte, of the Ministry of Commerce, together with M. Cams and M. Dumoulin, were tried for selling decorations wholesale, some of them as cheap as $4000. M. Chapgard, a druggist, took one at this bargain figure, and so did a decorator named Dumas, but M. Gossard, big wool merchant, paid three times as much.

In fact, many wealthy men, after receiving the decoration, never wore it nor mentioned it, and are said to have told their friends that they did not want the thing, but had felt obliged to buy and pay for it, in order to enjoy certain political favors in a business way.

The great Napoleon would turn in his porphyry sarcophagus if he knew that the medal for heroism that he founded in 1802 had fallen so low as to be forced by politicians upon rich tradesmen who toss it away in a drawer like tickets they are forced to buy for a policeman's ball.

New York Herald Tribune

26 April 1931

"Photographing Charlie: The Elusive King Charles of Screenland, Touring France in State, Agrees in Paris to Pose for a Wandering Photographer Who, He Learns, Is Also An Alumnus of Mack Sennett's Comedy College—and Finally Fulfills His Promise After Only a Week of Waiting."

By James E. Abbe

During the entire last week, my camera was set up in one of the sumptuous salons of the suite which CC occupied at the historic old Hotel de Crillon.

Togo, Charlie's Japanese valet, informed me that it was stumbled over by the most distinguished members of Parisian society, literati, diplomats, and whatnot, as well as by the Duke of Westminster on behalf of the British empire.

Charlie, himself, upon the day of his arrival, told me to set up, that he would pose for me at his first opportunity. This was because he had posed for me ten years on the set in Hollywood and we were both alumni of Mack Sennett's Comedy college.

While my camera waited stoically for Charlie, I, myself, sat in an outer salon next to the bilingual secretary, who responded, in one way or another, to a telephone call a minute for seven days.

Disposed as he was to be gracious to any and everybody in Paris, Charlie, after all, was only one man and could not be everywhere he was invited, or see everybody who wanted to see him. It devolved upon this efficient and diplomatic Mlle. Lachat to be considerate of all who telephoned without committing the elusive Charlot to anything.

Carl Robinson, who bears the title of Charlie's "personal manager," hovered around, receiving from the secretary a sotto voce interpretation of the applicants' requests and social standing and, as best he could, deciding who might penetrate as far as the outer salon to be given the once-over.

Liveried pageboys entered unannounced with one calling card after another and mail by the bundle.

As the days passed, I became more and more reconciled to waiting to photograph Charlie—reconciled to having been allowed such proximity to the most sought-after man in Paris.

Now and then I would break down at the sound of disappointed voices and saunter over to the big French window to gaze out over the balcony on the Place de la Concorde, where Louis XVI, Marie Antoinette, and their pals had been guillotined during the Revolution.

It was from the balcony that Charlot himself greeted his French subjects upon his arrival, and every day about noon I myself would hang over the rail to watch Charlie run the gauntlet of French admirers and newspaper photographers, after having just put me off until "later."

Merely having the price won't get you into this special suite in the Crillon. It reeks of tradition. General Pershing, Colonel House, the King of Egypt, Lloyd George, the Sultan of Morocco, the Bey of Tunis—to mention only a few latter-day celebrities—have occupied it.

At the time of Louis XVI it was reserved for the more important guests of the King.

Carl Robinson informed me that it was just one of Charlie's little unaccountable whims which prevented my camera, my lamps, and me from being thrown out onto the spot where better men and women than I had had their heads cut off.

Carl Robinson's title of "personal manager" is misleading, from what I observed. I guess no one has ever managed Charlie. Nevertheless, he is a privileged character, as far as the French are concerned, for being Charlie's right-hand man. Few persons have the distinction of not going to jail if they have socked a French *agent de police* on the jaw. When Charlie stepped off the train at the Gare de Lyon some ten thousand Parisians were waiting to greet him. A phalanx of picked police battered a path through the gesticulating mob for Charlie to get to his auto. Somehow the personal manager got separated from Charlie, and discovering a lieutenant of police barring his way with outstretched arms, he let the lieutenant have one on the jaw. Jaw, lieutenant, and all went down for the count. But only for the count of two.

By the time the infuriated lieutenant had caught up with his assailant, Carl was linked arm in arm with Charlie, and it was the lieutenant who did the apologizing.

One of the most important jobs of Charlie's personal staff is to prevent the most colorful instances of Charlie's trip from getting into the hands of press correspondents. Charlie is obligated to hold back at least 50,000 words of anecdotes for his own story of the trip, which he is to write at $1 a word.

A layman might think that from the grand manner in which Charlie and his entourage travel, that $50,000 wouldn't cover the cost of the trip. But all Charlie has to do is to accept breakfast, luncheon, and dinner dates, gifts from admirers, receipted bills from hotel managers and private cars on the trains, and what he will put out in actual cash might not be more than you or I would pay on an "all-expense" tour.

Lady Deterding, the wife of the Shell Oil King, who had the apartment next to Charlie's, gave a dinner in his honor one night. There were ninety guests. This must have cost as much as the Crillon Hotel did when it was purchased by M. de Crillon from the family of the Princess de Polignac in 1870.

The miracle of Charlie's visit abroad (up to now) is that he hasn't gotten married again. So far the English press has given much space to photographs of a beautiful bare-back English girl whom Charlie had selected for his next picture.

The front cover of a Berlin illustrated weekly was adorned with the head of an undeniably ravishing German creature who had been selected by Charlie for the same role.

Then, in Vienna, Charlie selected a Rumanian beauty, who has been in Paris all the last week, and according to the ever watchful press, has been undergoing numerous motion picture tests with a view to being Charlie's leading lady in his next picture.

If Charlie goes through with the trip as planned—does Spain, Russia, China, Japan, and few hundred other countries—one might assume that his next picture is going to be a story of the old Hippodrome chorus with each chorus girl a glorified foreign beauty.

The willingness of these prospective leading ladies to forsake their native lands, firesides, and whatnot on the chance of future fame, fortune, or even alimony, is evidenced by an incident at the front door of the Hotel de Crillon at 10 a.m. one day last week.

Out of the elevator stepped a young beauty in a gorgeous evening gown and wrap. Hall boys sprang to be of service. It seemed she had been wait-ing all night, outside Charlie's apartment in the hope of being "selected." Three of the boys procured her a taxi, and the press photographers, who were camped on the sidewalk the entire week, were so astonished at the apparition that they didn't even shoot when they saw the whites of her eyes.

City Lights opened in Belgium while Charlie was in Paris. The King and Queen were present. A two-column story of the opening appeared on the front page of Belgium's biggest daily paper the following morning. It was full of praise, complimentary comments of the King and Queen, and only a paragraph deploring the fact that Charlie had not made the three-hour train ride from Paris to appear at the performance in person.

However, King Albert, having heard that Charlie was extremely fatigued because of demands made upon his time when he had come abroad only for a rest, grabbed an airplane and came to Paris to congratulate Charlie in person.

King Albert received King Charles, at the request of the former, at the Belgian Embassy. That no taint of publicity might possibly be connected with the meeting, it was mutually agreed that no photographers be allowed in. That same dignified avoidance of documentary publicity was observed during the luncheon with Briand. We photographers were barred.

Even though I put in a week to get six photographs, at least I got to talk with Charlie on several occasions.

The first time was when he had just come in from having lunch with Briand and was all aglow with the latter's pet idea of a United States of Europe. Evidently the veteran diplomat had made Charlie feel absolutely at home on this almost state occasion, because Charlie said, "It wasn't at all the formal affair I'd feared it would be. As a matter of fact, it was so pleas-ant, I even enjoyed the food."

I was sitting in the salon with my camera, in conference with Togo, while Charlie was out getting his Légion d'Honneur decoration. It was the sixth day of my vigil. Togo was telling me that I had gone about it wrong to get Charlie to pose for me, that I should have come to him first. I was about convinced that Togo was right when Charlie walked into the salon through a secret and private entrance.

Charlie called us over to the window, naively produced a little leather case from his pocket, and opened it to show us the gorgeous Cross of the Legion of Honor, which is "le plus beau geste" that the French can make to an individual.

Turning to me, Charlie was almost blushing, "They say it is the first time it has been given to a foreign actor." Togo and I both congratulated him. Turning the cross over in his hand, as if it were a sacred relic, he noticed that it did not have his name engraved. For a second we were, all three, crestfallen. Then Charlie suddenly bethought him of a mailing tube, which he had under his arm. I held the cross while he extracted from the tube his diploma, which he unrolled. Then we all bucked up. For there it was in black and white—that Charlie Chaplin was a "Chevalier du Légion d'Honneur." "'Chevalier' is the first grade," Charlie said to me. "You have to be a Chevalier first, then if you are promoted you become an officer or a commander or something."

I thought to myself—well, anyhow, it's a start. For the first time since I have known him, I saw Charlie, himself, in the same light as his screen personality.

His expression and his ever-so-slight pantomime as he showed his valet and me his Cross of the Legion of Honor was identical with that of the little vagabond of the screen, who was so touched by the friendliness of the blind flower girl.

There is nothing particularly pathetic in not knowing how to read French, but as Charlie tried to decipher what was inscribed on the diploma I was impelled to come to his rescue—as everyone feels like doing at the sight of him in one of his screen predicaments.

Is it possible that Charlie's appeal is derived from the source that a famous French journalist, Marcel Espiau, stated in a recent article—that he is not an entertainer, but a symbol of his race throughout the ages, a race that still has its wailing wall, and which, on occasions when it has protested, has always done so with humility.

Charlie is known and loved by the French as the great poet of the screen, but it was as a Chevalier de Légion d'Honneur that he posed before my camera after he had handed Togo the insignia of his office to be locked up for safekeeping.

Judged by the standards of my Broadway and Hollywood days, the last week, devoted to making a half-dozen shots, has been a wash-out. And yet, in the eyes of local photographers, newspaper and magazine editors, I am considered "Photographer, by Appointment, to His Majesty King Charles of Screenland" with the privilege of displaying the Chaplin coat of arms on my bill heads, if any.

Appendix C

From the Archive Pressbooks

The Command Performance Debacle

Chaplin briefly mentions a British press story about his supposed refusal to take part in a command performance in Part III, a story he claimed had been greatly blown out of proportion. He declares the story "untrue, I having received only a telegram from a 'Mr. Black,' who requested me to appear at a vaudeville benefit which was termed 'a command performance' because Their Majesties would be present. This was not a royal command. It was the 'command' of Mr. Black, who has no official position with the royal household whatsoever."

The following news photo and reports are included to demonstrate the depth and breadth of this controversy as it was reported in the United States at the time. Representative articles have been chosen from a range of venues, illustrating a wide range of opinions on the subject. Just this small collection of articles shows as well the amount of press a figure such as Chaplin could garner over even a small misunderstanding such as this one.

John Bull Hit by a Chaplin Pie

DID THE JESTER SNUB THE KING?

Did Charles Spencer Chaplin refuse to give a "command" performance before King George?

"Nonsense!" declares the comedian. "I received no command from the King, but merely a request from the music-hall manager to appear in a charity show."

But London views the matter differently, we read, and Chaplin

The Smile He Brought to London

Before he slapped the British as "hypocrites"—Charlie Chaplin signing autographs for a group of London admirers.

is sharply criticized for not appearing at what his critics considered a "command" performance.

And Chaplin, London born, strikes back with bitter words that show that his European tour has not been so delightful as the stories of his triumphal progress from city to city would indicate. In an interview with the London *Express*, says the United Press correspondent, he assailed the British as "the greatest hypocrites in the world" at times, and said that Europe had bullied, misunderstood, and misinterpreted him. He also is quoted:

"They say I have a duty to England. I wonder just what that duty is? No one wanted me or cared for me in England seventeen years ago. I had to go to America for my chance, and I got it there. Only then did England take the slightest interest in me."

DECLARING that "patriotism is the greatest insanity the world has ever suffered," the comedian takes a fling at all Europe:

"I have been all over Europe in the last few months. Patriotism is rampant everywhere, and the result is going to be another war.

"I hope they send the old men to the front the next time, for it is the old men who are the real criminals in Europe to-day."

"Chaplin said that he had been so misunderstood that he did not care whether he ever made another picture," adds the correspondent, reverting to the "command" performance—

"Chaplin telegraphed George Black, director of the Palladium, explaining his rule never to appear on the stage, since he was associated with the screen, and enclosing a donation of $1,000 for the benefit fund—which he told Black was equivalent to his earnings in his last two years in England before going to America.

"'I am by way of being a student of history,' the actor said. 'I know that the jester always pays, for the king inevitably kicks

him down-stairs. The most famous Court clowns eventually are beheaded, but what happens to the monarch then? In nearly every case, kicking the jester has presaged the fall of the throne.'"

CHAPLIN'S retort attracts the notice of American editors.

Maybe he "was simply getting even with George Bernard Shaw," suggests *The Jersey Journal*, pointing out that "Shaw has a nifty way of using every suitable occasion (which means every occasion) for slamming the United States, where his works are probably as popular as they are in England."

"Being misunderstood, bullied, and misrepresented has been the fate of great men always," says the Manchester (N. H.) *Leader*—

"He is not the first man who has had to go from his native heath to find recognition.

"Another thing, he may be mistaken in his belief that he was as good an artist when he was struggling in London seventeen years ago as he is to-day.

"Probably, he finds the ground for his charge of hypocrisy against his countrymen in the unstinted applause that has been his portion on this trip.

"But that is unfair, for it is the way of the world to pay honor to those who have achieved notable success in any line. Moreover, it is but fair that the Europeans should do something of this sort, in order to counterbalance the plaudits Americans have been bestowing on foreign celebrities in recent months."

"There's a sting in Chaplin's comment that the thousand dollars he donated to the fund was equal to his earnings the last two years he was in England before coming to America to become a popular idol," says the Philadelphia *Record*:

"The dicer, the mustache, the baggy trousers, flappy shoes, and saucy cane were his make-up, then as now; and England had (and missed) first chance to appreciate and reward the mixture of satiric perception and sympathetic interpretation of Chaplin's clowning."

My Word!

—Thomas in the Detroit "News."

"Chaplin Refuses Command Showing"

9 May 1931

AP

Charlie Chaplin will stick to the silver screen like the shoemaker to his last and not even the invitation or "command" of Britain's King and Queen will lure him to the stage.

The Evening Standard, recording an interview with Chaplin at Juan les Pins, France, today said he had refused a royal command invitation to appear at a benefit vaudeville performance soon which their majesties will attend.

"I don't appear in public that way," the newspaper quoted Chaplin. "The last thing in the world I want to do is to make a stage appearance. It would be bad taste."

The Evening Standard said Chaplin was sending a check to the benefit, which has been arranged by a royal committee for aged and disabled vaudeville artists.

Most actors regard the invitations to appear at command performances, which receive their name from the wording of the invitations, as feathers in their caps and there have been very few refusals. It is not certain that either King George or Queen Mary expressed a wish to see Chaplin in person at the performance, although this may have been the case.

Chaplin is a British citizen. He has been represented as regarding the life of the British country gentleman as his ideal. He was given a tumultuous reception recently when arriving here from the United States.

"Chaplin Brands British as World's Greatest Hypocrites"

Springfield (MA) News

11 May 1931

Comedian Doubts that He Owes Anything to Native Land that Spurned Him in Days of Hardships

Charles Spencer Chaplin, comedian, in serious mood bitterly assailed the British as the "greatest hypocrites in the world" at times in an interview printed today in the *London Express*.

He was quoted as saying that Europe had bullied, misunderstood, and misinterpreted him. Chaplin, interviewed at Juan-les-Pins, France, struck sharply at his critics in England who flayed him for not appearing at a recent "command performance" in a London variety show charity affair.

"They say I have a duty to England," the interviewer quoted Chaplin as saying. "I wonder just what that duty is. No one wanted me or cared for me in England 17 years ago. I had to go to America for my chance and I got it there.

"Only then did England take the slightest interest in me. I asked a few friends to a party after my first night of *City Lights*, yet society seemed staggered, shocked, and upset at such a social debacle. Then down here, I sat one night patiently waited for the Prince of Monaco and it appears that I was insulting to the Duke of Connaught.

"Why are people bothering their heads about me? I am only a movie comedian, and they made a politician out of me, a material sort of fellow, which I am not."

Chaplin said that patriotism was "the greatest insanity the world has ever suffered."

"I have been all over Europe in the past few months," he said. "Patriotism is rampant everywhere, and the result is going to be another war. I hope they send the old men to the front the next time. For it is the old men who are criminals in Europe today."

* * *

Wichita (KS) Eagle
22 May 1931

Of course Charlie Chaplin has no regrets for refusing to perform before the King of England. He got so much more publicity the way it was.

"A Popular Act: Chaplin's European Performance"

San Francisco Call-Bulletin

14 May 1931

Chaplin's flare of temper in Europe has done him no harm in this country. He didn't know he was being invited to a "command" vaudeville performance before the King of England and refused. Then a little storm broke over his head and Charlie said just what he thought about Europe and his birthland. He reminded England that nobody paid any attention to him when he was a poor and obscure music hall performer and that he had to go to America to be successful.

All these years, perhaps, Charlie Chaplin has thought of himself as an Englishman. Now suddenly, he discovers that he's not an Englishman at all but an American. He thought London was his home; he went to London and found that home was where he's just come from. Does that make him sad or happy?

"Chaplin's Mistake"

New York Mirror

19 May 1931

Answering Michael Healy, who recently cheered Charles Spencer Chaplin's attitude against his English critics: Mr. Chaplin made the mistake of classing all British as English. There are three other countries in Britain besides England. I think it was rather sporting of Chaplin to slight King George for the faults of the Englishmen, his own countrymen. Perhaps the financial returns did not suit him, since it was a charity affair. Long live the King!—Scotty

* * *

"English Comedian Praises Chaplin for Not Playing in London Benefit Charlie Did Just Right in Declining Invitation and Giving $1000 Instead, He Says"

St. Paul Minnesota Pioneer Press

26 June 1931
By Grace Kingsley

Charlie Chaplin, I find, has the sympathy of most English actors when it comes to the matter of that much discussed so-called command performance in London, which Chaplin refused or neglected to attend.

I met Herbert Mundin, one of London's favorite comedians, recently and both he and his wife, known professionally as Kathleen Shaw, who have just come from the storm center, so to speak, say that Charlie did just right not to respond to the invitation of the stage producer who asked him to appear at the benefit performance involved.

"The man had said in the papers," they told me, "that it would be a great feather in his cap if he could get Chaplin to appear. But Chaplin was on a holiday, there was really no royal command at all, and we think that his donation of a thousand dollars to the benefit was a generous act. In no case could Chaplin have brought more money to the theater by his appearance, since it had all been sold out weeks beforehand.

Mundin, who has appeared opposite Beatrice Lillie in tow of the Charlot Revues, I found to be a most modest little man, who prefers to talk about others rather than himself. This is his first trip to California, and he expects to remain and go into pictures.

* * *

"Facts of the Case"

Charleston WV Gazette

21 June 1931

"I think you should know the facts," writes Beatrice Lillie, "about Charles Chaplin's alleged 'snubbing' of King George and Queen Mary.

"Chaplin was not summoned to a command performance, but to a benefit show at which the King and Queen would be present. When they desire a command performance they summon their favorite artists to Buckingham Palace.

"I have appeared at the command evenings, but when invited to perform at benefit shows I always sent a cheque with my regrets.

"Chaplin, who hasn't been a stage performer for 15 years and who was in France when asked, sent the committee a cheque for $1,000. I call that extremely handsome. I generally sent ten pounds ($50 to you, Mr. Barron.).

"Chaplin did not snub their majesties. Something ought to be done about it. Chaplin is too great an artist and sweet a man to be so slandered."

So there you are, Lady Peel.

Appendix D

Notes and Correspondence
Syd Chaplin's Contribution

Sydney Chaplin (1885-1965) was Charlie's half-brother and closest blood relative throughout much of his life. Their lives and fortunes intersected often and one of these times just happened to be during the 1931-32 tour. Syd was living here and there in continental Europe during this period, and when called by Charlie to join him on the tour, jumped at the chance. They met up in Nice in June 1931. Syd's contribution to *A Comedian Sees the World* cannot be overlooked. Along with the two representative letters about the trip he sent back to England to friend R. J. Minney (many of which appeared verbatim in *Everybody's Weekly*), Syd kept notes of the Bali adventure—notes he hoped would help Charlie to recall names, places, and people when it came time for him to write the travel narrative. Just these sample pieces of Syd's notes and correspondence give a whole other angle on the tour—a glimpse "behind the screen."

Syd Chaplin to R. J. Minney

9 March 1932
NYK Line on board *Maru*

My dear Jim,
Here I am again with five minutes to spare. My time has been so taken up
with pleasure that I have neglected my friends but not forgotten them. I
have been owing you a letter for so long that I can only pay the interest by
extending the length of the letter, which may not be so good "sez you." A
great deal of water has gone into stocks since I wrote you last or should I
say a great deal of food has passed under the "bridges." First, let me tell you
I have had a wonderful time with Charlie at St. Moritz. It was so unexpected. I was just getting ready to hibernate for the winter and figuring out
how I could reduce my debts by going off the Gold Standard or the end
of the pier when I received a telegram from he of the quarter to three feet,
asking if I would care to join him in the solidified water sports. So packing
my skates and skis in my Gladstone, I beat it for the country of high altitude and prices—as Charlie was footing the bill I went first class instead
of on the break rods. The first thing that happened on crossing the border
of Italy was to have my two beautiful cigarette lighters confiscated by the
customs as they are not allowed in the country. This lowered my opinion of
Michael Angelo to Zero. It left me with as much appreciation of him as the
British had for Wagner during the War. However, the rest of the journey
passed off without event and Charlie received me with open checkbook. I
found Charlie looking well and madly enthusiastic about skiing. It was his
first season and everyone told me of the great progress he had made. I was
invited to go with him and Mr Citröen and party on a skiing expedition
the next day. We started off in two of Mr. Citröen's special-built tractor cars
taking our lunch with us, which we thoroughly enjoyed in an out-of-the-
way farmhouse miles from anywhere and well off the beaten track of skiers.
Of course, we would be exclusive. This was my second time on skis and the
guide assured me I had nothing to fear. All I had to do was to keep my balance and put my trust in the Lord.
This was good advice, as the latter knew more about gravity than I did
having made it. Twelve of us started down and eleven arrived. After I came

to, I found myself buried in snow at the bottom of a ravine; the rest of the party had disappeared. I had visions of being left there for the night and frozen to death. I managed to pick myself up and continue on. I arrived an hour later at the station, just as the rest of the party were about to take the train back to St. Moritz. I was looking like a snowman; icicles were hanging from my nose and eyelashes. Everyone roared with laughter and I was the joke of the evening. I decided I had had enough of skiing and would confine my future activities to the bobsleigh, which I did. It's funny the different fears that people have. Charlie would not go down the bob run for a £1000 and no one could persuade him to and yet he would go on night skiing expeditions that I would not have for any sum and yet I have not the slightest fear of the curves in the bob run. Perhaps I have less ...? than he has. It is strange the amount of energy I developed while in St. Moritz. I don't know whether it was the altitude that suited me or whether it was due to the Fellows syrup of Hypophosphates I was taking, but I was untiring. Everyone would remark about my vitality; I would dance in the bar until two or three in the morning—rumbas and Tyrolean waltzes—until my partners dropped from exhaustion. There was one little German girl there and how she could *dance*. When we got together the floor would clear and our rumba would always finish up with a big round of applause. All the old men with whiskers would ask me where I got my energy from, so I started advertising the Syrup. It resulted in a run on the local chemist and depleted his stock and left him wondering what it was all about. My energy was a great joke to Charlie because on my arrival, I told him I did not think my heart would stand the altitude. From then on in the middle of one of my dervish whirls, Charlie would shout out "mind your poor heart, Syd." He had a wonderful time in the bar playing all sorts of practical jokes and pulling different stunts with the orchestra. Some of the best sports up there were with the members of nobility. They would enter into any kind of stunt we arranged. One night the Prince de Bourbon and I danced a waltz in a stooping position like two dwarves. I also danced an eccentric rumba with the Princess de Hesse. They all seemed to enter into the spirit of fun, but you could always tell the nouveau riche. They would sit perpendicular and parallel with their starched shirtfronts and talk Einstein.

I was sorry to leave St. Moritz, but Charlie decided to get back to America via the Orient as he was anxious to see Japan and did not want to make the journey when the weather was hot. So Kono, his Japanese secretary, was told to make all arrangements; the result is we are now comfortably installed in a suite on board the *Suwa Maru*. This is not a very large boat, only 10,500 tons, but English built and very steady—in fact remarkably so—as the waves are running very high, but there is scarcely any roll. All the staff are Japanese and do everything in their power to make us comfortable. The service is excellent and we look like we will be having an enjoyable trip. There are not many people on board. There is, however, one loud-speaking English couple who can be heard all over the dining saloon. They are the type that usually bring ridicule upon English people. This fellow has very prominent teeth and talks all the time about riding to the hounds what! what! And his wife has a set of false teeth that whistle. She reminds me of poor Harry Weldon when he used to say "s'no ussse." Charlie made me double up with laughter when we got back into the cabin. He made a set of prominent teeth with a piece of orange peel and then gave me an impromptu conversation between the couple. If he would only do it for the talkies, it would be worth a fortune. I have never laughed so much in my life. I wish Charlie would keep in the lighter mood always; he gets so serious—at the present moment he is writing an article on how to solve the Germany reparation problem. And his solution of the difficulty is really remarkable and so simple I cannot see why it has never been thought of before. He has put his proposition up to several bankers and financiers and not one can find an argument against it, but on the contrary think it unassailable. I cannot give you his idea in this letter; it would take too long and I want to post this at Port Said. It's strange that Charlie should interest himself in such serious subjects, but it would be still stranger if the world's financial problem was solved by a comedian. I noticed a few of the books in Charlie's cabin:

Behind the Scenes of International Finance by Paul Einzig
The Bank of International Settlement by Paul Einzig
The Economic Consequences of the Peace by J. M. Keynes
Reminiscence of the Russian Revolution by Phillip Price

In my cabin you still see:

The World's Best Humorous Anecdotes by Lawson
A Beachcomber in the Orient by Foster
Finding the Worth While in the Orient by Kirtland

Boy, I'm out for a good time. Let Charlie do the worrying.

We are getting off at Port Said and taking a look at the Pyramids and catching the boat again the next day. We have eighty Arabs aboard who also get off at Port Said. They are going to Mecca for the religious festival. They opened up conversation with Charlie and me. They spoke French and I did the interpreting for Charlie. I asked them where they were going and they said "Mecca," but I thought they said "America," so I told them they ought to have a lot of fun there and told them not to miss some of the night cabarets but to be careful of the booze, it was not so good. There was a chilly silence and then it suddenly dawned upon me. It made a big hit with Charlie. So did another remark I made at St. Moritz. Charlie was discussing "honors" with a Prince. The Prince remarked about Charlie's ribbon of the Légion d'Honneur and the Prince said he had the Cross of something or another from somebody and I chipped in and said all I had was the "double cross" and everyone had given me that. Well, you must be getting tired of reading this letter, so I will conclude by telling you that it is our intention to break our journey to Japan and proceed to Java and then to the Island of Bali. This is the island that Roosevelt has been raving about in the papers as being the last unspoiled paradise on earth, so Charlie is going to see what impression he gets from it. I am afraid Roosevelt has sealed its doom. There are two American artists on board who have been studying art in Rome and are now going to Bali for a year and they have very little money to do it on. They confessed to me that they had been inspired by the Roosevelt article, so it looks as though we may be the vanguard of the Army to follow. Well, Jimmy, I have done a hell of a lot of talking about my brother and myself and not a word about you. I suppose by now you have the new addition to the family. Heartiest congratulations. Send me one of the formula—and a photo, one of the baby, not the formula. How do you like your new house and how did the film turn out you wrote for B. . .? I hope it was a big success. Wheeler seems to have had no luck (not with the formula but with work). I have given my apartment to him and Dorothy while I am away. I think they will enjoy a stay there. I guess he will write and tell you all the news. I see poor Aubrey has been under the weather. I have just written him a long letter and I have a lot more to write, so will close with all good wishes and love to Edith and yourself.

Yours always, Sydney

P.S. My dear Jimmy,

You can use any of the material in this letter for your paper, but for god's sake, correct the grammar and spelling. I have not even troubled to go over it. Change it as you like, but don't change the facts. You understand, old dear. Give my love to Maxwell and a big kiss to Thorpe.

Drop me a line c/o Thomas Cook, Tokyo, Japan.

"Love Drama in Charlie Chaplin's Ship"

Everybody's Weekly

23 April 1932
By Syd Chaplin
Young Japanese Boy Shoots Himself, After Parting with Girl

While Charlie Chaplin, the world's most famous film star, was traveling with his brother Syd to Japan, a fellow passenger in the same ship figured in a most touching love drama, which is revealed below.

Who was it said "It is better to have loved and lost than never to have loved at all?"

A young Japanese boy returning home after a stay in Europe did not agree with one word of this sentiment. He had loved—loved madly. She was a French girl, and just before sailing, he found that she was only a "gold-digger"—nothing more. He had loved and lost. Life was intolerable, but he was bearing up. At the other end of the long journey was home—the family from whom he had been parted, waiting to greet him and to solace him.

Blinded for Life

Also on board the *Suwa Maru*, a Japanese liner carrying a mere handful of passengers, was Charlie Chaplin and his brother Syd. Charlie, after a long holiday spent in various parts of Europe, was returning to Hollywood.

All the passengers were startled one day. The Japanese youth, unable to struggle with his memories any longer, had decided to do away with himself. He shot himself in the head.

"But the bullet," Syd writes in a letter to a friend, "by a miracle, did not penetrate the skull. It passed between the outer skin and the bone and came out again—but not before it had blinded the poor fellow for life.

"He is now on his way back to his parents. Can you picture the homecoming? It is very sad to see him being led about the boat. The other day he was photographed, at his own wish, with Charlie and myself."

Craze for Coconut Milk

"This is a long, lazy journey. The passengers just idle their time away in deck chairs. But Charlie is busy most of the time writing. He has got a craze for the milk of coconuts and ordered a sack to be delivered on board in Ceylon. He is also keeping fit by running around the decks morning and evening.

"The other night the Captain invited us to a Japanese dinner on the top deck. Everything was cooked in correct Japanese fashion. Even the music was Japanese, and two of the stewards danced for our entertainment.

"Charlie and I sat for two solid hours in the Japanese manner, and, believe me, the feeling after a first day's horseback riding is nothing in comparison with the aches and cramps on rising from a Japanese squat. Japanese sitting, like skiing, should be learnt when young.

"Charlie is anxious to live in Japanese hotels in Japan. If so, I intend buying a chair for myself. I am also taking no chances of getting a splinter in my neck by using a block of wood for a pillow.

"I thought that Japanese meal was never going to end. They cook it right on the table in front of you and put in everything but the mountain of Fujiyama. They gave us chopsticks to eat with. Charlie had practiced before and was quite dexterous with them. But I was about as graceful as an elephant trying to thread a needle with boxing gloves on. Can you imagine trying to eat a pea with two sticks in one hand!

"Anyway, it was an amusing affair, and in spite of the fact that my legs are slightly warped, I thoroughly enjoyed it."

Sydney Chaplin Typescript Ms. (Bali)

Chaplin Archives, Montreux, Switzerland

We left on 4 March from Naples on *Suwa Maru*. Evelinoff and May came to see us off. Arrived Port Said. Motored through Cairo. Lunched at Shepheard's Hotel. Rushed around town shopping, white suits, tropical helmets, etc. Visited pyramids. Watched a man ascend and descend more than six minutes, very dangerous, stumble would be fatal. Photographed camels. Difficulty in purchasing movie camera. Everybody hunting Cairo. Dozen people and dozen camels arrive at Cook's office. Motored back to ship at night. Trip to Ceylon uneventful. Two American artists on board named Sitton and Johnson. Times exercise and running, etc. We partake first Japanese dinner. Stiffness after sitting in Japanese fashion for two hours. Stewards give Japanese dances. Your burlesque fan afterwards.

Photographs taken with the whole ship crew, stokers, stewards, and navigators. We arrived at Ceylon. Large crowd to meet us. British methods of using the whip on natives. We noticed the same thing in Cairo. We motored to Kandy. At dusk there is a full moon, which means Buddhist religious festival. This is our first impression of the tropics. All along the road we get the smell of spices and the perfume of the frangipane flower. We meet village procession and devil dancers. Dinner at Kandy. Crowd watching us eat through the window. After dinner, devil dances on the lawn. Midnight we take jinricksha ride around the lake. See tortoise crossing the road. The following morning, photographed devil dances, town, and temple. We are impressed by the handful of rice donation to the poor. Priest writes on wood. Offerings of flowers in temple. Motored back to Colombo. Visited tea and rubber factory. Leave Ceylon.

Arrived at Singapore. Drive around Singapore—should be called "Stinkapore." Visited natives' quarters. Guide would keep taking us to parks and municipal buildings. We are presented in native quarters with leis of flowers, same as they put around your neck in Honolulu. We visited Hindu temple and saw worshipping ceremonies. We were especially shown the golden horse with the swinging and detachable phallus. Drive to Seaview Hotel. We are the only customers. They switch off all our lights after serving us with drinks, because it is midnight—and so, we drank in the dark.

We sailed on 28 March on the *Van Lanesberg* for Java. We meet lady journalist abroad, armed with letters of introductions from crowned heads and presidents, etc. She is the one who pestered us to death at Bali. We arrived Batavia 30 March. Large crowd on dock. You are presented with wreath of welcome. We take tea at the Java Hotel with Hank Alsen, the cameraman. We drive to Bandoeng. Took a hot bath at the Praenger Hotel. This was the only hotel we found in Java where you could lie in the bath. All the others had Dutch dipper system. We dined at this hotel. You were very much impressed with the modern design, and complimented the manager. You and the manager standing outside in the center of the road, admiring the architecture in the pouring rain. He trying to be polite and getting soaked to the skin. You are wearing Mackintosh and entirely unconscious of predicament.

We motored to Garoet and stopped at Ngamplang Hotel. We stayed there that night. Wearied insects making strange noises entered the room, which suggests a new idea and picture. In the morning we found the hotel had a beautiful view over the mountains and valleys. We drive to Tjisoeroepan Hot Springs, Lake Leles, and Bagendit. We threw out money to crowds of kids. Girls entirely nude came running out of the lake to get their share. We take moving picture of the crowd scrambling for money. We dismiss car and take train to Djokja. There is no room in the carriages, so we sat in dining room all the way. We are smothered with smoke and dirt from the engine.

You decide not to travel again by train.

We stay at the Grand Hotel at Djokja.

Next morning we visit the Borobudur Temple. This is the famous temple that was covered up by the jungle for many years. You can get all the data you want about this temple from the library. We motored to Soerabaja. We arrived at night at the Orange Hotel. There is a large crowd waiting at the hotel. You make a speech over the radio in the hotel lobby and are presented with bouquets of flowers. We get a lot of amusement out of "Dutch wife" in bed.

The following morning, we take a KPM steamer and sail for Bali. We sit at the captain's table; he is quite a comedian. There is a Dutch opera singer on board also at our table. Every now and then he would burst out into song during the meal. He was very proud of his bass voice. We struggle with the Dutch rijsttafels. This is the mountain of food so beloved by the Dutch.

The following morning we arrived at Bali at the port of Boeleleng. There is a large crowd on the docks to meet us. You are surprised as you thought in Bali you would be unknown. We are met by Mr. Minas, the Armenian who owns the tour agency there. We are invited to the governor's house. In Bali, he is known as resident, and his name is Beeuwkes. We are entertained by governor and his wife and friends. I take photographs of group. We then motored to South Bali. You don't like the personality of Minas, who traveled with us in the car.

We arrive Den Pasar and stop at the Bali Hotel. The manager's name is Mr. B. Clalle. After we listen to the gamelan orchestra for the first time. Also see the girls dancing. Following are the few notes that may be useful to you:

The rajah who invited us to his palace is named Anak Agoeng Ngoerah Agoeng Agoeng Van Granjar. His position is the island's *Bestvurder*. The outstanding points about him were his large watch and very heavy golden chain, which he keeps looking at. His desire to sell all the family heirlooms. Everything—going so far as to bring them down to the hotel. His politeness was of picking his teeth and his capacity for belching, which on the islands is considered very good manners and a sign to all hosts that the food is truly appreciated. So every banquet eventually turns into a belching competition.

You also dined with the rajah and his wife at the assistant's resident's house in Den Pasar. The Dutch officials remain formally dressed in spite of the heat. But hear that you dislike formality. They made in etiquette to remove their coats at dinner. All the Dutch officials' wives are mountains of flesh with great capacities for rijsttafels, so different to the slim bodies of the natives.

At the rajah's palace, we saw the "*topeng*," which is the mask dance. All performances were very aristocratic. You can tell the breeding by the long fingernails on the left hand. There were beautiful golden embroidered costumes on the outside, and filthy dirty linen underneath, which they always seem anxious to show you by continually opening their covering robes.

We also saw the kris dance in which the dancers are supposed to be in a trance and are brought out of same by holy water thrown upon them by the priest. This is the dance that our journalist lady friend so rudely inter-rupted in order to get the pose for a photograph, and thereby destroying interest and suspense.

Just before the dance commenced, we noticed all the younger peo-ple vacating the front seats, while full-grown men took the pleasure. We were informed that they were placed there to protect us in case the danc-ers should attack us with their knives, which they were apt to do under the influence of their trance.

We finished up everything with the shadow-play. This is known as the *Wayang Kulit*. The names of the other Bali dances are as follows: The bar-ong, Lion dance, Witch dance. This is the dance we saw one night where they sacrifice the chicken before the witch's mask. The dance in which the actor plays the witch sometimes gets mad and becomes irresponsible of his actions. This is also the dance where they put over such a wonderful fire-work display.

There was also some good comedy works, but where three comedians, each in his turn, were supposed to be invisible; then you have the *legong* dance. This is danced by two or three girls and is a religious dance. This is the dance in which the girls use the wings on their arms. Girls do not dance this dance after they reach the age of puberty.

Then there is the *baris* dance. This is the warrior dance, only danced by men. There is also another dance, which is the Balinese modern conception of jazz. They say this dance was suggested and influenced by a visiting Mala Opera Company, circuses, and Chinese acrobats. I do not know the name of this dance, but you will find it mentioned in the book *Last Paradise* or the book about Bali, both of which you have with you.

There is another dance called the *sang hyang*. This is also a trance dance in which the men all shout in unison like a college yell. We saw the kris dance in the villages of Batoe and Boelan. We saw the legong dance, baris dance, and sang hyang dances in the village of Bedoeloe. This is the village where the two girls whom we photographed teaching other girls to dance. The village where we saw the priest using the whip on the villagers who stole the temple offerings is named Sebatoe.

Notes

Introduction

1. The Charles Chaplin Film Corporation Minutes Book for 9 December 1936, suggests that Chaplin's "honeymoon" tour to the Orient following *Modern Times* was also conducted for publicity purposes.

2. Actually, this strategy was one Chaplin used to great effect in such films as *The Bank* (1915) and *The Vagabond* (1916). What was new about it was Chaplin's foregrounding it in the opening credits ("A comedy with a smile—and perhaps a tear.") and then making his juxtapositions more explicit throughout the film.

3. Harris's testimony in William Hamlin's "The Funniest Thing That Charlie Chaplin Ever Did" included Chaplin's mistreatment of her during their first Christmas together when Harris had just been released from the hospital after treatment for a nervous condition. Chaplin failed to come home on Christmas Eve, after he had told her "he would be home and have dinner with me and help me trim the Christmas tree" (3). When he did arrive home in the early hours of the morning, he woke Harris up to castigate her for buying so many presents. On Christmas day, he arose very late and continued to yell at her for her overindulgence, stating that "he did not believe in such things" (n.p.). Such pronouncements must have seemed sacrilegious to working-class Americans.

4. The first commercially acceptable feature film to incorporate synchronized music, singing, and limited dialogue was, of course, Al Jolson's *The Jazz Singer* (1927).

5. Also, and perhaps more compelling, are the Charles Chaplin Film Corporation Minutes for 14 October 1930, in which Chaplin states "that inasmuch as the picture was not a talking motion picture, there was considerable doubt in his mind, as well as in the minds of others engaged in the motion picture business to whom he had talked, as to the reception with which a silent motion picture would be received by the theatre going public."

6. See Maland 98-105, especially 102, and Robinson, *Chaplin: His Life and Art* 375-76.

7. The document numbered twenty-three pages and was printed on cheap pulp paper. It was released to the public on 12 January 1927, just two days after the complaint was filed in Los Angeles. Among its more revealing claims is item 3 under part V: "defendant solicited, urged and demanded that plaintiff submit to, perform and commit such acts and things for the gratification of defendant's said abnormal, unnatural, perverted and degenerate sexual desires, as to be too revolting, indecent and immoral to set forth in detail in this complaint" (4).

8. Interestingly, extracts from the Charlie Chaplin Film Corporation Minutes Book show that Chaplin bought stock in London throughout 1932 (noted purchases are dated 11.1.32, 20.5.32, 17.11.32, and one previous purchase is discussed on 21.3.33) despite this financial turn of events.

9. Chaplin relates in "ACSTW" that "a message from Mahatma Ghandi stated that he would like to meet me, either at the Carlton Hotel or elsewhere" (pt. IV: 22).

10. Several pieces of correspondence in the Charlie Chaplin Archive attest to the wisdom of Chaplin's economic suggestions for the crisis. One written 14 December 1932, by chemist R. R. Snowden states that "some time ago I read of your plan for financially rehabilitating the world, and am astonished that the world leaders seem to have neglected it up to the present time. It looks to me like the most sensible and practicable plan yet offered. . . ." Another, sent 27 June 1932, by congressional candidate David Horsley, offers a similar approbation: "I have just read your article in the Examiner disclosing the plan you spoke of to the press on your arrival to solve the world's most pressing problem, i.e. the resumption of international trade. The plan appeals very much as it is both logical and practical."

11. In his first economic speech, which occurred in the House of Commons on 25 February at a dinner sponsored by Lady Astor, Chaplin said that "the limited amount of gold is not sufficient to serve an increasing population as a medium of exchange, especially with the rapidly decreasing man power in labor. Gold scales are too small. [. . .] Enlarge those scales to silver ones or something else" (pt. I: 88).

12. An extract from the Charles Chaplin Film Corporation Minutes Book, dated 1 January 1931, states that "in order to properly show, exploit and sell the picture CITY LIGHTS it is desirable, necessary, and best business judgment that Mr. Chaplin attend personally, openings at New York, London, Paris, Berlin and other cities."

13. "It is not difficult to reconstruct the great popularity and enthusiasm around the genius of our great patron 'Charlie'" (translation mine).

14. As of 3 December 1921, Alf Reeves mentions in a letter to Monta Bell that the book's chosen title was "The Hour of Success" (Charlie Chaplin Archive).

15. A sampling of newspaper reviews include the (1) *Allentown Record* of 17 February 1922, which states "Charlie Chaplin's book, *My Trip Abroad*, is the best dollar's worth of light—and not so light at that—reading I have come across for some time. It is a real human document" (n.p.); (2) *Cleveland Press*, 10 March 1922, which suggests that "few novels published recently contain as much real emotion and such thoughtful, sensitive observation as Charles Chaplin's account of his trip to Europe" (n.p.); and (3) *Indianapolis News*, 17 May 1922, a rare negative review that states "Charlie Chaplin [. . .] telling about his journey to Europe last year, does not show the genius he reveals on the screen. The careful reader will discover a side of Charlie that he never suspected. In fact, the careful reader will think the picture rather an unflattering one" (n.p.).

16. Robinson devotes an entire chapter to *My Trip Abroad* in his book *Chaplin: The Mirror of Opinion* (52-59). "A Comedian Sees the World," however, is not mentioned.

17. Monta Bell, 1891-1958. Bell worked as a reporter for the *Washington Post* and as editor and general manager of the *Washington Herald* at the time he was chosen to collaborate on *MTA*. In the same letter quoted above in which Bell indicates his progress on the book, he asks Chaplin for a job and signs a contract on 1 January 1922, and is on the job in time to watch some of the last days of Chaplin's filming of *Pay Day* in late February 1922. He was given a bit part in Chaplin's next film, *The Pilgrim*, and held the post of literary editor on *A Woman of Paris* before going off on his own to work as a director, first for Warner Brothers and later for MGM, Fox, and Universal.

18. Bell also received a Chaplin studios contract for his trouble, as supported by a letter from Alf Reeves to Bell, dated 3 December 1921, which mentions that Bell's contract was signed and sent to lawyer Nathan Burkan and that Bell was expected to begin work in January 1922 (Charlie Chaplin Archive).

19. *The Woman's Home Companion*, launched in 1873, was a pioneer in the dissemination of information to women. Allan Nevins wrote in November 1933 that *WHC* "has led, has counseled, and has encouraged women in their momentous upward climb of six busy decades" (136). This same issue featured stories and articles by no less than Booth Tarkington, Pearl S. Buck, Theodore Dreiser, and Eleanor Roosevelt. In the editorial of this issue, longtime editor-in-chief Gertrude Battles Lane writes that "constantly we strive to reflect the

changing world and particularly the broadening concerns of women" (4). A publishing pioneer in her own right, Miss Lane edited *WHC* from 1912 until her death in 1941, creating such features as "The Better Babies Bureau," the first magazine feature to present medical and health tips for mothers. At the time of her death, *WHC*'s circulation had climbed to 3.5 million, a record for a magazine of its type ("Gertrude B. Lane" 23).

20. Miss Willa Roberts, managing editor of *WHC* at the time of Chaplin's second overseas tour, is the person with whom Chaplin and his staff had the most contact over the course of the nearly three years of the "ACSTW" experience. An article from the *Little River News* in Ashtown, Arkansas, dated 24 June 1931, details her experiences defeating a group of male editors in her efforts to sign Chaplin for the book. After Chaplin released the news to the publishing world in early June that he would be writing a book abroad, Roberts made early progress in the race to sign him by being the only editor to use the transatlantic phone lines to begin her negotiations. She then traveled to Berlin and completed business with Chaplin in only four hours. Interviewed at the New York Pier on her return, Roberts noted that "'In all my experience with authors, I have never met one who was any more business-like than Chaplin'" (n.p.). This good working relationship was to turn sour later on.

21. A letter from Alf Reeves, Chaplin Studios manager, to Syd Chaplin, Charlie's brother, dated 30 March 1933, provides some indication of the reason why the series was never published in book form: [*WHC*] expect to have the entire story completed in their magazine before any other publication of it is made either here or abroad. She [Willa Roberts] says this is the publishing practice. If this is so, it will be quite some time before we will be able to publish it either in book form, or as a newspaper or magazine serial anywhere else, for it will run about six months in its serial form, which would thus bring it into next year for general release."

Part I

1. The only contract that exists for the serialization is entitled "Synopsis for Contract with *Woman's Home Companion* March 25, 1931." It reads:
50,000 word manuscript. Price $50,000. Formal contract to be signed on Charles Chaplin's return to Hollywood at which time he will receive $10,000, balance to be paid on completion of manuscript. Charles Chaplin's name not to appear in any other American magazine until after publication of the entire manuscript.
It's signed by Chaplin at the Hotel Crillon, Paris.

2. One of the illustrators for this installment was Walter Jack Duncan (1881-1941). Duncan received his training from the Art Students League in New York and got his first illustrating project in 1903 for *The Century*. He specialized in pen-and-ink and was known for his careful preliminary studies. He published a scholarly book entitled *First Aid in Pictorial Composition* in 1939.

3. In a 23 July 1932, article in the *Union Star* [Schenectady, NY], entitled "Chaplin Finds Writing Art Is Long," the reporter writes both about Chaplin's frustrations and Miss Roberts's details about Chaplin and his project:

Charlie Chaplin, as an author, is so painstaking and meticulous that the book which he started a year ago is still only half finished, and his next motion picture production will have to wait until the book is completed.

The first half of the book, comprising about 25,000 words, has just been submitted by Chaplin to Miss Willa Roberts, managing editor of the magazine, which will publish it in serial form.

"The book is not exactly an autobiography," Miss Roberts said, "but is a summary of the high lights [*sic*] of Mr. Chaplin's career. It is very well written, although the author insists that he is an 'unlettered man.'" The first half of the book includes some very striking incidents involving such figures as Einstein, Lady Astor, the Prince of Wales, Ramsay MacDonald, Brians the Prince of Monaco, Bernard Shaw, Lloyd George and others. The only motion picture star mentioned in the book is Marlene Dietrich.

Mr. Chaplin has a memory like a filing cabinet. Nothing escapes him. We have had some remarkable evidence of this in connection with the typist's copy sent to the author. In several cases, he noted the omission of commas or punctuation marks which had been altered. Like Bernard Shaw, he insists on typographical exactitude, and he objects to the slightest alteration of his original text.

Like Gene Tunney, he won't have any professional help in the writing. "I would rather prefer the text should be completely mine," he insisted, "even with mistakes in grammar, than to have it written on corrected by somebody else. It wouldn't be my story if anybody else tampered with it."

Personally, I find his literary style delightful, and I think he can have a real future as a writer if he wants to do so.

4. Burke, in *City of Encounters*, explains Karno's London Comedians and Chaplin's place in the organization:

In their prime [the music halls] made a special feature of sketch-companies and troupes, and it was in these that Charles gained his early experience. Fred Karno was the principal figure in this business. He had many companies, and in those companies many comedians, who later became stars, were given their first chance. He had *The Mumming Birds*, in which Charles played the drunken swell in the prompt-side box, opposite Jimmy Russell who played the bun-flinging schoolboy in the o.p. box. He had *The Dandy Thieves*. He had *Fred Karno's Farm*. He had *The Football Match*. And half a dozen more. Others of these troupes were The Six Brothers Luck, Lew Lake & Company, The Eight Lancashire Lads, The Casey Court Juveniles, Parke's Eton Boys, Joe Boganny's Lunatic Bakers, Phil Rees' Stable Lads, and Haley's Juveniles. In how many of these troupes Charles worked, I don't know. By different stories he must have worked in all of them, but, as I have said, he is not interested in the stories that are spread about him, and won't bother to give the facts which he alone can give. I know that he was a Casey Court boy and a Lancashire Lad and a Fred Karno comedian; and I think that is all.

The humour of these sketches was the monstrous-grotesque humour of the last days of Bartholomew Fair. It went out of fashion when American humour and heavily-anglicized French wit came in, and it only returned to favour when Charles unconsciously replied to the American invasion by taking it to America and infecting the whole world with it. [. . .] (160-61)

5. Chaplin toured London, Paris, and Berlin in September, 1921. The travel narrative *My Trip Abroad*, published by Harper and Brothers in 1922 and ghostwritten by Monta Bell, resulted from this tour.

6. From Chaplin's typescript draft (Charlie Chaplin Archive): "This is something new since the advent of the talkies and took three weeks of Lala-la-ing to arrange. After which another two weeks were necessary for recording it. I shall try to give you an idea of how this is done. Of course there are two ways—one, the sound is recorded with the photographing of the picture and the other, a picture is taken silently and the sound put in afterwards. "City Lights" was the latter.

There is a large room about 100' × 60'. At one end is a screen and the other a padded projection room. The orchestra sits in front of the screen. There are "fishing rods" on wheels but instead of a fish at the end of the line; there is a microphone. These are placed meticulously about the orchestra. On one side there is a small sound-proof room on wheels big enough for a man to sit on. Here the occupant controls the sound which is transmitted to the main recording room where it is actually produced on film and disc. Before recording; the picture is run and music and sound effected are rehearsed. The man in the box tells if you are playing too loud, or whether your noise effects are properly timed with the action of the picture. When everything is perfected, the sound operator signals to the Recording Room and then to the Projection Room: The Projection machine are inter-locked so that they synchronize: then the sound effects are played to suit the action. One reel at a time is completed which is immediately played back for your approval. Something may be out of time. Then you must do it over again. I had a scene where I swallow a whistle. The whistle was very difficult to synchronize. We took the scene some eighteen times. Either the whistle was a little too soon or too late. Shooting a pistol is another difficult action to follow, because it happens so suddenly and the noise of the shot is liable to break the recording needle."

7. A *New York Times* article dated 13 February 1931, indicates that Chaplin visited Sing-Sing Prison in Ossining, New York, with *City Lights* prior to his departure:

More than 1,800 prisoners at Sing Sing prison enjoyed a respite from the dull monotony of their existence this evening when Charlie Chaplin visited the prison as a guest of Warden Lewis E. Lawes and brought with him his latest picture, "City Lights." The film was shown to the prisoners in the new auditorium, and the Warden, his little daughter, Joan, and the members of Mr. Chaplin's party sat in a box.

After the showing, Mr. Chaplin made a brief talk to the prisoners in which he expressed happiness at being able to bring a little enjoyment into their lives and told of his pleasure at seeing them respond so appreciatively to his comedy. Warden Lawes described the evening's entertainment as the "biggest hit we've ever had."(20)

8. Kellner in *The Last Dandy*, claims that:

[Ralph Barton] had been one of the twenties' leading *bon vivants*, elegant in Charvet cravats and dove-gray spats, with the French Legion of Honor in his buttonhole, a cynic's wit on permanent tap, and a philanderer's reputation with women. Moreover, as the most popular artist of the decade whose roar had just dwindled to a whimper, he had a fat income. Two books of his own lay behind him; his drawings had appeared in half a dozen others; his illustrations and caricatures ran regularly in fashionable magazines; and apparently he never wanted for commissions. But his matinee idol's suave charm and effortless art masked persistent bouts of depression that success had only deepened. From the *fin de siècle* drollery of his first magazine cover, for *Judge* in 1914, to the grotesque Christmas shoppers on his last one, for *The New*

Yorker in 1930, Barton's career embraced the same fate that had befallen so many other wits and critics, from Jonathan Swift to H. L. Mencken; a darkening vision, an inability to laugh any longer at the foibles their work reflected. No career in that ridiculous period Carl Van Vechten called "The Splendid Drunken Twenties" was so emblematic of it, save F. Scott Fitzgerald's perhaps; no life reflected so sadly how the decade fed on its children. Complicated by private demons disguised as insomnia and creative blocks, and finally by an alienating paranoia, both his career and his life outspanned themselves. Five years before his suicide, Ralph Barton was featured in *Vanity Fair*'s Hall of Fame—a prestigious honor then—but nobody sent flowers to the small chapel at the Campbell Funeral Home in New York. (1)

9. Bartlett reports in "Charlie Chaplin's No-Man":
Born in Brooklyn, the son of the present Mrs. Richard K. Fox, owner of the *Police Gazette* and widow of the man who built up that well-known pink periodical in its palmy days. [. . .] Carl started his journalistic career, after a brief fling at banking, in Brooklyn. He worked on various New York papers, and then felt the urge to travel and went to Los Angeles. After working on the Los Angeles *Times* for a while, he got a job as press agent with a new moving-picture outfit specializing in animal pictures. [. . .] It was just then that the opportunity to go to work at the Chaplin studios came along, and Robinson has been Chaplin's man Friday ever since—sixteen years. (78)

Robinson, in fact, may be the one to thank for the "travel narrative as publicity vehicle" idea. According to studio records, he negotiated contracts for both *My Trip Abroad* and "CSTW." From an article entitled "Charlie Chaplin Reported Ready to Retire from Films as Actor" in the *St. Paul Pioneer Press*, 27 April 1932, the reporter relates that Robinson was in a venture with cameraman Rollie Totheroh to make a three-reel film of the Olympic Games in Los Angeles, including scenic and historic shots in California. Robinson also reported wanting to make a series of three-reelers, highlighting travel in the United States, so it seems clear that he had more than a passing interest in travel generally.

10. Chaplin's typescript draft (Charlie Chaplin Archive) adds the following: Donahue and Sir Malcolm Campbell would come to my cabin of an evening and tell anecdotes. Steve especially was a good [end of page 5] story teller. He would relate many experiences of his horse racing. One story I thought was very human and touching about a horse named _____ with which he had won the English Derby. It appeared this

horse was most eccentric when running in a race. He had a habit of stopping abruptly, almost throwing his jockey—at other times he would be leading then quit suddenly before the winning post. One day he would look beautifully groomed with his coat nice and shiny—the next day it would look dry and dull in spite of the groom's care. Then again at a trial canter, he would break the track record, and then the following morning he would hardly be able to move. Nobody knew what was the matter with him, not even the Veterinary. The day before the Derby, Steve went to the stable and found him looking unusually seedy. He thought he would notify the owner and the trainer, and advise them to scratch him for the big race. But later at practice, he broke another record. "So he was a complete enigma to all of us," said Steve. "At the start of the Derby he looked as though he was going to have another relapse," Steve said, He was very much worried as nothing could be done if this mood came over him. He was not the kind of a horse on which you could use the whip. Kindness was the only treatment he would respond to and so after two or three affectionate pats, he seemed to come out of his lethargy. We got off at a good start and kept in the middle of the bunch for a while. "Gradually the rest began to drop away from us and there were only four horses ahead, as we came into the stretch. If only he would last," continued Steve. "We are leading now. As we were half way in the stretch, I felt a change come over him. He commenced slowing up I whispered gently to him and again it had a magical effect. Just as a horse was nosing ahead of us, he leaped forward as if by about six weeks after the Derby, the owner commissioned a painter to do a portrait of him. One morning towards the completion of the picture, the painter went to the stable and found the horse lying in a pool of blood. A veterinary was summoned and discovered the horse had died of a hemorrhage. Upon a postmortem, it was revealed that he had been born with only one lung. This had accounted for all his peculiarities. Just think of the spirit of that animal, winning the Derby with such a handicap. It was the noblest horse he ever rode he concluded. Steve has an instinct for horses. He treats them like human beings. His canny insight into their temperament, and the intelligence he puts into a race, are the chief factors of his success."

11. A *New York Times* article, "Chaplin Off to Find His Boyhood London," dated 14 February 1931, mentions Campbell and his exploits:

"Another passenger was Captain Malcolm Campbell, British racing motorist, who made the world record of 245 miles an hour recently at Daytona Beach, Fla., in his ten-ton automobile, Blue Bird, which has to go five miles to get a start. It was brought to the Cunard pier at the foot of West Fourteenth Street and hoisted on board by a special derrick" (20). It appears that a lot of irony surrounded Chaplin's meeting of Malcolm Campbell on board the *Mauretania*. Chaplin mentions that they decided to split their celebrating, with Chaplin deciding to depart at Plymouth and Campbell at Southampton. As Leo Villa and Tony Gray report, after Chaplin departed, "the *Mauretania* got stuck in the mud, just off the Isle of Wight, and Campbell was taken off by special tender before the line could be refloated, so we didn't see the moment of his arrival back on English soil" (65). Also, another great irony was contained in the fact that "as soon as he landed in England, Campbell was informed that he was to be knighted" (65). As David Robinson relates, Chaplin expected to be knighted as well during his visit, but this never occurred. A press leak from the prime minister's office after Chaplin was finally knighted in 1975 showed that the only reason the honor was withheld in 1931 was due to "unfavorable publicity generated by the Northcliff press during the First World War" (427-28).

12. Sir Philip Albert Gustave David Sassoon, 3rd Bt (1888-1939), descended from Baghdadi Jews who had made a fortune in India from the opium trade, was one of the best-known and most glamorous figures in Britain. At twenty-three, Sassoon became the youngest member of Parliament, becoming a Unionist MP for Hythe in 1912. He was a patron of the arts, serving as chairman of the trustees of the National Gallery and a trustee of the Tate Gallery, the Wallace Collection, and the British School at Rome at various times. He was also considered the most eligible bachelor of the age and possibly the greatest host of his time. Trent House, the Sassoon family estate in Middlesex, came to him at his father's death in 1912 and soon became the venue for his entertaining.

13. Nancy Langhorne Astor (1879-1964). Born in America, Astor met and married Waldorf Astor, her second husband, in 1906. Early in their marriage, both became involved in feminist politics. They were also much under the influence of David Lloyd George and his 1909 social welfare budget. Astor was a pacifist who championed temperance, women's rights, and benefits for children. She was the first woman to serve in Parliament, which she did as a Conservative from 1919 to 1945.

14. In an article entitled, "Chaplin Fled from Shaw," the *New York Times* reported on 27 February 1931, that

> Ten years ago, when the literati were just beginning to discover that Charlie Chaplin was a "genius," the movie comedian mounted George Bernard Shaw's doorstep, saw the playwright's name staring boldly from a glittering brass plate, lost his courage, turned tail and ran.

Today he disclosed that he had confessed that misadventure to Mr. Shaw when they met for the first time, at a luncheon given by Viscountess Astor yesterday.

It was while he waited to ring Mr. Shaw's doorbell, Mr. Chaplin said, that a boy with an autograph book in his hand followed him up the steps. Mr. Chaplin turned quickly and the boy ran. In a moment Charlie was going after him.

"Why did you run away?" Mr. Shaw demanded.

"Purely a case of follow the leader," said Mr. Chaplin.

"'m nobody to be afraid of," Mr. Shaw replied, chuckling in his beard. (23

15. Amy Johnson (1903-41) was born in Hull, Humberside, in England and became an aviator in 1929. In 1930 she became the first woman to fly solo from England to Australia, which she did in her aircraft *Jason*, winning £10,000 from the London *Daily Mail*. In 1931 she flew to Japan via Moscow and back. She joined the Air Transport Auxiliary as a pilot in World War II and was lost after baling out of the plane over the Thames estuary.

16. Browne, in his memoir *Too Late to Lament*, wrote about Chaplin's visit to the Old Bailey:

Charlie Chaplin visited London. Lord Chief Justice Hewart, an old friend of my mother, and Mr. Justice Roche (as he was then), my father's favourite pupil, invited Chaplin and me to attend a trial at the Old Bailey and to have lunch with them afterwards in the Judges' Room. Charming, dapper, warm-voiced, widely-read, Chaplin had a swift intelligence, a passion for social justice and, though he had probably given more pleasure to more people than anyone who had ever lived, no hint of conceit. The case was one of vitriol-throwing. During our lunch our hosts cross-examined us. I had sat in court tormented by horror at the thing's dreadful decorum, its outer calm and inner agony, the hidden suffering of she who had so bitterly thrown the acid and of he who had so terribly received it in his face. Chaplin, a truer artist, had been interested primarily in the courtroom ritual; he shared his fellow-guest's pity for the human emotion behind the impersonal pageant but his pity was healed by the stage-values of the play. (314)

17. Ramsey MacDonald (1866-1937), a Scotsman, joined the Independent Labour Party in 1894, taking the post as leader of that party from 1911 to 1914 and from 1922 to 1931. He became the first Labour Party prime minister in 1924, holding the post from January to November in that year. In 1929 he

became prime minister again until the 1931 elections and then continued to lead his "National government" until 1935, when he retired.

18. A *Daily Mail* article entitled "Mr. Chaplin Spends the Whole Night Talking," details Chaplin's visit to Chequers:

Mr. Ramsay MacDonald asked me if I could possibly visit the kitchen, as he was afraid that if I did not do so, the whole domestic staff would be disorganized, as they were all so eager to see me. I went down stairs and spent a very delightful time talking to the staff.

The cook, a charming Manchester woman, was delighted to hear that I had lived in Hyde-road there. I signed autographs for the members of the staff and had a most pleasant time with them.

During the afternoon I had a sleep. The night before I had been too excited to sleep. To be candid, I think that Mr. Ramsay MacDonald had an afternoon nap himself.

He played one of two practical jokes on me. When I told him how fond I was of the feel of old books he pointed some out to me and suggested I should take them from the shelves. When I tried to do so I nearly tore my nails off as they were just dummies.

He also showed me a picture and covering the inscription with his hand said to me, "This is one of the most beautiful young women in English history." I said, "She is quite adorable," and then taking his hand away, I read from the inscription that it was a painting of Oliver Cromwell at the age of ten.

Mr. Chaplin showed great interest in *The Daily Mail* Spot the Stars Competition. "I think," he said, "this is a very novel and interesting contest, and it does not surprise me that so many of your readers have entered for it."

19. Princess Elizabeth Asquith Bibesco (1897-1945) was the daughter of Margo Asquith, who became famous for her writing. She is also well known for her affair with Katherine Mansfield. Two fellow writers have this to say about her:

Princess Bibesco delighted in a semi-ideal world—a world which, though having a counterpart in her experience, was to a great extent brought into being by her own temperament and, one might say, flair.
—Elizabeth Bowen

She is pasty and podgy, with the eyes of a currant bun, suddenly protruding with animation.
—Virginia Woolf

20. "Quaglino's is an attractive restaurant where one can dance to excellent music, both jazz and tango. The decorations are in excellent taste with low warm lighting. You can always be assured of meeting someone interesting here—a Prince of the realm, a politician or an actor" ("ACSTW" typescript draft).

21. Randolph Churchill (1911-68) was the son of Sir Winston Churchill and is probably best known for the two-volume biography he wrote of his father. However, he was a popular young journalist in life, also having a distinguished career in military intelligence in World War II.

22. Son of the famous First Earl of Birkenhead (1872-1930), who had just recently passed away when Chaplin met him in 1931 at Quaglino's. His father the earl was a Conservative MP since 1906, well known for his oratorical powers and wit.

23. David Lloyd George (1863-1945) was an Advanced Liberal for Caernarvon Boroughs since 1890, the same year he officially became a solicitor. He served as chancellor of the Exchequer from 1908 to 1915, becoming during this period a noted social reformer. At this time he passed the Old Age Pensions Act (1908) and the National Insurance Act (1911). He served as prime minister from 1916 to 1922 and was one of the big three at the signing of the Treaty of Versailles in 1918. He resigned from public office shortly following the 1931 elections.

24. David Kirkwood, the son of a laborer, was born in Glasgow, Scotland, in 1872. In 1891 Kirkwood was converted to socialism after reading *Looking Backward* by Edward Bellamy. The following year he joined the Amalgamated Society of Engineers (AEU). He joined the Independent Labour Party and served on the Glasgow Trade Council. He remained active in the AEU and was chief shop steward at the Beardmore Works (1914-15). On 25 March 1916, Kirkwood and other members of the Clyde Workers' Committee were arrested by the authorities under the Defense of the Realm Act. The men were court-martialed and sentenced to be deported from Glasgow. Kirkwood went to Edinburgh, but in January 1917 he traveled to Manchester to speak at the national conference of the Labour Party. On his return to Glasgow, he was rearrested and deported once more to Edinburgh. He remained there until he was freed on 30 May 1917. In the 1922 General Election Kirkwood was elected to the House of Commons for Dumbarton Burghs. He was one of the leaders of the Independent Labour Party in Parliament until joining the Labour Party in August 1933. He held his seat in Parliament until 1951, when he was created Baron Kirkwood. He died on 16 April 1955.

25. From Chaplin's typescript draft (Charlie Chaplin Archive):

Today is Sunday and I have arranged to meet my friend, Thomas Burke, the novelist and author of "Limehouse Nights," "The Wind and the Rain," etc. Ten years have intervened since I saw him last and it is surprising how little he has changed—so different from myself who has greyed-up in the interim.

Burke is always stimulating and we discussed every topic under the sun. I told him of my visit to Hanwell Schools and wondered whether Hanwell is the school he referred to in his book, "The Wind and the Rain," but it wasn't the same. I told him how thoroughly I enjoyed the visit to my school, how fascinating it was to go back into the past. Burke says he is afraid of the past. He hates to go back. He said he could never disassociate himself sufficiently to enjoy it. I agreed poverty does frighten one, but having lived in America for twenty years, I was sufficiently removed from its stigma.

I discussed his work, telling him that I thought "The Wind and the Rain" was his best book, because it revealed the soul of the artist. Later we went for a drive in the country and pulled up at some wayside inn where we partook of an English tea.

Part II

1. Chaplin's typescript draft adds this information:
My manager has shown me a newspaper with a derogatory story in it about myself. "Ha, Ha" I exclaim. "I am outstaying my welcome." "I think you have offended Beaverbrook in some way," my manager commented. "Beaverbrook. Who's Beaverbrook?" I enquired. He is the head of a syndicate of newspapers here in England and from what I gather he does not feel generously disposed towards you. However I am not perturbed about this; having developed the proverbial ducks feathers, I am no longer unfledged or vulnerable to their attacks. I have lived in Hollywood for seventeen years and having been married and divorced twice; and by this time, I am a seasoned old duck.

I am also informed that I had made enemies amongst some of the exhibitors. They felt they had been slighted. It is here I should like to explain myself and say that after working for ten years in the atmosphere of motion pictures, on an occasion of this sort it is a relief to get away from it. For those whom I have offended, I am sorry but if they reflect on my position and the circumstances, I feel sure they will understand and forgive any delinquency on my part. However, other things have cropped up also. There is a Trust in the British film industry, so I am told, who is dictating the price they will pay for my picture. Being an ultra-individualist and disliking Trusts of any kind, I give my London representatives carte blanche to fight them as they please. If their price had been fair and satisfactory, my manager contends, we would do business with them but they want to take advantage of their power. All this is very boresome. I wave it aside, telling him not to worry me with their business troubles and to go ahead and do as they please. At this stage I always shrug my shoulders and become complicated.

2. Chaplin was still using this anecdote in the late 1950s. It appears nearly verbatim in the text of the "Immortal Memory" speech he gave at the Charles Dickens birthday dinner in London on 7 February 1955 ("Immortal Memory" 112-14).

3. In an article dated 30 May 1931, and entitled "Charlie Chaplin's Favourite Dance Tune!" in *Home Chat*, one of Chaplin's episodes with Sari Maritza is recounted:

In "City Lights" there is a haunting melody which threads its way through the film. It is Charlie Chaplin's favourite dance tune, and Jean Butt tells you where you can buy it in record form.

Those of you who have seen Charlie Chaplin's famous talkie, "City Lights," will no doubt remember the haunting little melody which runs all through it. Once heard, it is difficult to forget, and I am going to tell you an interesting piece of news about it, taken from the Columbia advance notes.

"Violetera" is the name of the tune we hear all through the film. On the night of Charlie Chaplin's cabaret party at the Carlton Hotel it was played by Geraldo's Gaucho Tango Orchestra, specially engaged for the occasion to entertain Charlie and his friends. This orchestra has made the tango (coupled with "El Relicario") for Columbia, exactly as played at the Carlton, and it contains a vocal refrain in French.

It is said that as the orchestra began to play, and nobody took the floor, Charlie approached Sari Maritza—the well-known film star—and together they gave a perfect exhibition of the dance.

This will certainly be a most popular record, both for the charm of its melody and for the interest which attaches to it.

4. Chaplin reports in *My Autobiography* the way in which he and Barton spent part of their final day together:

Before leaving he [Barton] asked if I would go with him to visit his daughter, who had only a year previously taken the veil and was now in a Catholic convent in Hackney. She was his eldest daughter by his first wife. Ralph had often spoken about her, saying that since the age of fourteen she had felt the call to become a nun, although he and his wife had done everything they could to dissuade her. He showed me a photograph of her taken when she was sixteen, and I was instantly struck by her beauty: two large dark eyes, a full sensitive mouth and an engaging smile looked out of the picture.

Ralph explained that they had taken her round Paris to many dances and night clubs, hoping to wean her away from her ecclesiastic desire. They had introduced her to beaux and given her the gayest time, which she seemed to have enjoyed. But nothing could deter her from becoming a nun. Ralph had not seen her in eighteen months. She had now graduated from novicehood and had fully embraced the order.

The convent was a gloomy, dark building in the heart of a slum district in Hackney. When we arrived there, we were greeted by the Mother Superior and ushered into a small, dismal room. Here we sat and waited for what seemed an interminable time. Eventually his daughter entered. I was immediately struck with sadness, for she was just as beautiful as her picture. Only, when she smiled, two teeth were missing at the side.

The scene was incongruous: the three of us sitting in that small gloomy room, this debonair, urbane father of thirty-seven, his legs crossed, smoking a cigarette, and his daughter, this pretty young nun of nineteen, sitting across from us. I wanted to excuse myself and wait outside in the car. But neither would hear of it.

Although she was bright and vivacious, I could see that she was detached from life. Her actions were nervous and jerky and showed strain as she talked of her duties as a schoolteacher. "Young children are so difficult to teach," she said, 'but I'll get used to it.'

Ralph's eyes twinkled with pride as he talked to her and smoked his cigarette. Pagan that he was, I could see he rather enjoyed the idea of his daughter being a nun. (347)

5. Chaplin reports on his reception in Berlin during this tour in his book *My Trip Abroad*:

We go to the Adlon Hotel in Berlin and find that hostelry jammed, owing to the auto races which are being run off at this time. A different atmosphere here. It seems hard for me to relax and get the normal reaction to meeting people. They don't know me here. I have never been heard of. It interests me and I believe I resent it just a bit.

I notice how abrupt and polite the Germans are to foreigners, and I detect a tinge of bitterness, too. I am wondering about my pictures making their debut here. I question the power of my personality without its background of reputation.

I am feeling more restful under this disinterested treatment, but somehow I wish that my pictures had been shown here. The people at the hotel are very courteous. They have been told that I am the "white-headed boy and quite the guy in my home town." Their reactions are amusing. I am not very impressive-looking and they are finding it hard to believe.

There is quite a crowd in the lobby and a number of Americans and English. They are not long in finding me, and a number of English, French, and American reporters start making a fuss over me. The Germans just stand and look on, bewildered. (115)

6. At the Hotel Adlon in Berlin, Germany, where Chaplin wanted to stay in 1921 but wasn't able until 1931, the following event occurred, as related in Adlon's *Hotel Adlon*:

The news of [Chaplin's] coming had been spread abroad, and the pavement on Unter den Linden was covered by a dense mass of people through which he had to fight his way from the car to the hotel doors, shaking hands, signing albums, returning smiles and greetings and struggling frantically not to be trodden underfoot. His navigation light, as he was washed to and fro on the bosom of this human tide, was the pale-blue peaked cap of the Adlon porter, who finally managed to rescue him and thrust him to safety through the revolving door. But then, when it seemed that all was well, he suddenly stopped in the middle of the reception hall and gazed at himself in comical bewilderment. His trousers were coming down! Souvenir-hunting admirers had robbed him of every button. He could do nothing but clutch them and make hastily for the lift, using that shuffling gait that all the world knows. (193)

Interestingly, a line to the effect that the Adlon boasts "the lobby in which Chaplin dropped his trousers" is still used in Hotel Adlon publicity.

7. The British ambassador in Berlin, Sir Horace Rumbold, agreed that the Nazis believed in force as opposed to cooperation in solution of European problems. "In the eyes of the Nazis," he wrote, "Germany is like Prometheus bound, and Hitler, or the Nazi movement, is cast for the part of Hercules. This aspiration for freedom and for equality has come to stay, and is an element which every German Government must take into account. It is bound, in my

opinion, to exercise an influence on the conduct of Germany's foreign policy and has begun to exercise such an influence" (Gilbert 791).

8. Dr. Karl Vollmueller, poet and auto industrialist, had met Chaplin for the first time in Hollywood, where he worked in the early days of the film industry. He is noted for having worked on Dietrich's *The Blue Angel* (1930) (Gersch 37-38).

9. Erich Carow was, at the time of Chaplin's visit, the most beloved comic in Berlin. He appeared at his own club, a sort of musical variety slapstick club, "Der Lachbühne":

> Er spielt eine arme, aber unbeirrbare Figur, einen Künstler, der zum Faktotum erniedrigt wird, dreimal wegläuft mitten ins Publikum, bis er die Stellung annimmt; der dann die Leute hinauswerfen und endlich sogar boxen muß. Er hat bein allem genausoviel Angst und genausoviel verzweifelten Mut wie der mittlere Mensch, den die Ereignisse treffen, und meinstens denkt er an die täglichen fünzig Pfennig, für die er bestehen muß, was über ihn kommt. (qtd. in Gersch 44-45)

10. Chaplin's typescript draft (Charlie Chaplin Archive) includes this additional information:

> Before visiting the members of the Government, I was taken through the local police gaol. This was unlike any I had seen before. There were no iron bars, or riveted tanks, which are characteristic of the English and American gaols. But for the many wooden doors along the corridor, one would hardly suspect it being anything but an ordinary building. With the level of the eye, there is a small trap door about a half foot square which the warders open to look into the cells. We looked in one. I was surprised to see how big they were. They had six bunks with as many occupants and a mess table on one side where some of the prisoners were playing checkers, while the others were lazily reading newspapers. I was told that the majority of crimes were due to economic want and a great many were political offenders.
>
> After visiting the Administration Buildings, we were shown into the Police Museum. I have never in my life seen a more gruesome spectacle than the horrors of that museum. Upon entering you are hit in the face, metaphorically speaking, by enlarged colored photographs about 2 ½ × 2 feet, of murdered victims just as they were found by the police in all their gruesome detail. There were decapitated bodies; quartered limbs in trunks; crushed in skulls and horrors of every kind. Then in the section along the wall that you could not escape, was a gallery of sex-maniacs and beside them the pictures of their dead victims. Next, was the gallery

of suicides, both men, women and children, photographed in all their nightmarish methods of destruction. The whole scene was so revolting that I never got over it for days. It seemed unnecessary to keep recorded details of all this horror but they said it was a gallery for detectives to study the nature of crimes and that it represented classic forms of criminology. There were instruments and weapons of all kind. There were different gambling articles for the purpose of cheating, marked cards, loaded dice, etc. However, I was too horrified to remain long in that department so we quickly left, hoping to forget as quickly as possible the memory of such awful things.

11. This four-time Academy Award–nominated composer was born in 1896. After studying at the Berlin Hochschule for Musik and the Stern Conservatory, Friedrich Hollander began writing music for producer Max Reinhardt at his Berlin cabaret. In the post–World War I era, Hollander became a leading intellectual on the Berlin scene, leading a jazz band in Berlin, composing music, and directing scathing anti-Nazi satirical cabaret revues. A pianist and prolific composer, poet, actor, and director, Hollander also wrote and directed early sound films in Berlin. He was also the composer for Marlene Dietrich's now-classic 1929 film, *The Blue Angel*, which includes the famed standard "Falling in Love Again." After immigrating to the United States, Friedrich Hollander moved to Hollywood, where he composed music for more than 120 films. He died in Germany in 1976.

12. La Jana was born as Henriette Margarethe Hiebel in Vienna. She began her career at a child ballet for the Frankfurter Opera. Later she appeared in cabarets and revues as a dancer. She made her film debut in 1925 with *Wege zu Kraft und Schönheit*. Among her other films are *Die weisse Geisha* (1926), *Der Biberpelz* (1928), *Thérèse Raquin/Du sollst nicht ehebrechen* (28), *Gaunerliebchen* (1928), *Ritter der Nacht* (1928) and *Die Warschauer Zitadelle* (1929). She had her greatest successes with her sound films *Der Schlemihl* (1931), *Truxa* (1936) and especially in the two-parter *Der Tiger von Eschnapur* (1937) and *Das indische Grabmal* (1937). Her last movies were *Es leuchten die Sterne* (1938), *Menschen vom Varieté* (1939), and *Stern von Rio* (1940). She caught pneumonia and pleurisy during a Christmas tour, which led to her death at the age of thirty-five.

13. In her 1940 book *Charlie Chaplin*, von Ulm reports on this episode: Sir Philip [Sassoon] then accompanied Charlie and Kono to Potsdam as guests of Prince Henry of Prussia, nephew of the former Kaiser. [. . .] Charlie was frank in his disapproval of the huge seventeenth-century quadrangular pile. [. . .]

Prince Henry was amused.

"You're quite right, old man. They're rather hideous, but you'll have to blame old Wilhelm I for that. Frederick the Great thought the palace bad, too, and built himself a retreat in the eighteenth century which, I am sure you will agree with me, is very nice. Though he and Voltaire both lived in your acrobats' pedes."

They strolled across the Havel, into the terraced gardens of *Sans Souci* and Charlie immediately recognized the prototype of many self-conscious eastern American estates. Great was his glee over Voltaire's room, which Frederick had caused to be papered with parrots, when he had become weary of the latter's interminable talk.

Browsing among the personal relics of the great Frederick, Charlie felt the glories and the tragedies of the man, who, though he was Emperor, had the courage to be, also, a musician. [...]

Charlie was awed by the gardens in which man had captured nature, as any unformed material, and fashioned it into line and proportion and color. (295-96)

14. The *Yorkshire Evening Press* reported on 16 March 1931, that the photograph actually bore the dedication "'To Charlie Chaplin, the nautical economist.'"

15. Sigmund Freud wrote to Yvette Guilbert in 1931: "In the last few days, Chaplin has been in Vienna [...] but it was too cold for him here, and he left again quickly. He is undoubtedly a great artist; certainly he always portrays one and the same figure; only the weakly poor, helpless, clumsy youngster for whom, however, things turn out well in the end. Now do you think for this role he has to forget about his own ego? On the contrary, he always plays only himself as he was in his dismal youth. He cannot get away from those impressions and humiliations of that past period of his life. He is, so to speak, an exceptionally simple and transparent case. The idea that the achievements of artists are intimately bound up with their childhood memories, impressions, repressions and disappointments, has already brought in much enlightenment and has, for that reason, become very precious to us."

16. Oscar Straus (1870-1954) was born in Vienna, but became a naturalized French citizen in 1939. He was best known for composing operettas and comic operas, of which his most famous is *Der Tapfere Soldat* (1908).

17. In an article dated 24 March 1931, (unidentified newspaper) and entitled "Whether Chaplin Is Jew Causes Him to Cancel His Visit to Budapest," the reporter details what turns out to be an itinerary change at this time:

Another of those East European religious quarrels that has in the past cost many lives has unknowingly been kindled up by Charles Chaplin. All of Budapest is in a turmoil and as a result of the argument Chaplin had to cancel his visit here enroute from Vienna to Berlin.

Trouble started when a Jewish paper in Budapest wrote a highly laudatory article of the comedian, claiming him as a Jew and a representative of the fine things Jews have accomplished in the arts. Went on to say that Chaplin originally came from Eastern Europe and that his name once was Thronstein [*sic*].

Immediately the anti-Semite press, highly in majority, bit back with long articles abusing Chaplin and the type of Jew he represented as well as Jewish fans of the theatre.

Although no rioting or trouble, situation looked highly serious until Chaplin made his diplomatic move by not coming here. Incidents of even minor value to this one have in the past incited much rioting and pogroms in Hungary, Roumania and other countries in the Slavic circle of Europe.

18. On 19 March 1931, the *Record* [Troy, NY] reports on Chaplin's entrance in "Chaplin's 'Armada' Blocks All Traffic on Venice Canal":

Down the Grand Canal of Venice came Charlie Chaplin this afternoon in a triumphal procession reminiscent of the Pied Piper of Hamlin.

Big boats, little boats, motor boats, row boats, steam boats, ferry boats and gondolas, tagged along behind his motor launch, from which Charlie bowed and waved to throngs which the windows of famous old palaces along the banks. At the Daniels Hotel, he disembarked and was ushered to the choicest suite.

Police had their troubles unraveling the tangle of navigation around the front of the hotel so that traffic could be resumed.

19. Chaplin sought out another of his interests while in Paris, one that would lead to his *Monsieur Verdoux* almost fifteen years later. As Sadoul writes in *Vie de Charlot*: "Le singulier assassin [Landru] intéressait depuis longtemps Chaplin. Lors de son séjour à Paris, en 1931, il avait tenu à rencontrer des chroniqueurs judiciaries presents au process Landru, pour se faire raconter différents details sur l'affaire" (165).

20. Comtesse Anna Elizabeth de Brancoven (1876-1933) was a noted French poet and novelist of Romanian and Greek descent. Her first popular work was a collection of sensual and musical poems entitled *La Coeur innombrable* (1901).

21. A similar anecdote appeared in Chaplin's earlier book: "Then there were others thanking me for happiness given the senders. These came by the thou-

sand. One young soldier sent me four medals he had gotten during the big war. He said that he was sending them because I had never been properly recognized. His part was so small and mine so big, he said, that he wanted me to have his *Croix de Guerre*, his regimental and other medals" (*My Trip Abroad* 77-78).

22. Albert I (1875-1934), king of the Belgians (1909-34), nephew and successor of Leopold II. He married Elizabeth, a Bavarian princess, in 1900. In World War I his heroic resistance (1914) to the German invasion of Belgium greatly helped the Allied cause. The King and Queen did much to improve social conditions in Belgium and in the Belgian Congo. Albert's democratic and affable ways won him great regard at home and abroad. He died in a rock-climbing accident.

Part III

1. Wallace Morgan (1873-1948) drew the beautiful comic sketches for this installment of Chaplin negotiating the boar hunt. He got his career start as a newspaper artist at the turn of the twentieth century. Because this career required him to draw diverse subjects under pressure, he never needed models in later life. He was one of the official artists assigned to the American Expeditionary Forces during World War I and he taught at the Art Students League on and off, from 1905-29. He served as president of the Society of Illustrators from 1929 to 1936 and received many respected awards later in life.

2. In a 20 March 1931, article in the *New York Herald* Paris edition, an episode involving Lord and Lady Deterding is recounted:

Tonight Mr. Chaplin will be the guest of Sir Henri Deterding, the oil man, and Lady Deterding, who also are staying at the Crillon. They were guests of Mr. Chaplin during their recent visit to California and saw him make several scenes for "City Lights."

Unofficial advices last night stated Mr. Chaplin will be decorated with the Legion of Honor tomorrow. Mr. Robinson believes the comedian will leave Paris on Sunday, probably for Barcelona.

Mr. Chaplin as an artist, genius, actor and psychologist was lauded in the traditional center of French learning last night by two noted French scholars, Pierre Andrieu and Raoul Villedieu-Benoit.

So tremendous was the rush to hear the double illustrated lecture in the Amphitheatre Descartes of the Sorbonne that the audience, filling this room and overflowing far into the corridors, was transferred to the institution's largest hall, the Amphitheatre Richilieu.

Mr. Andrieu, praising Mr. Chaplin's artistry, traced his evolution as an actor from his days of pure comedy to those of a comic element mixed with pathos and deep knowledge of human nature.

Not only is the film star a great actor and artist, said M. Ville-dieu-Benoit, but he is a great psychologist.

To illustrate the savant's discussion, takes from many of the Chaplin films were projected, starting with the ancient, pie-throwing Mutual pictures of 1913 on up to "The Kid" and "The Circus."

3. Sem (Georges Goursat, 1863-1934) was born in the Dordogne region of France. He was attracted to the glamour of the big city and studied art in Paris. He was neither a fine artist, nor one whose drawing was held in high regard, but his skill in caricature was outstanding. He is especially known for his skilled portrayals of city life in Paris at the turn of the century.

4. *The Illustrated Sporting and Dramatic News* for 4 April 1931, reports in an article entitled "Charlie Hunts the Boar in France—in a Duke's Pink Coat" that Chaplin "followed the Duke's pack of boarhounds in Hallet Wood, part of the Forest of Eu." Accounts of Charlie Chaplin's success in riding to hounds vary from being well up in "a thrilling run of 20 miles in 3 ½ hours," unfortunately without killing the boar, "due to his inability to master his horse in covert."

5. Not mentioned here, but only in his later *My Autobiography* (1964) is Chaplin's lover, May Reeves. Their relationship was reported on at length in the press at the time. Noted gossipmonger, Louella Parsons, in a column published on 28 July 1931, offers her analysis of the affair: "A romance as hot as the rays of the July sun has just reached me via cable. Our old friend, Charlie Chaplin, king pin of the comics and regular Don Juan when it comes to falling in love, has again succumbed to love's young dream. Charlie, according to our cable advices, is infatuated with a beautiful Roumanian girl.

Unfortunately for Charlie's reputation as the perfect Romeo, our information is that the love is mostly on Charlie's side, the Roumanian beauty being admittedly in love with a slick haired youth who might be cast as a gigolo if he were in Hollywood.

Having had many experiences in matters of the heart with such beauties as Lita Grey Chaplin, Mildred Harris, Pola Negri, Peggy Joyce, et cetera, et cetera, Charlie has, like Alexander, cut the Gordian knot. He has, putting it in simple language, promised the said youth to make another Valentino of him.

The lad with visions of the glamour and glory that surrounded the adored Rudolph, has let Charlie occupy the center of the stage. So not every one is happy, the boy, the girl and the other side of the triangle, the world's greatest comedian.

Happiness means to Charlie contentment in affairs of the heart and when the screen clown is in love the sky is the limit. Ordinarily as thrifty as a Scotch banker, Charlie forgets money when he is basking in the sunlight of some fair charmer's smiles. So just to prove to the Roumanian beauty how little money means, he has built a costly home in Juan Les Pins adjoining the lady's humble abode.

6. A *Continental Daily Telegraph* article dated 19 August 1931, and entitled "Millionaire's Wife as Film Star," suggests that Mrs. Gould had an ulterior motive for making sure that Chaplin became the Goulds' guest:

The reason of the film star's visit, it is understood, is to make a last effort to secure the consent of Mr. Frank J. Gould, the American millionaire, to permit beautiful Mrs. Frank Jay Gould to appear in a super motion picture.

Mr. Chaplin is endeavoring to find a way to make use of what he believes to be the wonderful picture talents of Mrs. Gould. He offered Mr. Gould to have different scenarios written by half-a-dozen of the world's best authors and so secure a suitable and satisfactory medium in which Mrs. Gould could appear. So far Mr. Gould is adamant. It is understood that one condition he made when he married Mrs. Gould was that she should never appear on the stage in a professional capacity.

In fact, this difference of opinion on the matter soon led to the couple's divorce.

7. An article entitled "April 1 Joke on Chaplin," dated 3 April 1931, in Edinburgh's *Scotsman*, relates one of Syd's typical practical jokes on the trip:

Charlie Chaplin found out to-day that it was April 1. He lunched with his brother Sydney and a large number of friends at a hotel, and one item on the menu was Charlie's favourite dish, "crepes suzette," the fascinating little rolled pancakes which are served with blazing rum.

When the dish arrived Charlie took three, and began to tell everyone of the excellent pancakes he had eaten in all the four corners of the world. "Ah!" said his brother Sydney, "just eat these, Charlie; I've bet you've never tasted any like them." Charlie struggled with them for some time before he discovered that they were made of cheesecloth covered with batter. It then gradually dawned on him that he had forgotten the date. "These are too hard on a man," he said, and then joined heartily in the laughter until he was otherwise occupied with some real "crepes suzette."

8. Chaplin provides this additional information in his typescript draft (Charlie Chaplin Archive), perhaps one of his wittiest parts of the work as a whole:

The casino life I found dull and silly but one could meet several nice people who had attractive homes and they would entertain in a nice way. I later discovered there were many lives to live there—the social, the intellectual and the bohemian, and of course the "casinian" to use my own eulogism.

Since staying here, I have made a discovery. The Riviera has a tendency to inspire ladies—I might say, middle-aged women, with a maternal feeling. Several were pointed out to me, who had adopted sons—young men between the ages of 19 and 25 who were usually young men of Latin origin and who had been left exposed to the bitter cruelties of the indifferent world. These yearning affectionate mothers with all the tenderness of their maternal heart would adopt these children. They were grand inspiring sights to see, mother and son dancing to the strains of a pleading tango. It has become quite a vogue lately to adopt these handsome young sons. I often thought it was singular that these adopting mothers only yearned for boys and never for little girls. It seemed that the old gentlemen were more interested in the latter. I suppose it is the law of opposites that ladies should like sons and gentlemen should like daughters. I hadn't been on the Riviera long before I felt that I should adopt one myself. Strange how one gets inspired with this paternal feeling. Maternity and Paternity is prevalent everywhere. One would occasionally see some old gentleman's adopted daughter running away with play with a mother's adopted son and how concerned the parents would be on finding their little children playing around the gambling tables. The parents would never like their offspring to mix with other children. Such a thing would cause them great anxiety, yet occasionally the little ones would play, not realizing the grief they were causing their fond parents. Due to this sort of disobedience parents would sometimes release from their legal charge and then the little boy would be homeless again. These tragedies are frequent on the Riviera, the land of adopted sons and daughters.

9. Von Ulm reports:

Another renewal of friendship delighted him; it was with Elsa Maxwell, that unique impresarianne of the party whose originality had resulted in changing dull and stately receptions and balls into wacky gatherings somewhat resembling mild riots, but, withal, a lot of fun. Miss Maxwell, short, stout and pudding-featured, impeccably frocked by Europe's famous couturiers—and still a frump—is a triumph of personality over bank balance. She ruthlessly jarred American society loose from its fond convictions that three generations of dubiously gotten wealth presupposed charm and other ingredients for social superiority. She convinced them that personal achievement in the arts, and professional distinction, or even just being amusing, were more logical entrance cards to the charmed circle in a supposedly democratic country than mere riches.

On the barren canvases of parties, Elsa Maxwell splashed—and still splashes—lavish color. As a beginning she flung her repertoire of songs (of her own composition) not to the favored few, the artists who revel in an occasional abandonment to Rabelaisian humor as a divagation from the effete pursuits, but to the stuffed shirts who could take her downright, spontaneous hell-raising—or go home. They did not go home. (319-20)

10. Sir Oswald Ernald Mosely (1896-1980), Sixth Baronet, was an English politician and founder of the British Union of Fascists. He was a member of Parliament for Smethwick from 1926 to 1931 and then chancellor of the Duchy of Lancaster in the Labour government from 1929 to 1931, resigning to form the "New Party," which eventually merged with the British Union of Fascists in 1932. He generally opposed free trade and affiliated himself with Nazi Germany.

11. The *Western Evening Herald*, in an article dated 10 April 1931, and entitled "Royalty Kept Waiting," relates that "An unfortunate hitch occurred at the first night of 'City Lights' at Monte Carlo":

The Duke of Connaught had graciously accepted an invitation to be present and arrived at the appointed hour, but Mr. Charles Chaplin did not arrive until an hour later.

The Duke, however, took the incident in the best part, and his welcome of the film star when he did arrive lacked nothing in warmness.

12. Prince Louis Honoré Charles Antoine Grimaldi, (1870 -1949) was the ruler of Monaco from 1922 to 1949 and is largely remembered as nearly running the principality into the ground, despite the great success he achieved as a military man prior to his reign, where he even received the Légion d'Honneur medal in 1908. His reign included the establishment of Prince Louis II Stadium, the Monaco Football Club, and new management for the shadily run Monte Carlo Casino, but then World War II intervened. The Grimaldi family found itself divided between loyalties to France, the Vichy government, and even Italy and her Fascists, leading to near dissolution by the communist faction of the occupying Allies at the close of the war.

13. Emil Ludwig (1881-1948). An article in the *Boston Globe*, entitled "Tragic Comedians" and dated 6 September 1931, provides more information on this meeting:

Mr. Emil Ludwig, that inexhaustible writer of biography after the mode, was astonished recently when he paid visit to Charlie Chaplin on the Riviera. This emotion was due to discovery that the artist, whose portrayals of outcast poverty have won him fame and fortune, is quite as simple and unaffectedly natural in life as he is in his role; that he is alert to the things of the spirit and to the vital movements of world affairs, and that he is a man of profound sadness.

Capable of embittered ferocity towards institutions, Charlie views the men and women who live and move beneath them with serene pity of acceptance and with quick sympathy. It is possible for this singular humorist to remark, one minute: "Suffering is beautiful, don't you think?"; and the next: "Ideals are dangerous things, from which, too often, nothing comes. Ideals? They are usually false." And he means that, too.

One instant he may explain that his model is Anatole France, the genial French mocker, who saw in life neither right nor wrong, but only the illusions born of human frailties; another minute this king of pantomime can lose himself in contemplation of a danseuse, performing courageously before an array of tables almost entirely empty in an enormous restaurant, and he can exclaim: "Look! How gripping when she bowed to the empty tables. I must open a picture that way: There will be a street singer who will sing up to a house full of windows, and later one will see that it is only a dead wall with nothing—no faces, no nods, nothing—to hear and acknowledge the singing."

14. The *Lancashire Daily Post* reports on "Charlie Chaplin's Reading" on 27 February 21931:

The Mysterious Universe by Sir James Jeans (Cambridge)

The Messiah Jesus and John the Baptist by Dr. Robert Eisler (Methuen)

The Conquest of Happiness by Bertrand Russell (Allen and Unwin)

The Treasurer's Report and Other Aspects of Community Singing by Robert Benchley (Harpers)

Brother and Sister by Leonard Frank (Davies)

Other titles are revealed in Syd's letter to R. J. Minney, 9 March 1932:

I noticed a few of the books in Charlie's cabin,

Behind the Scenes of International Finance by Paul Einzig

The Bank of International Settlement by Paul Einzig

The Economic Consequences of the Peace by J. M. Keynes

Reminiscence of the Russian Revolution by Phillip Price

15. Sadakichi Hartmann, critic and poet (1864-1944), was half Japanese

and half German. His play *Last Thirty Days of Christ* "embodies a rare and, to the strictly orthodox, sacrilegious vein of satire. It portrays Jesus as the mystic, the lone philosopher in an age of materialism, eons ahead of his own disciples, an 'old soul' far above the understanding of his closest followers. But it shows him as a cynic, also, divining the sycophancy of his disciples" (Von Ulm 281-82).

16. Chaplin recounts in his autobiography that:

I now saw H. G. Wells frequently. He had an apartment in Baker Street. When I visited him there, he had four lady secretaries inundated in books of reference, checking and making notes from encyclopedias, technical books, documents and papers. "That's *The Anatomy of Money*, my new book," said he. "Quite an industry."

"It strikes me they're doing most of the work," I remarked jokingly. What appeared to be large biscuit tins were ranged on a high shelf around his library, each labeled "Biographical Material," "Personal Letters," "Philosophy," "Scientific Data," and so forth.

After dinner, friends arrived, among them Professor Laski, who was still very young-looking. Harold was a most brilliant orator. I heard him speak to the American Bar Association in California, and he talked unhesitantly and brilliantly for an hour without a note. At H. G.'s flat that night, Harold told me of the amazing innovations in the philosophy of socialism. He said that the slightest acceleration in speed translates into terrific social differences. The conversation was most interesting until H. G.'s bedtime, which, with little subtlety, he indicated by looking at the guests, then at his watch, until everybody left. (*My Autobiography* 348)

17. Paul Morand (1888-1976) is the son of a painter and a dramatic author. At twenty-four, he became an attaché of the French embassy in London. At twenty-nine, he published his first novel, *Mercure de France*. His novel *Milady* was his masterpiece. However, he made some unwise political choices and attached himself to the Vichy government, becoming an ambassador to Bucharest. After the war, he was decommissioned and retired to Montreux, Switzerland. However, with the passage of time, his collaborator status was forgotten and he was elected to l'Académie française in 1968.

18. A *Herald Dispatch* [Huntington, WV] article dated 30 April 1931, and titled "Aimee, Charlie Go Sightseeing," confirms that McPherson, the famous Glendale, California, evangelist (Angelus Temple), met up with Chaplin in Marseilles: "While attempting to evade the public eye here by changing her residence four times, she bumped into Charlie Chaplin, the film comedian,

and when they learned that their plans to visit the same resort coincided, they boarded the same train for Juan-les-Pins." Gerith Von Ulm, ostensibly through Chaplin's valet, Kono, reports that the two spent several days together. After an initial dinner at which Chaplin regaled McPherson with such lines as "Religion—orthodox religion—is based on fear, fear of doing something on earth which will keep them out of heaven. My God, they miss out on all the glorious freedom of life in order to reach a mythical heaven where they can walk on golden streets and play a harp—a bait of pure boredom, if you ask me," (330-31), he set out night after night thereafter until McPherson's departure, "to the colorful, picturesque waterfront of Marseilles" (331).

19. Frank Harris (1856-1931). Irish writer Harris ran away to America in 1871 and then returned to London in 1876 to become a journalist. He was known in this field for his sensational headlines. Although he is most remembered for his excellent biography of Oscar Wilde, he encountered the most controversy for his four-volume autobiography, *My Life and Loves*, which was banned for pornography. He accompanied Chaplin on his first tour of Sing Sing in 1921.

Part IV

1. Harry D'Abbadie D'Arrast was born in Argentina, educated in Paris and England, and highly decorated for service in World War I. He met George Fitzmaurice, the director, following the war and followed him back to Hollywood, circa 1922. D'Arrast was known for his boyish good looks, charm, and grace. Chaplin offered him a position as technical adviser on *A Woman of Paris* and D'Arrast continued in his employ on *The Gold Rush* before beginning his own directorial career. Although he made only eight films, *A Gentleman of Paris, Laughter*, and *Topaze* among them, they are remembered for their stylishness, their wit, and photographic beauty.

It is likely that Chaplin stayed overnight at D'Arrast's family estate, Château d'Echauz, in the tiny village of St. Etienne de Baigorry in the Basque country.

2. Elsa Maxwell relates in her autobiography:

The first time I saw Chaplin, he gave an unforgettable one-man show at Biarritz in 1928 [*sic*]. Jean Patou had hired a fleet of motorboats to take a party of guests to a bullfight at Bayonne, but the excursion was canceled by a violent hurricane that blew up suddenly. The storm knocked out the electric lights and several women showed signs of panic as the wind and the rain mounted in fury. Patou's house was on the water and everyone was wondering apprehensively whether it was safe to remain, until Chaplin took charge of the situation.

"It's nonsense to sit around like this," Chaplin said to me. "Let's amuse ourselves. Play something from *Carmen* and I'll take it from there."

With absolutely no preparation, Chaplin proceeded to give an enthralling pantomime of a bullfight in the flickering candlelight. He impersonated, in turn, a frenzied spectator, the bull, a picador, a gored horse, and the matador. Each characterization was so perfect and the continuity had such dramatic purity that there was a collective gasp when he made the matador's final thrust at the bull. With a subtle shrug, Chaplin abruptly changed the mood and improvised a tragic triangle in which a husband murdered his wife and her lover, then committed suicide. Chaplin's artistry held us spellbound for three hours, by the watch. It was not until he finished that we realized the hurricane had long since subsided. (233)

3. Two instances indicating Chaplin's altruistic nature were reported in the press at this time. The *Camberwell & Peckham Times*, reported on 5 September 1931, in "Charlie Chaplin's Gift," for instance, that:

Charlie Chaplin has a soft spot in his heart for the men who work in the Borough Market. He has written to Mr. W. Blackman, secretary of the Borough Market sports, enclosing a cheque for £20, to be spent on buying a suit of clothes, an overcoat, and a gold watch to go to the winners of the basket carrying competition at Herne Hill next week. The watch has to be inscribed with the winner's name and will be marked "From Charlie Chaplin. London Market Sports, 1931." Nearly 60 entries have been received from men, representing all the London markets, for the basket-carrying competition, and 672 baskets will be required to equip them all for the contest.

Yet again, in the *Sunday Dispatch* of 11 October 1931, reports in "Karno Comrades" that:

there is all the romantic irony of an O. Henry plot in the story of how Charlie Chaplin met a colleague after twenty years. With his cousin Aubrey, Chaplin spent a day revisiting old haunts at Lambeth. On returning they walked through the Strand and passed a pavement artist. Charlie grinned as he noticed a crayon drawing of himself. Suddenly he stopped and gripped Aubrey's arm. "Just go back and ask that artist fellow if his name is Dando." Aubrey did so. The man's name was Dando. Charlie strode over in a flash. Their hands met in a tight grip—these two who used to act together. They were both members of Fred Karno's Mumming Birds. Dando's name was Arthur Webb. A piece of crinkly paper passed to Dando "just to celebrate the reunion."

4. In an article entitled "Chaplin to Witness 'Fun' of Elections," by Ferdinand Kuhn Jr., dated 9 October 1932 (Charlie Chaplin Archive pressbook, no source listed), he reports that:

Charlie Chaplin and Ramsay MacDonald had an unexpected midnight meeting Monday just as the Prime Minister, pale and tired, was walking home from the House of Commons. Somehow Mr. MacDonald was gloomy. His cabinet had decided to plunge into a general election, and as an old campaigner he did not enjoy the prospect. He knew that the strain of past struggles would be nothing compared with the responsibility of leading the so-called National party, all of whose component elements were pulling in opposite directions.

But Chaplin was grinning happily. "I had thought of leaving England in a few days," he told the Prime Minister, "but now that there is going to be an election, I'm going to stay and see the fun."

Not being a candidate or party leader, Charlie was perfectly right in looking forward to "fun." From the sightseer's viewpoint—and from the newspaper correspondent's, too—this election is going to be more fun than any since the famous knock-down, drag-out fight which Dickens described so cruelly a century ago. It may be as Lord Derby said this week, "The most jealous election in British history," but it is going to have its lighter sides. [...]"

5. It was during this few weeks when Chaplin made his oft-quoted critique of the European situation, quoted here in the 5 September 1931, *Burlington Post* [Iowa], in an article entitled "Wisdom from the Mouth of a Jester": "When importuned on patriotic grounds to participate in some public function, contrary to his practice, he replied: 'Patriotism is the greatest form of insanity the world ever suffered. It is rampant everywhere and what is going to be the result?—another war. I hope they send the old men to the front next time, for they are the real criminals of Europe today.'"

6. Painter Augustus John writes that:

It was at the Morrells that I once met Charlie Chaplin. He found it difficult, I think, to preserve his natural cheerfulness amidst the habitual gloom of the Bloomsburyites who formed the rest of the party, but his spirit was more than equal to those adverse conditions: he was not one to be silenced and he had the hearty backing of his hostess to count on.

While he was speaking on social conditions in a strain which seemed to me familiar and sympathetic, I was impelled to slap him on the back, saying "Charlie, why, you're nothing but a dear old anarchist!" Recovering, he replied, "Yes, that's about it." Although he agreed that London was his proper habitat, he admitted to being enticed by the powerful lure of Hollywood. Recalling his early days and the vicissitudes of his family, all rolling stones of the music hall, he mentioned that his mother had been courted by a lord: "Oh," drawled Ottoline, much interested, "which lord?" "Ah, I'm not going to tell you," replied Charlie. (84-85)

7. Chaplin presents a different version of the story in *My Autobiography*: For company, I bought a rabbit, and wherever I stayed I would smuggle it into my room unknown to the landlady. It was an endearing little thing, though not housebroken. Its fur looked so white and clean that it belied its pungent odor. I kept it in a wooden cage hidden under the bed. The landlady would cheerfully enter the room with my breakfast, until she contacted the odor; then she would leave, looking worried and confused. The moment she was gone I would release the rabbit and it would lope around the room.

Before long I had it trained to run to its box every time there was a knock at the door. If the landlady discovered my secret I would have the rabbit perform this trick, which usually won her heart, and she would put up with us for the week.

But in Tonypandy, Wales, after I showed my trick, the landlady smiled cryptically and made no comment; but when I returned from the theatre that night my pet had gone. When I inquired about it, the landlady merely shook her head. "It must have run away or someone must have stolen it." She had in her own way handled the problem efficaciously. (83)

8. The Douglas Plan was based on the work of Clifford Hugh Douglas (1879-1952), an English engineer and social economist, educated at Cambridge University. Having devised the economic theory of Social Credit in 1924, in which he applied engineering methodology to economics, Douglas believed the economic system was organized to create unnecessary scarcity of products and services in order to maximize profits for the powerful, without any of that profit ending up in the hands and pocketbooks of the workers. To remedy the problem, he proposed a twofold plan. First he proposed the establishment of a National Dividend to distribute money equally to all citizens (over and above their wages) and second employ a price adjustment mechanism, the Just Price, which would prevent any threat of inflation. Individual

freedom as provided by economic freedom was Douglas's central goal. See also Martin-Nielsen.

9. The 4 November 1931, issue of *Performer* reports on Chaplin's initiation: Sunday was a red letter night in the records of the Grand Order of Water Rats, for Charlie Chaplin was initiated into the brotherhood of the Order, in the presence of one of the biggest attendances of officers and Rats ever experienced for such a ceremony.

Had space permitted the gathering would have been even greater, for though the time of the initiation had been kept secret many more than could be accommodated called up at the Water Rats' Club and had to be tactfully denied admission. Telegrams were also received from many Rats who were unable to be present.

The initiation ceremony was impressively carried through by King Rat Will Hay, Chief Precentor Fred Russell and the officers of the Lodge—after which formality was discarded, and there ensued one of those real jolly nights in the celebration of which the Rats stand pre-eminent among all organizations.

Into these proceedings of informal nature Charlie Chaplin entered with zest and spirit taking an active part in anything that happened; meantime exchanging confidences and reminiscences with those of the company of whom he remembered of yore. For, as he remarked, there were many there that night who were stars when he (Mr. Chaplin) had but just stepped onto the music hall stage—and many whose work he retained a lively recollection of from the time when he was one of the Eight Lancashire Lads. The time passed rapidly and pleasantly, and not least for the new member, who clearly welcomed the opportunity of being, not a famous film star, the center of adulation, but just Charlie Chaplin among associates in the great business of entertaining the public. So strongly did this effect him that towards the close of the evening, he assured the company that it had been the jolliest and happiest time he had spent since he had been back to England.

10. Walska, in her memoir *Always Room at the Top*, relates her Chaplin encounter in St. Moritz:

Ten days! With some friends, I went for the winter sports to—St. Moritz. [. . .] What a pity it got dark after four o'clock. But then the pastries were so good at Hanselmann's!

An after-dinner philosophical conversation with Charlie Chaplin easily compensated for the shortness of the day. And I had as a flirt the handsomest man Great Britain has produced! He was so very handsome! And his mentality did not overtire him at all! Wonderful—there was no possibility of getting into a discussion with him. We skated together. He skated badly but his skating suit was so becoming to him! (330)

11. A *Los Angeles Times* article, dated 27 May 1932, and entitled "Chaplin's Prank Sends Naples Policeman to Jail" details at least one of Chaplin's activities while in Naples:

Because Charlie Chaplin engaged in one of his characteristic pranks on his recent tour of Europe, a Naples policeman had to spend five days in his native "cooler" and now wants to come to Hollywood—if Charlie will give him a job.

Alf Reeves, business manager for Chaplin, learned about it yesterday in a letter from the poliziotto.

In a spirit of fun, it seems, Charlie posed between two policemen, mocking an expression of surprise at his "arrest." Photographs of the funny pose found their way to the press and were widely published. Then the superior of the two poliziottos was reprimanded and sentenced.

12. According to Syd Chaplin's notes for the Asian leg of the tour (Charlie Chaplin Archive), he and Charlie noticed "British methods of using the whip on natives. We noticed the same thing in Cairo."

13. According to Syd Chaplin's notes (Charlie Chaplin Archive), Chaplin was "very much impressed with the modern design and compliment the manager. [He] and the manager [stood] outside in the center of the road admiring the architecture in the pouring rain. [The manager was] trying to be polite and getting soak[ed] to the skin. [Chaplin was] wearing a MacIntosh and entirely unconscious of predicament."

14. According to Syd Chaplin's notes (Charlie Chaplin Archive), Chaplin "made a speech over the radio in the hotel [Orange Hotel] lobby" here.

Part V

1. His work still revered and collected today, Peter Helck (1893-1988) was the illustrator for this installment. Like the other illustrators for the series, Helck was also a student at the Art Students League in New York City. Known especially for his studies of automobiles, Helck acquired this passion and expertise during four years abroad in which he did some British motor advertising. He was author-illustrator of two books, *The Checkered Flag* and *Great Auto Races*.

2. According to Syd Chaplin's notes (Charlie Chaplin Archive), the young men were Sitton and Johnson.

3. Al Hirschfeld (1903-2003) and his wife Florence lived in Bali during this period because it was a cheap place to be an artist. Florence wrote an extensive article on Chaplin's visit, entitled "Charlie Chaplin, Balinese." In one passage, she relates that:

> Chaplin entered into the spirit of the place and ate rice with his fingers from dishes made of banana leaves, squatted on the ground to watch cockfights, and would go any distance to see a native dance or hear an orchestra. His understanding of the dancing and music was amazing. The music is entirely different from the white man's, and persons who have long been in Bali find it difficult to interpret, yet Chaplin went away from the performances humming entire passages with unerring instinct. And his imitations of the dancers would pack a Broadway house. (n.p.)

4. Walter Spies was born in Russia on 14 September 1898, so he was about twenty-five years old when he came to Indonesia in 1923, and about twenty-nine years old when he moved to Bali in 1927. In almost everybody's opinion, Walter Spies was the greatest and certainly the most flamboyant painter to live in Bali, where his name has become a legend. After World War I, he was thrown into the creative maelstrom of the Weimar Republic, embracing the German artistic avant-garde. Lover of the great German film director, Frederich Murnau, Spies was in close contact with Otto Dix and Oskar Kokoschka, who both influenced his painting. In a letter to his father in 1919, Walter writes that he wishes to free himself of indoctrination and prejudices about taste and beauty and paint freely like a child, with the skill of Chagall and Klee. Bali was to give him the freedom to realize his wish.

5. According to Syd Chaplin's notes (Charlie Chaplin Archive), in the kris dance, "the dancers are supposed to be in a trance and are brought out of same by holy water thrown upon them by the priest. [. . .] Just before this dance commenced, we noticed all the younger people vacating the front seats while full-grown men took the pleasure. We were informed that they were placed there to protect us in case the dancers should attack us with their knives which they were apt to do under the [influence] of their trance."

6. Donald Richie writes that:

> Prime Minister Inukai was one of Japan's foremost liberals. He had long fought for parliamentary democracy and had initiated a policy of friendly relations with China that would, it was hoped, somewhat counter Japan's military adventures in that country.

> It was only many years later that Chaplin learned of the connection between his own experiences and the assassination. At the trial of those

who had killed the prime minister, Lieutenant Seishi Koga, the leader, testified that there had been plans for another assassination—that of Charlie Chaplin.

The famous comedian was to have met Inukai on May 15 and both he and the prime minister were to have been killed. During the proceedings, the judge asked Koga what the significance of killing Chaplin was to have been. The young man answered (in the words of Hugh Byas, from whom this account is taken) that "Chaplin is a popular figure in the United States and the darling of the capitalist class. We believed that killing him would cause a war with America." Japanese sources, however, say the assassination of the comedian was merely to cause such confusion that the coup d'état could be more easily consolidated. (110-11)

7. Takejirô Ôtani (1877-1969). With his twin brother Matsujirô Shirai, he founded Shôchiku, a kabuki production company in 1895 (named as such in 1902). Samuel Leiter, personal communication, 24 November 2013.

Appendix B

1. "The Legion was founded as a military institution, as the names of its ranks indicate, and the members were distributed around the country in different regional groups. It was intended as a framework for civilian society.

This new order, established on the initiative of the First Consul Bonaparte, was to consist of a corps d'élite that would combine the courage of servicemen and the talents of civilians, and would form the basis of a new society to serve the nation.

On 14 floréal year X (4 May 1802), Bonaparte declared to the Council of States 'If we award honors to civilians or military men, then we would need to set up two separate orders—but there is only one Nation. However, if we only gave honors for military exploits, that would be even worse, because it would make the Nation appear worthless.'"

Works Cited

Adlon, Hedda. *Hotel Adlon: The Life and Death of a Great Hotel.* Trans. and ed. Norman Denny. New York: Horizon Press, 1960. Print.

"Aimee, Charlie Go Sightseeing." *Herald Dispatch* (30 April 1931): n. p. Charlie Chaplin Archive pressbooks. Print.

Alexandre, Maxime, et al. "Hands Off Love." *Transition* Sept. 1927: 1–11. Print.

"April 1 Joke on Chaplin." *Scotsman* (3 April 1931): n. p. Charlie Chaplin Archive pressbooks. Print.

Bartlett, Charles. "Charlie Chaplin's No-Man." *American Magazine* October 1931. Charlie Chaplin Archive pressbooks. Print.

Bell, Monta. Letter to Charles Chaplin. MS. November. Charlie Chaplin Archive.

Bercovici, Konrad. "A Day with Charlie Chaplin." *Harper's Monthly Magazine* Dec. 1928: 42–49. Print.

Bewsher, Paul. "Mr. Chaplin Spends the Whole Night Talking." *Daily Mail* 23 February 1931. Charlie Chaplin Archive pressbooks. Print.

Browne, Maurice. *Too Late to Lament: An Autobiography.* Bloomington, IN: Indiana UP, 1956. Print.

Burke, Thomas. *City of Encounters: A London Divertissement.* Boston: Little, Brown & Co., 1932. Print.

Chaplin, Charlie, dir. *City Lights.* Perf. Charlie Chaplin and Virginia Cherrill. United Artists, 1931. Film.

——. "A Comedian Sees the World." *Women's Home Companion* Sept 1933: 7-10, 80, 86-89; Oct. 1933: 15-17, 102, 104, 106, 108; Nov. 1933: 15-17, 100, 102, 104, 113, 115, 116, 119; Dec. 1933: 21-23, 36, 38, 42, 44; Jan. 1934: 21-23, 86. Print.

——. "A Comedian Sees the World" MS. Charlie Chaplin Archive.

——. "A Comedian Sees the World" TS. Charlie Chaplin Archive.

——, dir. *The Countess from Hong Kong.* Perf. Marlon Brando and Sophia Loren. Universal, 1967. Film.

——. "Depression #1" TS. Charlie Chaplin Archive.

——, dir. *The Great Dictator.* Perf. Charlie Chaplin, Paulette Goddard, and Jack Oakie. United Artists, 1940. Film.

——. *Hallo Europa!* Leipzig: Paul List Verlag, 1928. Print.

——. "The Immortal Memory of Charles Dickens." *Dickensian* 51.315 (1955): 112–14. Print.

——, dir. *The Kid.* Perf. Charlie Chaplin and Jackie Coogan. First National, 1921. Film.

——. *A King in New York.* Perf. Charlie Chaplin and Dawn Addams. Attica-Archway, 1957. Film.

——. *Limelight.* Perf. Charlie Chaplin and Claire Bloom. United Artists, 1952. Film.

——. *Mes Voyages.* Trans. P. A. Hourey. Paris: Kra, Editeur, 1928. Print.

——, dir. *Modern Times.* Perf. Charlie Chaplin and Paulette Goddard. United Artists, 1936. Film.

——, dir. *Monsieur Verdoux.* Perf. Charlie Chaplin and Martha Raye. United Artists, 1947. Film.

——. "Monta Bell" TS. May 24, 1960. Charlie Chaplin Archive.

——. *My Autobiography.* New York: Simon and Schuster, 1964. Print.

——. *My Trip Abroad.* New York: Harper and Brothers, 1922. Print.

——. *My Wonderful Visit.* London: Hurst & Blackett, Ltd., 1922. Print.

——, dir. *Woman of Paris.* Perf. Edna Purviance and Adolph Menjou. United Artists, 1923. Film.

Chaplin, Charles, Jr. *My Father, Charlie Chaplin.* New York: Random House, 1960. Print.

Chaplin, Sydney J. Untitled TS (1932 Southeast Asian Travel Notes). Charlie Chaplin Archive.

——. Letter to R. J. Minney. MS. 9 March 1932. Charlie Chaplin Archive.

"Chaplin Finds Writing Art Is Long." *Union Star* (23 July 1932): n.p. Charlie Chaplin Archive pressbook. Print.

"Chaplin Fled from Shaw." *New York Times* (27 Feb. 1931): 23. Print.

"Chaplin Made Social Lion." *New York Herald Paris Edition* (20 March 1931): n.p. Charlie Chaplin Archive pressbook. Print.

"Chaplin off to Find His Boyhood London." *New York Times* (14 Feb. 1931): 20. Print.

"Chaplin Visits Sing-Sing: Exhibits New Films for Prisoners and Gives a Brief Talk." *New York Times* (13 Feb. 1931): 20. Print.

"Chaplin's 'Armada' Blocks All Traffic on Venice Canal." *The Record* (19 March 1931): n.p. Charlie Chaplin Archive pressbook. Print.

"Chaplin's Prank Sends Naples Policeman to Jail." *Los Angeles Times* (27 May 1932): n. p. Charlie Chaplin Archive pressbooks. Print.

"Charlie Chaplin as Author." *Indianapolis News* (17 May 1922): n.p. Charlie Chaplin Archive pressbooks. Print.

Charlie Chaplin Film Corporation Minutes. (14 Oct. 1930; 1 Jan. 1931; 11 Jan. 1932; 20 May 1932; 21 Mar. 1933): n. p. Charlie Chaplin Archive, Bologna, Italy. Print.

Charlie Chaplin's Divorce Case (Uncensored). The Superior Court of the State of California, Los Angeles, CA, n.d. Print.

"Charlie Chaplin's Favourite Dance Tune!" *Home Chat* (31 May 1931): n.p. Charlie Chaplin Archive pressbook. Print.

"Charlie Chaplin's First Book, *My Trip Abroad*, Will Be Published in February." *Allentown Record* (17 Feb. 1922): n.p. Charlie Chaplin Archive pressbooks. Print.

"Charlie Chaplin's Gift." *Camberwell & Peckham Times* (5 Sept. 1931): n. p. Charlie Chaplin Archive pressbook. Print.

"Charlie Chaplin's *My Trip Abroad*." *Cleveland Press* (10 March 1922): n.p. Charlie Chaplin Archive pressbooks. Print.

"Charlie Chaplin's *My Trip Abroad*." *Cleveland Press* 10 March 1922, n.p. Print.

"Charlie Hunts the Boar in France—in a Duke's Pink Coat." *The Illustrated Sporting and Dramatic News* (4 April 1931): n. p. Charlie Chaplin Archive pressbooks. Print.

"A Comedian Sees the World" contract TS. *Woman's Home Companion* to Charles Chaplin. 25 March 1931. Charlie Chaplin Archive.

Eastment, P. C. Letter to Charles Chaplin. MS. 19 October 1921. Charlie Chaplin Archive.

——. Letter to Charles Chaplin. MS. 16 February 1922. Charlie Chaplin Archive.

Evelinoff, Boris. Letter to Arthur Kelly. MS. 12 December 1935. Charlie Chaplin Archive.

——. Letter to Charles Chaplin. MS. 12 December 1935. Charlie Chaplin Archive.

Farmer, Harcourt. "Is the Charlie Chaplin Vogue Passing?" *Theatre* 30 (Oct. 1919): 249. Print.

Fiaccarini, Anna, and Cecilia Cenciarelli. "Charlie Chaplin as Author." *Limelight: Documents and Essays from Chaplin Archives.* Ed. Anna Fiaccarini, Peter von Bagh, and Cecilia Cenciarelli. Bologna: Cineteca di Bologna, 2002. 22-25. Print.

Foster, Harry L. *A Beachcomber in the Orient.* New York: Dodd, Mead and Company, 1923. Print.

Gehring, Wes D. *Charlie Chaplin: A Bio-Bibliography*. Westport, CT: Greenwood, 1983. Print.

Gersch, Wolfgang. *Chaplin in Berlin: Illustrierte Miniatur nach Berliner Zeitungen von 1931*. Berlin: Parthas Verlag, 1999. Print.

"Gertrude Battles Lane, Noted Editor, Dies." *New York Times* 26 Sept. 1941: 23.

Gilbert, Martin. *A History of the Twentieth Century*. Vol. One, *1900–1933*. New York: William Morrow and Co., Inc., 1997. Print.

Hamlin, William. "The Funniest Thing That Charlie Chaplin Ever Did." *San Francisco Sunday Chronicle* (n.d.); 3. Print.

Hirschfeld, Florence. "Charlie Chaplin, Balinese." *New York Herald* 12 June 1932. Charlie Chaplin Archive pressbooks. Print.

"Historique: La Légion d'honneur." *La Grande Chancellerie de la Légion d'honneur*. 20 April 2006. <http://www.legiondhonneur.fr/shared/fr/histoire/fhisto.html>.

Horsley, David. Letter to Charlie Chaplin. 27 June 1932. Charlie Chaplin Archive, Bologna, Italy.

John, Augustus. *Chiaroscuro: Fragments of Autobiography*. New York: Pellegrini & Cudahy, 1952. Print.

"Karno Comrades." *Sunday Dispatch* (11 Oct. 1931): n. p. Charlie Chaplin Archive pressbooks. Print.

Kellner, Bruce. *The Last Dandy: Ralph Barton, American Artist, 1891-1931*. Columbia, MO: U of Missouri P, 1991. Print.

Kirtland, Lucian Swift. *Finding the Worth While in the Orient*. London: George G. Harrap & Co., Ltd., 1928. Print.

Kuhn, Ferdinand, Jr. "Chaplin to Witness 'Fun' of Elections." 9 October 1932. Charlie Chaplin Archive pressbook, no source listed. Print.

Lane, Gertrude Battles. "Going Like Sixty." *Woman's Home Companion* (Nov. 1933): 4.

Lewis, Tracy Hammond. "Charlie Chaplin Introspects." *New York Telegraph* 24 Feb. 1922: n.p. Charlie Chaplin Archive pressbook. Print.

Lyons, Timothy J. *Charles Chaplin: A Guide to References and Resources*. Boston: G. K. Hall, 1979.

Maland, Charles. *Chaplin and American Culture: The Evolution of a Star Image*. Princeton, NJ: Princeton UP, 1989. Print.

Martin-Nielsen, Janet. "An Engineer's View of an Ideal Society." *Spontaneous Generations* 1.1 (2007): 95–100. Print.

Maxwell, Elsa. *R.S.V.P.: Elsa Maxwell's Own Story*. Boston: Little, Brown and Co., 1954. Print.

"Millionaire's Wife as Film Star." *Continental Daily Telegraph* (19 August 1931): n. p. Charlie Chaplin Archive pressbooks. Print.

Nevins, Allan. "60 Years after." *Woman's Home Companion* Nov. 1933: 24-25, 135-36. Print.

Parsons, Louella. "A Romance as Hot as the Rays of the July Sun.." *Milwaukee Sentinel* (28 July 1931): n. p. Charlie Chaplin Archive pressbooks. Print.

Powell, Hickman. *Bali: The Last Paradise.* New York: Dodd, Mead & Co., 1930. Print.

Quigley, Carroll. *Tragedy and Hope: A History of the World in Our Time.* New York: The Macmillan Company, 1966. Print.

Reeves, Alf. Letter to Charles Chaplin. MS. 6 Dec. 1921. Charlie Chaplin Archive, Bologna, Italy.

———. Letter to Monta Bell. MS. 3 Dec. 1921. Charlie Chaplin Archive.

————. Letter to Sydney Chaplin. MS. 30 March 1933. Charlie Chaplin Archive.

Reeves, May, and Claire Goll. *The Intimate Charlie Chaplin.* Ed. and trans. Constance Brown Kuriyama. Jefferson, NC: McFarland & Co., Inc., 2001. Print.

Richie, Donald. *The Honorable Visitors.* Rutland, VT: Charles E. Tuttle Co., 1994. Print.

Robinson, David. *Chaplin: His Life and Art.* New York: McGraw-Hill, 1985. Print.

———. *Chaplin: The Mirror of Opinion.* London: Secker & Warburg, 1983. Print.

"Royalty Kept Waiting." *Western Evening Herald* (10 April 1931): n. p. Charlie Chaplin Archive pressbooks. Print.

Sadoul, Georges. *Vie de Charlot: Charles Chaplin ses Films et son Temps.* Paris: Éditeurs François Réunis, 1952. Print.

Snowden, R. R. Letter to Charlie Chaplin. 14 Dec. 1932. MS. Charlie Chaplin Archive, Bologna, Italy.

"Sunday Was a Red Letter Night in the Records of the Grand Order of Water Rats." *Performer* (4 Nov. 1931): n. p. Charlie Chaplin Archive pressbooks. Print.

Tidden, Fritz. "A Personally Conducted Tour." *Moving Picture World* 25 Mar. 1922: n.p. Charlie Chaplin Archive pressbooks. Print.

"Tragic Comedians." *Boston Globe* (6 Sept. 1931): n. p. Charlie Chaplin Archive pressbooks. Print.

Villa, Leo, and Tony Gray. *The Record Breakers: Sir Malcolm and Donald Campbell, Land and Water Speed Kings of the 20th Century.* London: Paul Hamlyn, 1969. Print.

228 · Works Cited

Von Ulm, Gerith. *Charlie Chaplin: King of Tragedy.* Caldwell, ID: The Caxton Printers, Ltd., 1940. Print.

Walska, Ganna. *Always Room at the Top.* New York: Richard R. Smith, 1943. Print.

"Wisdom from the Mouth of a Jester." *Burlington Post* (5 Sept. 1931): n. p. Charlie Chaplin Archive pressbooks. Print.

"Woman Defeats Men Editors in Race for Chaplin Book." *Little River News* (24 June 1931): n. p. Charlie Chaplin archive pressbook. Print.

"The World Crisis in Dumb Show." *New York Times* 15 April 1932: n.p. Charlie Chaplin archive pressbook. Print.

Index

Abbe, James (1883–1975), 160–65
Albers, Hans (1891–1960), 146
Albert I, King of the Belgians (1875–1934), 18, 71–73, 146, 163, 208*n22*
Alsem, Hank (Alsen), 184
Andrieu, Pierre (1849–1935), 208–9*n2*
Astor, Nancy Langhorne (1879–1964), 34–37, 44, 145, 148, 188*n11*, 196*n13*
Austin, Charlie (1878–1944), 118–20, 148

Baker, Josephine (1906–1975), 156, 158
Balinese dances: kris dance, 137, 185, 221*n5*; topeng dance, 185; wayang kulit (shadow-play), 186; witch dance, 186; legong dance, 186; baris dance, 186; sang byang dance, 186
Ballard Institute, London, UK, 148
Bank, The (1915), 187*n2*
Barton, Ralph (1891–1931), 30, 31, 34, 36–37, 43, 45, 47, 49–51, 145*n8*, 193*n8*, 201–2*n4*; Chaplin's invitation to Europe, 29; depression of, 30; departure for America, 54; suicide, 54, 194*n8*

Beaverbrook, Lord (William Maxwell Aitken) (1879–1964), 200*n1*
Bell, Monta (1891–1958), 8, 9–11, 189*n14*, 189*n17*, 189*n18*, 192*n5*
Berthelot, Pierre, 68, 155, 158
Bessodes, Victorine, 157
Bibesco, Princess Elizabeth Asquith (1897–1945), 42, 198*n19*
Birkenhead, Second Earl of (Frederick Smith) (1907–1975), 43, 145, 199*n22*
Borobudur Temple, Magelang Regency, Indonesia, 129, 149, 184
Brancoven, Comtesse Anna Elizabeth de (1876–1933), 207*n20*
Briand, Aristide (1862–1932), 64, 67, 68, 70, 146, 163
Brissac, Duke de (Twelfth), 105
Brüning, Heinrich (1885–1970), 6
Burke, Thomas (1886–1945), 145, 191*n4*, 200*n25*

Cami, Pierre Henri (1884–1958), 67, 154
Campbell, Sir Malcolm (1885–1948), 30–31, 194*n10*, 195–96*n11*
Carlton Hotel, London, UK, 31, 33, 145; *City Lights* afterparty, 53–54
Carow, Erich (Garro) (1893–1956), 56–57, 146, 204*n9*

Carpentier, Georges (1894–1975), 158

Catial, Dr. C. L., 109–10, 148

Chaplin, Aubrey, 180, 216*n3*

Chaplin, Charlie (1889–1977): London/Paris/Berlin trip (1921), 1, 24, 153, 192*n5*, 202–3*n5*; fame/popularity, 2, 65–66, 114–115; Chaplin/Harris divorce, 2, 187*n3*; U.S. tax debt, 3; *My Trip Abroad* (1922), 3, 7, 8–9, 11, 189*n14*, 189*n15*, 189*n16*, 189*n17*, 192*n5*; "A Comedian Sees the World" (1933–1934), 3, 4, 7, 11, 13–16, 150–51, 154, 175, 190*n21*; *My Autobiography* (1964), 8, 16–17; "economic policy" (27 June 1933), 11, 16, 150, 188*n10*; writing process, 13–16, 19, 191*n3*; signing *Woman's Home Companion* contract, 14, 190*n20*; tea ceremony (Japan), 16, 142–43; development of social consciousness, 17; London childhood, 23–24, 34, 38–39; English music hall, 24; meeting Hetty Kelly, 24–26; signing Mutual contract, New York, NY (1916), 26–27; visit to Kennington, 34; art as propaganda, 36; "soul of a tourist," 37; political speech at Lady Astor's, 44–45; visit to Hanwell school, London, UK, 46–48; unfinished Napoleon project, 49; visit to Chartwell, 49–51; *City Lights* premiere, London, UK, 51–53; visit to Netherlands, 55; Rotterdam bridge with Chaplin figure, 55; visit to Berlin, Germany, 55; Hotel Adlon, 55; tea with members of the Reichstag, Berlin, Germany, 57; visit to Sans Souci Palace, Potsdam, Germany, 58; discussion with Einstein on financial crisis and gold standard, 61–62; tripartite economic solution, 62; visit to Vienna, Austria, 62–63; trip to Venice, Italy, 64–67; visit to Paris, France, 67–73; performer in Eight Lancashire Lads, London Hippodrome, 70–71; participation in boar hunt, Normandy, France, 79–83; visit to French Riviera, 83–96; *City Lights* premiere in Monaco controversy, 86; royal command performance debacle, 86–87, 147, 167–73; thoughts on his literary education, 88; discovery by Mack Sennett, 89–92; first job as director, 92; visit to Algeria, 96–97; Los Angeles slumming adventure (as Mr. Gale), 98–102; discussion of writing with Frank Harris, 102–3; visit to Biarritz, Spain, 105–6; visit to San Sebastian, Spain, 106; at bullfight, 106–8, 147; discussion with Gandhi on politics, 111–12; in Amarillo, TX (1916), 114–15; with *Sherlock Holmes* touring company, 115–16; visit to Lancashire, UK, 116; discussion of politics in Lancashire, 117; visit to St. Moritz, Switzerland, 120–23; learning to ski, 120, 122–23, 177; visit to Rome, Italy, 124–26; volunteering for the Third Liberty Loan campaign (1918), 124; visit to Ceylon

(Sri Lanka), 126–27; visit to Singapore, 127, 139; visit to Java, 128; visit to Bali, 131–39; discussion of American versus Balinese morality, 134–35; visit to Tokyo, Japan, 139; return to America, 143–44; succumbs to dengue fever, 149; receives Officier de l'Instruction Publique, Paris, France (1921), 153–54; "patriotism," 170, 217n5; English or American, 170, 171; stock purchases, 188n8; thoughts on gold standard, 188n11; *Woman's Home Companion* contract, 190n1; Karno performer, 191–92n4; knighthood, 196n11; Beaverbrook situation, 200n1; London exhibitors' problem, 200n1; visit to police gaol and museum, Berlin, Germany, 204–5n10; cancellation of Budapest visit, 206–7n17; thoughts on Riviera casino life, 211n8; visit with Aimee Semple McPherson, 214–15n18; altruism, 216n3; on Balinese music, 221n3

Chaplin, Hannah Harriet Pedlingham Hill (1865–1928), 34

Chaplin, Lita Grey (1908–1995): Chaplin/Grey divorce, 2–3

Chaplin, Sydney J. (1885–1965), 14, 83–84, 124, 126, 131, 139, 140, 146, 149, 175–86, 190n21, 210n7, 220n12, 220n13, 220n14, 220n2, 221n5

Chartwell, Westerham, UK, 4, 49–51, 145, 148

Chequers, Wycombe, Buckinghamshire, UK, 4, 41, 145, 198n18

Chevalier, Maurice (1888–1972), 147

Churchill, Randolph (1911–1968), 42–43, 145, 199n21

Churchill, Sir Winston Leonard Spencer (1874–1965), 4, 49–51, 53–54, 145, 147, 148; visit with Chaplin in Los Angeles, CA, 49

City Lights (1931), 2, 3, 7, 163, 170, 188n12, 193n7, 201n3; Los Angeles premiere, 28–29; London, UK, premiere, 51–53, 145; London premiere afterparty, 53–54; musical soundtrack, premiere in Monaco controversy, 86, 147, 212n11; musical soundtrack, 192–93n6

Cochet, Henri (1901–1987), 147

Conference on war reparations, Geneva, Switzerland (16 June–9 July 1932), 7

Connaught and Strathearn, Duke of (Prince Arthur William Patrick Albert) (1850–1942), 85–86, 146, 170, 212n11

Countess from Hong Kong, A (1967), 18

Court of Arbitration, The Hague, 6

Dando, Arthur, 19, 216–17n3

D'Arrast, Harry D'Abbadie (1897–1968), 105, 147, 215n1

Day's Pleasure, A (1919), 1–2

Deterding, Lady, 75, 162

Deterding, Sir Henri Wilhelm August (1866–1939), 208n2

Devil dancers, Kandy, Sri Lanka, 126

Dietrich, Marlene (1901–1992), 58, 146

Donaghue, Steve (1884–1945), 194–95n10

Douglas, Clifford Hugh (1879–1952), 218n8

Douglas Plan, 116, 218–19*n8*
Dressler, Marie (1868–1934), 124
Dryden, Wheeler (1892–1957), 179
Duncan, Walter Jack (1881–1941), 191*n2*
"Dutch wife," 128–29

Eight Lancashire Lads, 70–71
Einstein, Albert (1879–1955): meeting with Chaplin, Berlin, Germany, 16, 59–62, 146; *City Lights* premiere, Los Angeles, CA, 29; visit to Chaplin's residence, Beverly Hills, CA, 59–60
Elvin, Joe (1862–1935), 119, 120
Espiau, Marcel (1899–1971), 164
Evelinoff, Boris, 8, 183

Fairbanks, Douglas, Sr. (1883–1939), 11, 120, 124, 149
Film industry: sound technology, 2
Financial crisis: Europe (1931), 4, 5; Germany, 6, 61–62; Hungary, 6
Flower, Sir Archibald Dennis (1865–1950), 116
Folies Bérgeres, Paris, France, 70, 146
Freud, Sigmund (1856–1939), 206*n15*

Gandhi, Mahatma (Mohandas Karamchand) (1869–1948), 5, 51, 109–12, 148, 188*n9*; arrest, 6
George M. Cohan Theatre, New York, NY, 2
George V, King (1865–1936), 169
Gold standard, 4, 61, 188*n11*; Britain goes off, 5
Gould, Edith, 210*n6*
Gould, Frank J. (1877–1956), 83–85, 146, 210*n6*

Grand Order of Water Rats: Chaplin initiation (November 1931), 19, 119–20, 148, 219*n9*
Great Dictator, The (1940), 17, 18
Grimaldi, Prince Louis Honoré Charles Antoine (1870–1949), 86, 147, 170, 212*n12*

Hanwell school, London, UK, 46–48, 145, 200*n25*
Harris, Frank (1856–1931), 94–103, 147, 215*n19*
Harris, Mildred (1901–1944): Chaplin/Harris divorce, 2, 187*n3*
Hartmann, Sadakichi (1864–1944), 89, 213–14*n15*
Hay, Will (1888–1949), 120, 219*n9*
Helck, Peter (1893–1988), 220*n1*
Henry, Prince of Prussia (Prinz Albert Wilhelm Heinrich von Preußen) (1862–1929), 58, 146, 205–6*n13*
Hirschfeld, Al (1903–2003), 14, 133, 134, 221*n3*
Hirschfeld, Florence, 133, 134, 221*n3*
Hitler, Adolf (1889–1945), 7; rejection of war reparations, 3–4; directive against Jews (9–16 March 1931), 5–6
Holländer, Friedrich (1896–1976), 58, 205*n11*
Hotel Adlon, Berlin, Germany, 55, 202*n5*, 203*n6*
Hotel Crillon, Paris, France, 75
House of Commons, London, UK, 108–9, 145, 188*n11*
Hunter, Catherine, 13–14

Inukai, Ken (Takeru) (1896–1960), 140–41, 150
Inukai, Tsuyoshi (1855–1932):

assassination, 7, 141, 150,
221–22*n6*

Jackson, Alfred Edwin, 70
Jazz Singer, The (1927), 187*n4*
John, Augustus (1878–1961), 112,
113, 217–18*n6*
Johnson, Amy (1903–1941), 36,
197*n15*

Kabuki-za Theatre, Tokyo, Japan,
142, 150
Karno, Fred (1866–1941), 192*n4*;
Karno's London Comedians,
191*n4*
Kasuaga prison, Tokyo, Japan, 150
Kelly, Arthur, 8, 27–28
Kelly, Hetty, 18, 24–26; death of,
27–28
Kessel, Adam (1866–1946) (wrongly
named Charles), 89
Kid, The (1921), 1, 7, 153
King in New York, A (1957), 18
Kirkwood, David (1891–1955), 44,
145, 199*n24*
Kono, Toraichi (1888–1971), 30,
(Togo) 160, 163, 164, 178,
205*n13*

La Jana ("G") (Henriette Margarethe
"Henny" Hiebel) (1905–1940),
58, 62, 205*n12*
Landru, Henri (1869–1922), 207*n19*
Lane, Gertrude Battles (1874–1941),
189–90*n19*
Lanvin, Jeanne (1867–1946), 157
League of Nations, 4, 6
Légion d'Honneur medal, 146, 153,
163, 208*n2*, 222*n1*
Le Guilloux, Mathurin, 158
Lillie, Beatrice (1894–1989), 172–73
Limelight (1952), 18–19

Little Tramp persona, 1, 11; differs
from *My Autobiography* persona,
17; creation of, 91
Lloyd George, David (1863–1945),
43–44, 45, 145, 199*n23*
Los Angeles Theatre, Los Angeles,
CA, 2
Ludwig, Emil (1881–1948), 87–92,
147, 212–13*n13*

MacDonald, Alister (1898–1993),
41, 42
MacDonald, Ramsay (1866–1937), 4,
41–42, 148, 197–98*n17*, 198*n18*,
217*n4*
Madame Tussaud's, Paris, France, 148
Maeterlinck, Maurice (1862–1949),
87, 147
Making a Living (1914), 90
Maritza, Sari (1910–1987), 54,
201*n3*
Maxwell, Elsa (1883–1963), 85, 146,
211–12*n9*, 215–16*n2*
McPherson, Aimee Semple (1890–
1944), 147, 214–15*n18*
Minney, R. J. (1895–1979), 175, 176–80
Modern Times (1936), 17, 18
Monsieur Verdoux (1947), 17, 207*n19*
Moore, Grace (1898–1947), 147
Morand, Paul (1888–1976), 96,
214*n17*
Morgan, Wallace (1873–1948), 208*n1*
Morrell, Lady Ottoline Violet Anne
(1873–1938), 112, 148, 217–18*n6*
Mosely, Sir Oswald Ernald, Baronet
(1896–1980), 85, 212*n13*
Mundin, Herbert (1898–1939), 172
Mussolini, Benito (1883–1945), 124

Napoleon's tomb, Paris, France, 67
Nazi party, 4, 6; economic
philosophy, 203–4*n7*

Noailles, Countess Anna Mathieu de (1876–1933), 68, 70, 146, 157
Normand, Mabel (1892–1930), 90, 91

O'Gorman, Joe, 119, 120
Old Bailey prison, London, UK, 40, 145, 197n16
Ôtani, Takejirö (1877–1969), 142, 222n7

Patou, Jean (1887–1936), 105, 215n2
Pay Day (1922), 189n17
Pickford, Mary (1892–1979), 11, 124
Pilgrim, The (1923), 189n17
Praenger Hotel, Java, 184

Quaglino's, London, UK, 42, 199n20

Reeves, Alfred (1876–1946), 14, 189n14, 189n18, 190n21
Reeves, May, 18, 183, 209–10n5
Reichstag, Berlin, Germany, 57, 146
Roberts, Willa, 11, 146, 150–51, 190n20, 190n21, 191n3; signing Chaplin contract, 14
Robey, George (1869–1954), 118, 145
Robinson, Carlyle (1887–1966), 9, 13, 30, 149, 160, 161, 194n9, 208n2
Roosevelt, André (1879–1962), 179
Round Table conference, St. James Palace, London, UK (8 September–1 December, 1931), 6
Rumbold, Sir Horace George Montagu, Ninth Baronet (1869–1941), 4, 56, 146, 203n7
Ruotte, Marcel, 159
Russell, Fred (1862–1957), 120, 219n9

Saitō, Makoto (Satai) (1858–1936), 7
Sem (Georges Goursat, 1863–1934), 75–76, 79, 209n3
Sassoon, Sir Philip Albert Gustave David, Third Baronet (1888–1939), 17, 34, 43–44, 58, 62, 85, 145, 196n12, 205n13
Sennett, Mack (1880–1960), 89–92
Shakespeare, William: monuments in Stratford-upon-Avon, UK, 116
Shaw, George Bernard (1856–1950), 35–36, 52, 145, 196–97n14
Shirai, Matsujirö, 222n7
Shôchiki Cinema, Tokyo, Japan, 142, 222n7
Sing-sing prison, Ossining, NY. 193n
Sorel, Cecile (1873–1966), 156
Spies, Walter (1895–1942), 135–38, 221n4
Sterling, Ford (1882–1939), 90
Stock market crash (October 24, 1929), 4
Strachey, Lytton (1880–1932), 112–13
Straus, Oscar (1870–1954), 64, 146, 206n16
Sumo wrestling, Tokyo, Japan, 140–41, 150
Sunnyside (1919), 1,

Tjipanas Hot Springs, Garoet, Java, 129, 149, 184
Trovat, Michael de, 147

U.S. Federal Reserve, 4,

Vagabond, The (1916), 187n2
Villedieu-Benoit, Raoul, 208–9n2
Von Vollmueller, Karl (1878–1948), 56, 57, 146, 204n8

Wales, Prince of (Edward VIII)
(1894–1972), 147, 148

Wandsworth gaol, London, UK,
40–41, 145

War reparations: Germany rescinded,
7

Wells, H. G. (1866–1946), 92–94,
147, 214*n16*

Westminster, Second Duke of (Hugh
Richard Arthur Grosvenor)
(1879–1953), 67, 75–83, 146

Wilson, Woodrow (1856–1924), 124

Wirth, Dr. Karl Joseph (1879–1956),
6, 146

Woman of Paris, A (1924), 189*n17*

Woman's Home Companion, 11, 14,
146, 189*n19*, 190*n21*; Chaplin
contract, 190*n1*

Workmen's apartments, Vienna,
Austria, 63–64, 146

Workmen's Theatre, Berlin, Germany,
57–58